CONTEMPORARY THEORIES
OF KNOWLEDGE

CONTEMPORARY THEORIES

of

KNOWLEDGE

JOHN L. POLLOCK
University of Arizona

HUTCHINSON
LONDON   MELBOURNE   SYDNEY   AUCKLAND   JOHANNESBURG

Hutchinson Education

An imprint of Century Hutchinson Ltd

62–65 Chandos Place, London WC2N 4NW

Century Hutchinson Australia Pty Ltd
P O Box 496, 16–22 Church Street, Hawthorn,
Victoria 3122, Australia

Century Hutchinson New Zealand Ltd
P O Box 40–086, Glenfield, Auckland 10,
New Zealand

Century Hutchinson South Africa (Pty) Ltd
P O Box 337, Berglvei 2012, South Africa

First published in the United States of America
by Rowman & Littlefield Publishers 1986

First published in Great Britain in 1987

Printed in the United States of America

ISBN 0 09 172931 9

FOR CAROLE

CONTENTS

PREFACE AND
ACKNOWLEDGMENTS

This book is intended to play two roles. On the one hand, it is a textbook. It is intended as an introduction to the theory of knowledge for readers with some intellectual sophistication but without an extensive knowledge of philosophy. On the other hand, it is an attempt to say what is true in epistemology, and in this latter guise it is aimed as much at the professional philosopher as at the student. The book endeavors to play both roles by taking its principal task to be that of mapping out the logical geography of epistemology in a way that enables the reader to see how the issues and theories fit together. A taxonomy of epistemological theories is constructed, and then the different kinds of theories are discussed in terms of their place in the taxonomy. I have done my best to present each general variety of epistemological theory in the best possible light. Then I have tried to raise only those objections to the theories that reflect very general features of them. I have tried to avoid raising objections that might be met by tinkering with details. In this way I have been led to reject all of the more familiar kinds of epistemological theories (foundations theories, coherence theories, probabilist theories, and reliabilist theories). That exhausts most of the logical geography of epistemology and leaves us with only a small verdant landscape to explore—the region of what I call 'nondoxastic internalist theories'. These are theories that insist that the justifiability of a belief is a function exclusively of the internal states of the believer, but also insist that we must include more than the believer's beliefs among those internal states. In particular, the believer's perceptual states and memory states can be relevant to what he is justified in believing, even when he has no beliefs about what perceptual states and memory states he is in.

One of my main concerns in this book is to integrate epistemology into a naturalistic view of man as a kind of biological information processor. I have tried to do this by exploring how we might build an intelligent machine that is capable of interacting with its environment and surviving in a hostile world. Very general constraints having to do with limited computational powers lead naturally to a machine many of whose features reproduce initially surprising aspects of human epistemology. The epistemology of such a machine will almost automatically be a variety of the kind of nondoxastic internalism that I have described.

To a certain extent this book grew out of two journal articles: "Epistemic Norms" (*Synthese*) and "My Brother, the Machine" (*Nous*). The former provides the positive theory of the book, and some material from the latter provides, in a sense, the theoretical underpinning for the positive theory. Jointly, they comprise chapter five. The rest of the book consists of a discussion of competing theories and was written as more or less an introduction to chapter five. In the end, the discussion of competing theories became as important as the the positive theory because of the light the discussion throws on the general structure of epistemology and epistemological problems.

This book has profited from philosophical discussion of its topics with many of my colleagues and students. Those who stand out most prominently in my mind are Keith Lehrer, Alvin Goldman, Stephen Schiffer, Stewart Cohen, John Carroll, George Smith, Bob Audi, and Hilary Kornblith. Others too numerous to mention have helped me in clarifying my thoughts on various aspects of the material and have helped me avoid errors I would otherwise have fallen into.

CONTEMPORARY THEORIES
OF KNOWLEDGE

1
THE PROBLEMS OF KNOWLEDGE

*I*T ALL BEGAN *that cold Wednesday night. I was sitting alone in my office watching the rain come down on the deserted streets outside, when the phone rang. It was Harry's wife, and she sounded terrified. They had been having a late supper alone in their apartment when suddenly the front door came crashing in and six hooded men burst into the room. The men were armed and they made Harry and Anne lay face down on the floor while they went through Harry's pockets. When they found his driver's license one of them carefully scrutinized Harry's face, comparing it with the official photograph and then muttered, "It's him all right." The leader of the intruders produced a hypodermic needle and injected Harry with something that made him lose consciousness almost immediately. For some reason they only tied and gagged Anne. Two of the men left the room and returned with a stretcher and white coats. They put Harry on the stretcher, donned the white coats, and trundled him out of the apartment, leaving Anne lying on the floor. She managed to squirm to the window in time to see them put Harry in an ambulance and drive away.*

By the time she called me, Anne was coming apart at the seams. It had taken her several hours to get out of her bonds, and then she called the police. To her consternation, instead of uniformed officers, two plain clothed officials arrived and, without even looking over the scene, they proceeded to tell her that there was nothing they could do and if she knew what was good for her she would keep her mouth shut. If she raised a fuss they would put out the word that she was a psycho and she would never see her husband again.

Not knowing what else to do, Anne called me. She had had the presence of mind to note down the number of the ambulance, and I had no great difficulty tracing it to a private clinic at the outskirts of town. When I arrived at the clinic I was surprised to find it locked up like a fortress. There were guards at the gate and it was surrounded by a massive wall. My commando training stood me in good stead as I negotiated the 20 foot wall, avoided the barbed wire, and silenced the guard dogs on the other side. The ground floor windows were all barred, but I managed to wriggle up a drainpipe and get in through a secondstory window that someone had left ajar. I found myself in a laboratory. Hearing muffled sounds next door I peeked through the keyhole and saw what appeared to be a complete operating room and a surgical team laboring over Harry. He was covered with a sheet from the neck down and they seemed to be connecting tubes and wires to him. I stifled a gasp when I realized that they had removed the top of Harry's skull. To my considerable consternation, one of the surgeons reached into the open top of Harry's head and eased his brain out, placing it in a stainless steel bowl. The tubes and wires I had noted earlier were connected to the now disembodied brain. The surgeons carried the bloody mass carefully to some kind of tank and lowered it in. My first thought was that I had stumbled on a covey of futuristic Satanists who got their kicks from vivisection. My second thought was that Harry was an insurance agent. Maybe this was their way of getting even for the increases in their malpractice insurance rates. If they did this every Wednesday night, their rates were no higher than they should be!

My speculations were interrupted when the lights suddenly came on in my darkened hidey hole and I found myself looking up at the scariest group of medical men I had ever seen. They manhandled me into the next room and strapped me down on an operating table. I thought, "Oh, oh, I'm for it now!" The doctors huddled at the other end of the room, but I couldn't turn my head far enough to see what they were doing. They were mumbling among themselves, probably deciding my fate. A door opened and I heard a woman's voice. The deferential manner assumed by the medical malpractitioners made it obvious who was boss. I strained to see this mysterious woman but she hovered just out of my view. Then, to my astonishment, she walked up and stood over me and I realized it was my secretary, Margot. I began to wish I had given her that Christmas bonus after all.

It was Margot, but it was a different Margot than I had ever seen. She was wallowing in the heady wine of authority as she bent over me. " Well Mike, you thought you were so smart, tracking Harry here to the clinic," she said. Even now she had the sexiest voice I have ever heard, but I wasn't really thinking about that. She went on, "It was all a trick just to get you here. You saw what happened to Harry. He's not really dead, you know. These gentlemen are the premier neuroscientists in the world today. They have developed a surgical procedure whereby they remove the brain from the body but keep it alive in a vat of nutrient. The Food and Drug Administration wouldn't approve the procedure, but we'll show them. You see all the wires going to Harry's brain? They connect him up with a powerful computer. The computer monitors the output of his motor cortex and provides input to the sensory cortex in such a way that everything appears perfectly normal to Harry. It produces a fictitious mental life that merges perfectly into his past life so that he is unaware that anything has happened to him. He thinks he is shaving right now and getting ready to go to the office and stick it to another neurosurgeon. But actually, he's just a brain in a vat."

"Once we have our procedure perfected we're going after the head of the Food and Drug Administration, but we needed some experimental subjects first. Harry was easy. In order to really test our computer program we need someone who leads a more interesting and varied life—someone like you!" I was starting to squirm. The surgeons had drawn around me and were looking on *with malevolent gleams in their eyes. The biggest brute, a man with a pockmarked face and one beady eye staring out from under his stringy black hair, was fondling a razor sharp scalpel in his still-bloody hands and looking like he could barely restrain his excitement. But Margot gazed down at me and murmured in that incredible voice, "I'll bet you think we're going to operate on you and remove your brain just like we removed Harry's, don't you? But you have nothing to worry about. We're not going to remove your brain. We already did—three months ago!"*

With that they let me go. I found my way back to my office in a daze. For some reason, I haven't told anybody about this. I can't make up my mind. I am racked by the suspicion that I am really a brain in a vat and all this I see around me is just a figment of the computer. After all, how could I tell? If the computer program really works, no matter what I do, everything will seem normal. Maybe nothing I see is real. It's driving me crazy. I've even considered checking into that clinic voluntarily and asking them to remove my brain just so that I can be sure.

1. Skeptical Problems

Mike is luckier than most brain-in-a-vat victims. He at least has a clue to his precarious situation—Margot told him he is a brain in a vat. Of course, it could all be contrived. Perhaps he is not a brain in a vat after all. There is no way he can be sure. Meditating about this case, it may occur to you that you might be a brain in a vat, too. If you are, there is no way you could ever find out. Nor, it seems, is there any way you can be sure you are not a brain in a vat, because everything would seem just the same to you in either case. But if you cannot be sure you are not a brain in a vat, how can you trust the evidence of your senses? You have no way of knowing that they are not figments of a computer. It seems that you cannot *really* know anything about the world around you. It could all be an illusion. You cannot rule out the possibility that you are a brain in a vat, and without being able to rule out that possibility, knowledge of the material world is impossible.

This is a typical example of a skeptical problem. Skeptical problems seem to show that we cannot have the kinds of knowledge we are convinced we have. Such problems have played a central role in epistemology. It is easy to become caught up in the task of refuting the skeptic, and at one time time epistemologists took that to be their principal goal. Descartes was concerned with finding beliefs that he could not reasonably doubt and to which he could appeal in justifying all the rest of his beliefs, and Hume was nonplussed by his inability to answer his own skeptical dilemma about induction. In the *Critique of Pure Reason*, Kant wrote:

> It still remains a scandal to philosophy . . . that the existence of things outside of us . . . must be accepted merely on *faith*, and that, if anyone thinks good to doubt their existence, we are unable to counter his doubts by any satisfactory proof.[1]

But contemporary epistemology takes a different attitude toward skepticism. If we consider a variety of skepticism that confines itself to some limited class of beliefs, it *might* be possible to answer the skeptic by showing that those beliefs can be securely defended by appeal to other beliefs not among those deemed problematic. But for any very general kind of skepticism, that is impossible in principle. Every argument must proceed from some premises, and if the skeptic calls all relevant premises into doubt at the same time then there is no way to reason with him. The whole enterprise of refuting the skeptic is ill-founded, because he will not allow us anything with which to work.

The proper treatment of skeptical arguments requires looking at them in a different light. We come to philosophy with a large stock of beliefs. Initially, we regard them all as knowledge, but then we discover that they conflict. They cannot all be true because some are inconsistent with others. One instance of this general phenomenon is represented by skeptical arguments. Starting from premises in which we are initially confident, the skeptical argument leads us to the conclusion that we cannot possibly have certain kinds of knowledge. But we are also initially confident that we do have such knowledge. Thus our original confidently held beliefs form an inconsistent set. We cannot reasonably continue to hold them all.

Upon discovering that our system of beliefs is inconsistent, the initial reaction might be that we should throw them all away and start over again. But that will not solve the problem. The skeptic is not just questioning our beliefs. He is also questioning the cognitive processes by which we arrive at our beliefs, and if we start all over again we will still be employing the same cognitive processes. We cannot dispense with *both* the beliefs and the cognitive processes, because then we would have nothing with which to begin again. As Otto Neurath [1932] put it in an often-quoted passage, "We are like sailors who must rebuild their ship upon the open sea."[2] We must start with the beliefs and cognitive processes we have and repair them "from within" as best we can. The legitimacy of beginning with what we already have was urged by G. E. Moore in a famous passage:

> I can prove now, for instance, that two human hands exist. How? By holding up my two hands, and saying, as I make a certain gesture with

1. Kant [1958], p. 34. This passage is quoted by G. E. Moore [1959], p. 126.

2. "Wie Schiffer sind wir, die ihr Schiff auf offener See umbauen müssen." This passage has been immortalized by Quine [1960], who refers to it repeatedly.

the right hand, "Here is one hand," and adding, as I make a certain gesture with the left, "and here is another." . . . But now I am perfectly well aware that, in spite of all that I have said, many philosophers will still feel that I have not given any satisfactory proof of the point in question. . . . If I had proved the propositions which I used as *premisses* in my two proofs, then they would perhaps admit that I had proved the existence of external things. . . . They want a proof of what I assert *now* when I hold up my hands and say "Here's one hand and here's another." . . . They think that, if I cannot give such extra proofs, then the proofs that I have given are not conclusive proofs at all. . . . Such a view, though it has been very common among philosophers, can, I think, be shown to be wrong. . . . I can know things which I cannot prove; and among things which I certainly did know, . . . were the premisses of my two proofs. I should say, therefore, that those, if any, who are dissatisfied with these proofs merely on the ground that I did not know their premisses, have no good reason for their dissatisfaction. ([1959], p. 144ff.)

If we reflect upon our beliefs, we will find that we are more confident of some than of others. It is reasonable to place more reliance on those beliefs in which we have greater confidence, and when beliefs come in conflict we decide which to reject by considering which we are least certain of. If we have to reject something, it is reasonable to reject those beliefs we regard as most doubtful.[3] Now consider how these observations apply to skeptical arguments. An argument begins from premises and draws a conclusion:

$$P_1$$

$$P_2$$

.

.

.

$$P_n$$

———————————

Therefore, Q.

Presented with an argument whose premises we believe, the natural reaction is to accept the conclusion, even if the conclusion is the denial of something else we initially believe. But that is not always the reasonable response to an argument. In the above argument, Q is a deductive consequence of $P_1, \ldots, P_n$, but all that really shows is that we cannot reasonably continue to believe all of $P_1, \ldots, P_n$ and $\sim Q$. The validity of the argument does not establish which of these beliefs should be rejected, because we can convert the argument into an

3. This is what John Rawls [1971] calls "the method of reflective equilibrium".

equally valid argument for the denial of any one of the premises. For instance, the following is also a valid argument:

$$P_2$$
$$\bullet$$
$$\bullet$$
$$\bullet$$
$$P_n$$
$$\sim Q$$

Therefore, $\sim P_1$.

Faced with a skeptical argument, we believe all of the premises $P_1, \ldots, P_n$, but we also believe $\sim Q$ (the denial of the conclusion, the conclusion being that we do not have the knowledge described). The argument establishes that we must reject one of these beliefs, but it does not tell us which we should reject. To determine that, we must reflect upon how certain we are of each of these beliefs and reject the one of which we are least certain. In typical skeptical arguments, we invariably find that we are more certain of the knowledge seemingly denied us than we are of some of the premises. Thus it is not reasonable to adopt the skeptical conclusion that we do not have that knowledge. The rational stance is instead to deny one or more of the premises. In other words, a typical skeptical argument is best viewed as a *reductio ad absurdum* of its premises, rather than as a proof of its conclusion.[4]

This lesson has been assimilated by contemporary epistemologists who, for the most part, no longer regard their task as that of disproving skepticism. But this is not to deny that skeptical problems are still important to epistemology. They are important for what they show about knowledge rather than because they make us doubt that we have knowledge. The task of the contemporary epistemologist is to *understand* knowledge. For this he need not refute the skeptic—we already know that the skeptic is wrong. Nevertheless, important conclusions about the nature of knowledge and epistemic justification can be gleaned from the investigation of skeptical arguments. This is because such an argument constitutes a *reductio ad absurdum* of its

4. There is no logical necessity that this should be the case. It is conceivable that there should be a skeptical argument whose premises we believe more firmly than we believe that we have the putative knowledge the argument denies us. The claim I am making here is a contingent one about those skeptical arguments that have actually been advanced in philosophy.

premises, and its premises consist of things we initially believe about knowledge and justification. Thus in deciding which of those premises is wrong we are learning something new about knowledge and correcting mistaken beliefs with which we begin. In short, the task of the epistemologist is not to show *that* the skeptic is wrong but to explain *why* he is wrong. The difference between these endeavors is that in the latter we can take it as a premise that we have various kinds of knowledge (i.e., we can assume ~Q) and see what that requires. For example, we might ask, "Given that we have perceptual knowledge, what must the relationship be between our perceptual beliefs and our sensory experience?" The fact that we do have perceptual knowledge will impose important constraints on that relationship and can lead us to significant conclusions about epistemic justification. This reasoning has the form, "We do have such-and-such knowledge; we could not have that knowledge if so-and-so were the case; therefore, so-and-so is not the case." This kind of reasoning is very common in contemporary epistemology. Note that such reasoning results from contraposing the premises and conclusion of a skeptical argument.

2. Knowledge and Justification

Epistemology is "the theory of knowledge" and would seem most naturally to have knowledge as its principal focus. But that is not entirely accurate. The theory of knowledge is an attempt to answer the question, "How do you know?", but this is a question about *how* one knows, and not about knowing per se. In asking how a person knows something we are typically asking for his grounds for believing it. We want to know what *justifies* him in holding his belief. Thus epistemology has traditionally focused on epistemic justification more than on knowledge. Epistemology might better be called 'doxastology'.

A justified belief is one that it is "epistemically permissible" to hold. Epistemic justification is a normative notion. It pertains to what you *should* or *should not* believe. But it is a uniquely epistemic normative notion. Epistemic permissibility must be distinguished from both moral and prudential permissibility. For example, because beliefs can have important consequences for the believer, it may be prudent to hold beliefs for which you have inadequate evidence. For instance, it is popularly alleged that lobsters do not feel pain when they are dunked alive into boiling water. It is extremely doubtful that anyone has good reason to believe that, but it may be prudentially rational to hold that belief because otherwise one would deprive oneself of the gustatory delight of eating boiled lobsters. Conversely, it may be imprudent to hold beliefs for which you have unimpeachable evidence. Consider Helen, who has overwhelming evidence that her father is Jack the Ripper. It may be that if she admitted this to herself it would be psychologically crushing. In such cases people sometimes do not believe what the evidence overwhelmingly supports. That is prudentially reasonable but epistemically unreasonable. Thus epistemic reasonableness is not the same thing as prudential reasonableness. Epistemic reasonableness is also distinct from moral reasonableness. It is unclear whether moral considerations can be meaningfully applied to beliefs. If not, then epistemic justification is obviously distinct from moral permissibility. If belief does fall within the purview of morality then presumably a belief can be made morally impermissible, for example, if one were to promise someone never to think ill of him. But clearly the moral permissibility of such a belief is totally unrelated to its epistemic permissibility. Consequently, epistemic justification is normative, but it must be distinguished from other familiar normative concepts.

Epistemic justification governs what you should or should not believe. Rules describing the circumstances under which it is epistemically permissible to hold beliefs are called *epistemic norms*. An important task of recent epistemology has been that of describing the epistemic norms governing various kinds of belief. For instance, philosophers have sought accounts of the circumstances under which it is epistemically permissible to believe, on the basis of sense perception, that there are physical objects of different sorts standing in various spatial relations to the perceiver. In part, epistemologists have tried to elicit the nature of the epistemic norms governing this kind of knowledge by looking at skeptical arguments purporting to show that perceptual knowledge is impossible. We know, contrary to the skeptic, that perceptual knowledge *is* possible, and that allows us to draw conclusions about the epistemic norms governing perceptual knowledge. This will be a recurring theme throughout the book.

If the central question of epistemology concerns the justification of belief rather than knowledge, why is the discipline called 'epistemology'? The explanation lies in the fact that there appear to be important connections between knowledge and justification. I have already noted that the question "How do you know?" can generally be construed as meaning "What justifies you in believing?", but we can reasonably ask why it can be construed in that way. To answer this question, epistemologists have spent a great deal of time laboring over the connections between knowledge and justification. It has been generally acknowledged that epistemic justification is a necessary condition for knowledge.[5] Consensus is rare in philosophy, but from the early part of this century until 1963 it was almost universally agreed that knowledge was the same thing as justified true belief. That is, a person knows something, P, if and only if (1) he believes it, (2) it is true, and (3) his belief is justified. But in 1963, Edmund Gettier published his seminal paper "Is Justified True Belief Knowledge?" in which he showed to everyone's astonishment that this identification is incorrect.[6] He did this by presenting counterexamples. In one of his examples we consider Smith, who believes falsely but with good reason that Jones owns a Ford. Smith has no idea where Brown is, but he arbitrarily picks Barcelona and infers from the putative fact that Jones owns a Ford that either Jones owns a Ford or Brown is in Barcelona. It happens by chance that Brown is in Barcelona, so this disjunction is true. Furthermore, as Smith has good reason to believe that Jones owns a Ford, he is justified in believing this disjunction. But as his evidence does not pertain to the true disjunct of the disjunction, we would not regard Smith as *knowing* that it is true that either Smith owns a Ford or Brown is in Barcelona.

The general reaction to Gettier's examples has been to concede that a fourth condition must be added to the analysis of 'S knows that P'. The search for this fourth condition has become known as the *Gettier problem*. The Gettier problem is a seductive sort of problem. When they first encountered it, most epistemologists were convinced that it must have a simple solution. Simple conditions were found that handled the original Gettier counterexamples, but new counterexamples emerged almost immediately. More and more complicated counterexamples were followed by more and more complicated fourth conditions. At the present time, the Gettier problem has become mired in complexity and few philosophers now expect it to have a simple solution. Nevertheless, having gotten hooked on the problem epistemologists are loathe to let it go, so it remains a frequent topic in contemporary epistemology. It must be emphasized, however, that it is basically a side issue.[7] The central topic of epistemology is epistemic justification rather than knowledge. For this reason the Gettier problem is not discussed in the main part of this book, although it is discussed briefly in the appendix. Its solution is not an essential part of the construction of an epistemological theory. On the contrary, I

5. Not quite all philosophers acknowledge this. See Peter Unger [1967] and Joseph Margolis [1973].

6. Remarkably, a counterexample to the traditional analysis can also be found in Bertrand Russell [1912], p. 132, but that went overlooked.

7. This is persuasively documented from an historical perspective by Mark Kaplan [1985].

take an epistemological theory to be a theory about how it is possible to acquire various kinds of knowledge, and this is most basically a theory about epistemic justification.

It is useful to distinguish two potentially different concepts of epistemic justification. I have taken the fundamental problem of epistemology to be that of deciding what to believe. Epistemic justification, as I use the term, is concerned with this problem. Considerations of epistemic justification guide us in determining what to believe. We might call this the 'belief-guiding' or 'reason-guiding' sense of 'justification'. Correlatively, epistemic norms are norms prescribing how to form beliefs. It is common in contemporary epistemology to find philosophers explaining instead that what they mean by 'justification' is, roughly, 'what is required for knowledge'. That, of course, is not very clear, because knowledge requires more than justification. For instance, it requires truth. Still, there may be a kind of justification that is required for knowledge and is distinct from the reason-guiding kind of justification. Whether this is so will be addressed at some length in the appendix. I will ultimately affirm that there is a strong sense of 'objective justification' required for knowledge that is distinct from, but definable in terms of, reason-guiding justification. But for now it must be emphasized that the topic of the main body of this book is reason-guiding justification, not "what is required for knowledge". This will be important at various stages of the argument where it is urged that particular theories could not play a reason-guiding role.

3. Areas of Knowledge

We know many kinds of things, and there appear to be important differences between the ways we know them. We can subdivide knowledge into different "areas", according to these epistemological differences. Knowledge based directly upon sense perception, or "perceptual knowledge", comprises one area. Knowledge possessed by virtue of remembering previously acquired knowledge comprises another. Inductive generalizations comprise a third. Knowledge of other minds, a priori knowledge, and moral knowledge comprise other areas. Knowledge in different areas will share some common features but will also exhibit important differences.

3.1   Perceptual Knowledge

The *problem of perception* is that of explaining how perceptual knowledge is possible. We all agree that sense perception can lead to justified beliefs about the world around us. But the details remain obscure. The skeptical argument with which this chapter began can be regarded as an assault on the possibility of perceptual knowledge. It seems that our perceptual experience could be precisely what it is without the world being at all what it appears to be (we might be brains in vats!). How then is it possible to acquire knowledge of the material world by relying upon sense perception?

The focus of the present book is "meta-epistemology". That is, it is more concerned with describing and contrasting *kinds* of epistemological theories than it is with addressing specific epistemological problems. The broad categories of epistemological theories that will be discussed will be enumerated in the next section. But one way of contrasting theories is by comparing what they have to say about specific epistemological problems, and the sample problem to which I will return repeatedly is the problem of perception. More has been written in epistemology about perceptual knowledge than about any other kind of knowledge. This is partly because the psychological facts are clearer. Specifically, we know that such knowledge is acquired in response to the activation of our sense organs, the most important of which is vision. This enables us to formulate the problem of perception as that of explaining how we can acquire justified beliefs about the external world on the basis of the output of our sense organs. This seemingly unremarkable formulation contrasts sharply with the formulation of epistemological problems concerning other areas of knowledge, as we will now see.

3.2   *A Priori Knowledge*

In contrast to perceptual knowledge, even the very basic psychological facts about other areas of knowledge tend to be obscure. It is clear that sense perception is the source of perceptual knowledge, but for some areas of knowledge the source is quite mysterious. A priori knowledge comprises one of the most problematic areas. A priori knowledge is usually defined as "what is known independently of experience", or perhaps as "what known on the basis of reason alone". But it must be acknowledged that these are not very helpful definitions and they should not be taken too seriously. Rather, we recognize that there is a certain class of knowledge that seems importantly different from other kinds of knowledge and we give it a label—'a priori knowledge'. The class is characterized by its stereotypes. These include most prominently knowledge of mathematical and logical truths. It is very difficult to say in even a superficial way what is involved psychologically in the acquisition of a priori knowledge. For instance, consider mathematical knowledge. We know that mathematical proof is an important factor in mathematical knowledge. The nature of mathematical proof is itself fraught with difficulty, but an even more obscure aspect of mathematical knowledge arises from the observation that any substantive proof (i.e., any proof of something other than a principle of logic) must start from premises already established. Where do the basic premises of mathematics come from? A once-popular view was that they are arbitrary axioms laid down by convention and that they "implicitly define" mathematical concepts.[8] Such a "conventionalist" view was attractive because it seemed to reduce a priori knowledge to something much easier to understand. But conventionalism lost its plausibility, partly because of Gödel's theorem. A rough formulation of Gödel's theorem is that given any set of axioms for mathematics, there are theorems we can prove in "real mathematics" that cannot be deduced from those axioms. This seems to show that we have more mathematical knowledge than we could have if conventionalism were true.[9] Today conventionalism has few supporters.

Ordinarily, the downfall of one theory heralds the apparent success of another. Theories are rarely overturned except in the face of seemingly better theories. But in the case of a priori knowledge, no better theory has appeared on the horizon. Other than conventionalism, the only kind of theory that has occurred to people is what might be called 'a priori intuitionism'.[10] According to this theory, basic a priori truths are "self-evident". We have the power to "intuit" that they are true. This putative faculty of a priori intuition has been described variously by different philosophers. Bertrand Russell described it as the power to directly intuit relations between universals.[11] Other authors have tried to describe it in a more ontologically neutral way.[12] But notice that the claim that we have such a faculty at all is really a psychological claim. Furthermore, although it is one that psychologists have not directly addressed, it must be regarded as being at least somewhat suspect. If there is any such faculty of a priori intuition, it tends to elude introspection. I would not claim at this point that there definitely is no such faculty, or that a priori intuitionism is a false theory, but it must be acknowledged that the psychological facts surrounding a priori knowledge are obscure. This makes it

8. See, for example, Ayer [1946].

9. For a detailed discussion of conventionalism and its relationship to Gödel's theorem, see Pollock [1974], chapter ten.

10. This is to be distinguished from the philosophy of mathematics known as "mathematical intuitionism" and defended by such people as Brouwer and Heyting. There is no close connection between these two kinds of intuitionism.

11. See Bertrand Russell [1912].

12. I took this course in Pollock [1974].

difficult to either formulate or evaluate philosophical theories of a priori knowledge.

3.3 *Moral Knowledge*

A priori knowledge is not the only area in which the psychological facts are obscure. Moral knowledge is at least as problematic. There is not even a consensus that moral knowledge exists. Although some moral philosophers are convinced that there is such a thing as moral knowledge, at least as many are adamant that there is not. The latter philosophers maintain that moral language plays a unique role that does not involve expressing truths. It has been urged, for example, that moral language expresses sentiments, or approval and disapproval, or some other kind of psychological attitude distinct from belief.[13] In any such "nonobjective" moral theory there is no such thing as an epistemological problem of moral knowledge, because if there are no moral truths then there can be no moral knowledge.

Suppose we set aside nonobjective views and assume that there is such a thing as moral knowledge. Then we are faced with explaining how we can acquire that knowledge. One possible view is analogous to a priori intuitionism. According to *ethical intuitionism*, we have a faculty of moral intuition that makes some moral truths self-evident, and then other moral truths can be defended on the basis of the self-evident ones.[14] But there is no general agreement that we have a psychological faculty of moral intuition. Ethical intuitionism is not popular in contemporary philosophy. There are alternative theories, but none of them are very popular either. In fact, in contemporary ethics there is little work even being attempted in moral epistemology. The psychological foundations of putative moral knowledge are in disarray. But without a better understanding of the psychological facts surrounding moral reasoning it is hard to get a philosophical theory of moral knowledge off the ground.

3.4 *Memory*

Much of what we know, we know by remembering. This has suggested to some epistemologists that memory is a source of knowledge. According to this view, remembering involves a psychological state—what we might call "apparent memory"—that plays a role in memory analogous to the role sense perception plays in perceptual

---

13. See for example A. J. Ayer [1946] and Charles Stevenson [1944].

14. The most important proponents of ethical intuitionism are H. A. Prichard [1950], Sir David Ross [1930], and G. E. Moore [1903].

knowledge.[15] Other philosophers have disputed this claim, insisting that memory introduces no new source of knowledge. Instead, they maintain, memory is just the exercise of previously acquired knowledge, and the source of remembered knowledge is whatever the source of the knowledge was when it was first acquired.[16] The debate here is in part over what occurs psychologically in remembering. Is there an introspectible state of apparent memory that distinguishes remembering something from simply believing it? Philosophers do not agree, and psychologists have done little to resolve the issue. But even if the psychological facts were resolved in favor of apparent memory, the philosophical question would remain whether apparent memory somehow licenses belief in what one presently remembers, or whether instead the justification of current memories is the same as the justification of those same beliefs when they were originally acquired.

Memory comprises an area of knowledge in the same sense that perceptual knowledge and a priori knowledge do, but memory also has a more pervasive significance for meta-epistemology. One of the main ways in which epistemological theories differ from one another is in their account of reasoning and its relationship to epistemic justification. Memory plays a fundamental role in reasoning. When we reason in accordance with any even slightly complicated argument, we do not hold the entire argument in mind at the same time. We attend to each step individually and rely upon memory to tell us that we got to that step in some reasonable way. A correct epistemological account of memory must make this legitimate. Thus the nature of memory knowledge will play a pivotal role in the formulation of alternative epistemological theories. For this reason, memory will be discussed at some length in the next chapter.

3.5 Induction

Knowledge of inductive generalizations comprises a kind of knowledge importantly different from the varieties of knowledge described so far. Induction is distinguished not by its source but by its method. The simplest kind of induction is *enumerative induction*, wherein we examine a sample of objects of some kind, A, observe that all the A's in the sample have another property, B, and infer on that basis that all A's are B. A related kind of induction is *statistical induction*, where instead of observing that all the A's in our sample are B we observe

15. I defended this view in Pollock [1974], chapter seven.
16. This view was defended by Norman Malcolm [1963], pp. 229–30, and Robert Squires [1969].

that some proportion m/n of them are B's and then infer that the probability of an arbitrary A being a B is approximately m/n. The way we reason in enumerative and statistical induction is fairly clear in bold outline, but the fine details have been remarkably resistant to accurate description.

Induction has exercised philosophers because of two different kinds of worries. The *traditional problem of induction* is Hume's problem. Hume's concern was to justify induction. He observed that the premises of an inductive argument do not logically entail the conclusion. We may observe that all the members of a limited sample of A's are B, but that does not logically entail that *all* A's are B. What justifies us in drawing a conclusion about all A's on the basis of such a limited observation? Hume took his problem to be that of answering the skeptic—a task at which he confessed defeat. In light of our earlier discussion of the role of skeptical arguments in contemporary epistemology, we can dismiss the traditional problem in the form given it by Hume. There is neither a need nor the possibility of proving the skeptic wrong. You can never *prove* the skeptic wrong because he does not leave you with enough ammunition to undertake such a task. But there is no reason why we should have to prove the skeptic wrong. We already know that he is wrong. One of the things we are certain about right from the beginning is that we can acquire knowledge of general truths on the basis of induction.

Although we had best not follow Hume in his attempt to refute the skeptic, this does not mean that there is nothing useful to be mined from Hume's skeptical argument. That argument went as follows:

(1) The premises of an inductive argument do not logically entail the conclusion of the argument.

(2) If the premises of an argument do not logically entail the conclusion, then the argument can provide us with no justification for believing the conclusion.

Therefore, induction cannot justify belief in its conclusions.

We are quite certain that the conclusion of this skeptical argument is wrong, so we had best re-examine the premises. Both premises may seem initially reasonable, but we are typically not as certain about either of them as we are that inductive knowledge is possible. Thus the skeptical argument is best viewed as a *reductio ad absurdum* of its premises. What remains is to decide which premise is false and diagnose the way in which it goes wrong.

For a while in the early part of the twentieth century it was popular to deny (1), maintaining that inductive reasoning turned upon an implicit premise affirming "the uniformity of nature". According to this premise, nature is uniform in the sense that generalizations holding at one time hold at all times. The intention was for this principle of the uniformity of nature to be sufficiently strong that, when conjoined with the inductive evidence, it would provide us with premises logically entailing the inductive generalization.[17] This attempt at meeting the skeptic is now recognized to have failed for two different reasons. First, no one was ever successful at formulating a principle of the uniformity of nature that was strong enough to provide the requisite entailment but was not obviously false. After all, nature is not *always* uniform—some generalizations hold in limited settings but fail in more general settings. Second, even if a principle of the uniformity of nature could be formulated, it would be a generalization about the way the world is, and so it seems that the only way one could become justified in believing the principle would be by induction. That would be circular if inductive reasoning turned upon our first justifying the principle of the uniformity of nature.

If the conclusion of the skeptical argument is false and the first premise is true then the second premise must be false. Denying (2) is the option taken by most contemporary epistemologists. It is generally recognized now that induction illustrates the existence of reasons that do not logically entail their conclusions. Such reasons are *defeasible* in the sense that, while they can justify us in believing their conclusions, that justification can be "defeated" by acquiring further relevant information. In the case of induction, if we observe that all the A's in our sample are B, this may provisionally justify us in believing that all A's are B. But if we subsequently encounter another A and note that it is not a B, that is sufficient to defeat the original justification and it makes it totally unreasonable to continue believing that all A's are B. Thus the skeptical argument about induction points to the existence of defeasible reasons in epistemology. In my opinion, that is one of the most important discoveries of contemporary epistemology; it will be discussed at some length in the next chapter.

Even if we dismiss skepticism regarding induction, we can resurrect Hume's problem in a new guise. While there is no need to justify induction in the sense of proving that inductive reasoning is epistemologically legitimate, it may still be possible to justify induction in another sense. The question arises whether inductive reasoning is a fundamental and irreducible component of our framework of reasons and reasoning.[18] If it is then no further justification can be demanded, but if it is not then it may be possible to base inductive

17. See Bertrand Russell, [1912], chapter VI, and C. I. Lewis [1956], chapter XI.
18. This view was endorsed and popularized by P. F. Strawson [1952]. I defended it myself in Pollock [1974], but I have since rejected it for the reasons described here.

reasoning on simpler and more basic kinds of reasoning. There is reason to think that the latter alternative may be the correct one. Principles of induction seem simple until we try to formulate them precisely; then they become extremely complicated and it is never clear whether we have got them quite right. I will illustrate some of the difficulties below. What is to be noted here is that if correct principles of induction are really that complicated, and we have that much trouble telling whether we have formulated them correctly, then it is unlikely that they are formulations of basic epistemic norms we follow directly in our reasoning. Instead, it seems likely that they reflect the application of simpler epistemic norms to cases having enough internal complexity to render the application logically and mathematically convoluted. I have argued elsewhere (Pollock [1984a]) that this is indeed the correct explanation for the complexity surrounding inductive reasoning.

Leaving aside the problem of justifying induction, much philosophical labor has also gone into what Nelson Goodman [1955] dubbed *the new riddle of induction*. This is the problem of giving an accurate formulation of principles of induction. Goodman's main interest was in just one aspect of this problem, but it is a multi-faceted problem. The aspect that concerned Goodman was the *problem of projectibility*. This is best illustrated by thinking first about deductive inferences. Rules of deductive inference apply equally to all propositions and properties. For example, we can infer Q from (P & Q) regardless of what P and Q are. The traditional view of induction took it to be like deduction in applying equally to all properties, but Goodman startled the world of philosophy by showing that there are restrictions on the use of inductive reasoning. Goodman's examples were highly contrived, but quite simple examples are available. For instance, having observed a sample of ravens, you might note that all the ravens you have observed have been observed. Obviously, that gives you no reason to believe that all ravens have been observed. Other examples can be constructed using disjunctions. Suppose, for example, that you would like to confirm inductively that all moose have whiskers. The natural way to proceed would involve collecting a sample of moose and examining them for whiskers. The trouble is, moose are big unruly creatures, and it would be nicer if we could avoid dealing with them. Why not, then, proceed as follows? Consider the disjunctive property of being either a mouse or a moose. We can safely collect a sample of mice-or-moose by just collecting a sample of mice. Upon examining them we find that they are all bewhiskered. That would seem to inductively confirm that everything that is either a mouse or a moose is bewhiskered, and the latter entails that all moose are bewhiskered. So we have a safe way of making inductive generalizations about moose. But obviously, this is absurd. It would be unobjectionable if we could reason inductively about mice-or-moose in the same way we can reason inductively about mice—by collecting an arbitrary sample and generalizing on the basis of it. But we cannot do that. To confirm a generalization about mice-or-moose we must confirm separate generalizations about mice and about moose.[19] To use Goodman's terminology, the property of being either a mouse or a moose is *unprojectible*. Simple rules of inductive reasoning only apply to projectible properties. Thus, in order to give a precise account of inductive reasoning, we need a criterion of projectibility. It has proven remarkably difficult to find such a criterion.

Projectibility is not the only source of difficulty in formulating precise rules of induction. In the case of statistical induction, even the precise form that the conclusion should take is doubtful. If we observe that out of n A's our sample contains m B's, we conclude that the probability of an arbitrary A being a B is *approximately* m/n. That means that the probability lies in some interval around m/n, but how narrow an interval? Untutored intuition does not seem to give us any guidance on this at all.

Another difficulty in formulating rules of induction concerns the circumstances under which inductive reasoning is defeated by peculiarities of the sample. Discovering that the sample is "biased" can disqualify it. It is easy enough to give examples of this phenomenon. For instance, suppose we want to determine the proportion of voters in Indianapolis, who will vote for the Republican gubernatorial candidate in the next election, and we do this by polling a randomly chosen sample of voters. We find that a startling 87 percent of them intend to vote Republican. Prima facie, that gives us a reason for thinking that approximately 87 percent of all voters will vote for the Republican candidate. But if we then discover that, purely by chance, our sample consisted exclusively of voters in their twenties, that would defeat the reasoning. It is easy to illustrate such "fair sample defeaters", but it is much harder to give a general characterization of them. Again, untutored intuition tends to lead us astray.

These difficulties in formulating correct principles of inductive reasoning illustrate that interesting epistemological problems remain even if we dismiss the Humean problem of answering the skeptic. We would like to have an accurate description of the epistemic norms governing induction, and we would like to know whether these norms are fundamental to our system of reasons and reasoning or whether they are derived from simpler and more basic epistemic norms.

---

19. For a fuller discussion of projectibility and the unprojectibility of disjunctions, see Pollock [198?c].

4. Theories of Knowledge

The preceding brief discussion of different areas of knowledge illustrates some of the epistemological problems that have excited philosophical interest in those areas. Each area has its own unique problems, and although there may be similarities between the problems that arise in different areas, the differences are as important as the similarities. On the other hand, there are also more general epistemological problems that arise in all areas of knowledge. These concern the nature and legitimacy of defeasible reasoning, the issue of whether knowledge has "foundations", the source of epistemic norms, and so on. We can describe broad categories of epistemological theories in terms of the solutions they propose to these general problems. Theories of knowledge can be classified in several different ways. First, we can distinguish between "doxastic" and "nondoxastic" theories.

4.1 Doxastic Theories

Until quite recently, it was customarily assumed by epistemologists that the justifiability of a belief is a function exclusively of what beliefs one holds—of one's "doxastic state". To say this is to say that if one holds precisely the same beliefs in two possible circumstances, then no matter how those circumstances differ with respect to things other than what one believes, there will be no difference in what beliefs are justified under those circumstances. I will call this the *doxastic assumption*, and an epistemological theory conforming to this assumption will be called a *doxastic theory*. The doxastic assumption is a very natural one, and no one even considered denying it until fairly recently. The rationale for it is something like the following: all our information about the world is encapsulated in beliefs. It seems that in deciding what to believe, we *cannot* take account of anything except insofar as we have beliefs about it. Consequently, nothing can enter into the determination of epistemic justification except our beliefs. Thus all an epistemological theory can do is tell us how our overall doxastic state determines which of our beliefs can be justified.[20]

The general category of doxastic theories is exhausted by two mutually exclusive subcategories—the foundations theories and the coherence theories.

---

20. This objection to nondoxastic theories is raised by Michael Williams [1977]. It is also pressed by Laurence Bonjour [1978], 10ff. Sosa [1981] mentions the objection, but dismisses it.

4.1.1   *Foundations Theories*

Foundations theories are distinguished by the view that knowledge has "foundations". The foundations theorist begins with the psychological observation that all knowledge comes to us through our senses. Our senses provide our only contact with the world around us. Our simplest beliefs about the world are in direct response to sensory input, and then we reason from those simple beliefs to more complicated beliefs (for example, inductive generalizations) that cannot be acquired on the basis of single instances of sense perception. This psychological picture of belief formation suggests a parallel philosophical account of epistemic justification according to which those simple beliefs resulting directly from sense perception form an epistemological foundation and all other beliefs must be justified ultimately by appeal to these *epistemologically basic beliefs*. The basic beliefs themselves are not supposed to stand in need of justification. They are in some sense "self-justifying". One is automatically justified in such a belief merely by virtue of having it. It is typically proposed that epistemologically basic beliefs are beliefs reporting the contents of perceptual states, for example, "There is a red rectangular blob in the upper left-hand corner of my visual field."

To complete this picture and build a concrete foundations theory, two things are needed. First, we must have an account of the epistemologically basic beliefs. This must include an account of which beliefs are epistemologically basic, and an account of the sense in which they are self-justifying. Second, we must have an account of "epistemic ascent"—the way in which nonbasic beliefs are justified by appeal to basic beliefs. A number of different answers have been proposed for each of these questions, and they will be examined in detail in the next chapter.

4.1.2   *Coherence Theories*

What distinguishes foundations theories from other doxastic theories is that they give some limited class of beliefs (the epistemologically basic beliefs) a privileged role in epistemic justification. The basic beliefs justify other beliefs without standing in need of justification themselves. Coherence theories deny that there is any such privileged class of beliefs. According to coherence theories, the justifiability of a belief is still a function of one's total doxastic state, but all beliefs are on an epistemological par with one another. This is to characterize coherence theories negatively—in terms of what they deny. Positively, a coherence theory owes us an account of what determines whether a belief is justified. If a belief is not justified by its relationship to a privileged class of basic beliefs, then it must be justified by its relationship to other, ordinary, run-of-the-mill beliefs (after all, that's all there are). Those beliefs are justified by their relationship to further ordinary beliefs, and so on. Instead of justificatory relations being anchored in a foundation, they must meander in and out through our entire network of beliefs. What makes a belief justified is the way it "coheres" with the rest of one's beliefs. Of course, to make this precise we need a precise account of the coherence relation. Different ways of spelling out coherence yield different coherence theories. These theories will be examined in chapter three.

4.2   *Nondoxastic Theories*

Nondoxastic theories deny the doxastic assumption. Any reasonable epistemological theory will make the justifiability of a belief a function at least partly of what other beliefs one holds, but nondoxastic theories insist that other considerations also enter into the determination of whether a belief can be justified. The naturalness of the doxastic assumption makes it seem initially puzzling how any nondoxastic considerations could be relevant, but one of the main contentions of this book will be that the doxastic assumption is false. It will follow that nondoxastic considerations must be relevant, but it remains puzzling how they can be relevant. Two kinds of answers have been proposed for this question. They are reflected by the internalism/externalism distinction.

4.2.1   *Internalism*

Foundationalism takes as its starting point the observation that our knowledge of the world comes to us through perception, broadly construed, and attempts to accommodate that by positing the existence of self-justifying epistemologically basic beliefs reporting our perceptual states. I will argue that all foundations theories are false for the simple reason that we rarely have any epistemologically basic beliefs, and never have enough to provide a foundation for the rest of our knowledge. That can be taken to motivate coherence theories, which give no special place to beliefs pertaining to perception. But I will argue that all coherence theories fail for a related reason—they are unable to accommodate perception as the basic source of our knowledge of the world. In determining whether a belief is justified, importance must be attached to perceptual states, but this cannot be accomplished by looking at *beliefs about* perceptual states. This suggests that justification must be partly a function of the perceptual states themselves and not just a function of our beliefs about the perceptual states. This sort of view is called *direct realism*, and a version of direct realism will be defended in this book.

The intuition behind the doxastic assumption is that in deciding what to believe, we cannot take account of anything except insofar as we have beliefs about it. That has to be wrong because the only kinds of doxastic theories are foundations theories and coherence theories, and they are all false. Explaining how the doxastic assumption goes wrong will occupy a large part of chapter five. I will not try to give the details here, but the general idea will be that we do not literally "decide" what to believe. That is to over-intellectualize the process of belief acquisition. Belief acquisition is determined by cognitive processes that have access to more than just our beliefs. Beliefs and perceptual states are alike in being "internal states". These are, roughly, states of ourselves to which we have "direct access", and our cognitive processes can appeal to internal states in general—not just to beliefs. This suggests that the justifiability of a belief should be a function of our internal states. This is the thesis of *internalism*. Beliefs are internal states, so doxastic theories are internalist theories, but there are also internalist theories that appeal to more than what we believe so not all internalist theories are doxastic theories.

The idea behind internalism is that the justifiedness of a belief is determined by whether it was arrived at or is currently sustained by "correct cognitive processes". The view is that being justified in holding a belief consists of conforming to epistemic norms, where the latter tell you "how to" acquire new beliefs and reject old ones. In other words, epistemic norms describe which cognitive processes are correct and which are incorrect, and being justified consists of "making the right moves". The internalist makes the further assumption that the correctness of an epistemic move (a cognitive process) is an inherent feature of it. For example, it might be claimed that reasoning in accordance with *modus ponens* is always correct, whereas arriving at beliefs through wishful thinking is always incorrect. This is implied by the claim that the justifiability of a belief is a function of one's internal states, because what that means is that we can vary everything about the situation other than the internal states without affecting which beliefs are justifiable. In particular, varying contingent properties of the cognitive processes themselves will not affect whether a belief is justified. This is might be called *cognitive essentialism*. According to cognitive essentialism, the epistemic correctness of a cognitive process is an essential feature of that process and is not affected by contingent facts such as the reliability of the process in the actual world.

I have defined internalism in terms of the notion of an internal state, but that notion stands in need of considerable clarification. That will be undertaken in chapter five.

4.2.2 *Externalism*

Externalism is the denial of internalism. According to externalism, more than just the internal states of the believer enter into the justification of beliefs. A wide variety of externalist theories are possible. What we might call *process externalism* agrees with the internalist that the epistemic worth of a belief should be determined by the cognitive processes from which it issues, but it denies cognitive essentialism according to which the correctness of a cognitive process is an essential property of it. It insists instead that the same cognitive process could be correct in some circumstances and incorrect in others. A view of this sort is represented by the *process reliabilist* who proposes that cognitive processes should be evaluated in terms of their reliability in producing true beliefs.

Reliabilist theories stand in marked contrast to more traditional epistemological theories. The reliability of a cognitive process is a contingent matter. For example, a cognitive process on which we place great reliance is color vision. Color vision is reasonably reliable in the normal environment of earth-bound human beings. But if we lived in an environment in which the colors of our light sources varied erratically, color vision would be unreliable. The reliability of a cognitive process cannot be assessed a priori. It depends upon contingent matters of fact. Thus reliabilism makes epistemic justification turn on contingent matters of fact. Cognitive essentialism is false on this view.

A different kind of externalist theory is *probabilism*, which assesses beliefs in terms of their probability of being true. Probabilism makes no explicit appeal to the cognitive pedigree of a belief, although the probability of a belief being true can of course be indirectly influenced by the cognitive processes from which it derives. Probabilism has been quite influential in the philosophy of science, where it is part of what is called 'Bayesian epistemology'. It has had little influence on epistemology outside of the philosophy of science, but it deserves a careful discussion and will be treated at length in chapter four.

One of the attractions of externalist theories is that they hold out promise for integrating epistemic norms into a naturalistic picture of man. Contemporary philosophers have been attracted by the conception of man as a creature of the world—a biological machine that thinks. Epistemic norms should emerge from his psychological construction, but their very normativity has seemed to make them resistant to such an account. Philosophers raised on the naturalistic fallacy in ethics are prone to suppose that naturalistic theories of normative concepts are impossible. But if epistemic relations can be reduced to considerations of probability or reliability, or to some other naturalistic concept, this obstacle dissolves. Externalist theories have seemed to provide the only possible candidates for naturalistic reductions of epistemic norms, so this has made them attractive in the eyes of many philosophers.

Externalist theories are automatically nondoxastic theories. That is, they take the justifiability of a belief to be a function of more than just one's total doxastic state. This will prove to be a source of difficulty for externalist theories. I will argue that nondoxastic internalist theories can escape the objection that in deciding what to believe, you cannot take account of anything except insofar as you have beliefs about it. They can do that by maintaining that in the requisite sense you can take account of other internal states. But you cannot similarly take account of external states, and that will prove to be the ultimate downfall of externalism. But this cannot be argued convincingly until chapter five.

4.3   Plan of the Book

The categories of epistemological theories are related to each other as follows:

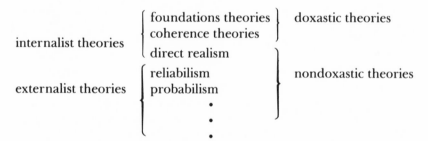

The plan of the rest of this book is as follows: Chapter two will attempt to construct the most plausible kind of foundations theory possible. The ultimate conclusion of chapter two will be that all foundations theories are false. If all foundations theories are false but the doxastic assumption is true then some coherence theory must be true. Chapter three will take up the general discussion of coherence theories, distinguishing between a number of different varieties, narrowing the class of feasible candidates to just a few and then rejecting them all. It follows that all doxastic theories are false. The way in which those theories fail will suggest that the solution may lie in direct realism, and that theory will be sketched at the end of chapter three. Its full defense, however, will await chapter five. Chapter four will discuss several kinds of externalist theories in detail. Reasons will be given for regarding externalist theories as an attractive alternative to more traditional internalist theories, but detailed objections will also be raised to existing externalist theories. These objections will dispose of those externalist theories that have actually been proposed in the literature, but the possibility will remain that some other kind of externalist theory might be true. Chapter five will attempt to tie it all together. Chapter five will explore the nature of epistemic norms, and will use the resulting account to propound a general refutation of externalism and a defense of direct realism. It will be urged that a proper understanding of epistemic norms makes them amenable to a naturalistic account, but not an externalist account. We will thus be led to a kind of naturalistic internalism.

2

FOUNDATIONS THEORIES

1. Motivation

U NTIL QUITE RECENTLY, the most popular epistemological theories
were all foundations theories.[1] Foundations theories are distinguished from other doxastic theories by the fact that they take a
limited class of "epistemologically basic" beliefs to have a privileged
epistemic status. It is supposed that basic beliefs do not stand in need
of justification—they are "self-justifying". Nonbasic beliefs, on the
other hand, are all supposed to be justified by appeal to basic beliefs.
Thus the basic beliefs provide a foundation for epistemic justification.

The simple motivation for foundations theories is the psychological
observation that we have various ways of sensing the world, and all
knowledge comes to us via those senses. The foundationalist takes this
to mean that our senses provide us with what are then identified as
epistemologically basic beliefs. We arrive at other beliefs by reasoning
(construed broadly). Reasoning, it seems, can only justify us in holding a belief if we are already justified in holding the beliefs from
which we reason, so reasoning cannot provide an ultimate source of
justification. Only perception can do that. We thus acquire the picture
of our beliefs forming a kind of pyramid, with the basic beliefs
provided by perception forming the foundation, and all other justified beliefs being supported by reasoning that traces back ultimately
to the basic beliefs (see Fig. 2.1).

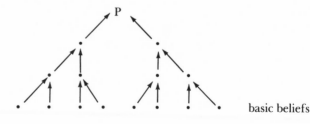

basic beliefs

Figure 2.1

1. Examples of foundations theories can be found in Rudolf Carnap [1967], C. I.
Lewis [1946], Nelson Goodman [1951], Roderick Chisholm [1966], [1977], and [1981],
and in my [1974].

26

The foundationalist picture seems to derive rather directly from psychological truisms, and this gives it considerable force. But the picture must be filled out in two respects before we have anything that deserves to be regarded as a concrete epistemological theory. First, we must know more about the basic beliefs. What kinds of beliefs are basic, and what suits them for such a privileged role? Second, we must know more about the way nonbasic beliefs are supported through reasoning from the basic beliefs. These two broad topics will be the subjects of the next two sections.

2. Basic Beliefs

It is the existence of epistemologically basic beliefs that distinguishes foundations theories from coherence theories. Basic beliefs must be justified independently of reasoning—if a belief can only be justified through reasoning, its justification is dependent on the justification of the beliefs from which the reasoning proceeds, and hence, by definition, it is not a basic belief. It seems that the only beliefs that are not held on the basis of reasoning are those held directly on the basis of various kinds of perception. Thus basic beliefs must be perceptual beliefs, in a sense yet to be made precise. But if basic beliefs are to provide a foundation, they must themselves have a secure epistemic status. Can such a status be granted to perceptual beliefs?

The beliefs we normally regard as the immediate result of perception are beliefs about physical objects. For example, I see that the door is open, I hear someone climbing the stairs, I smell the fish frying, I feel (proprioceptively sense) that my fist is clenched, and so on. An undeniable feature of such beliefs is that they can be mistaken. At the very least, we can be fooled by unusual perceptual environments. For example, if I see a red shirt in green light I may think it is black. Furthermore, our perceptual beliefs are strongly influenced by our expectations. If I expect to see my brother sitting behind his desk, I may (at least momentarily) think I do see him if his chair is occupied by someone who resembles him only vaguely. There are many possible sources of perceptual error. Ordinary perceptual beliefs cannot be taken for granted. If they are fallible, it seems that they stand as much in need of justification as any other beliefs, and hence cannot provide the stopping point for justificatory appeals.

The traditional response of the foundationalist has been to deny that basic beliefs are *ordinary* perceptual beliefs. Instead, the foundationalist retreats to a weaker kind of belief. Basic beliefs must be perceptual beliefs *in some sense*, but they need not be beliefs about physical objects. I can be mistaken about what color something is, but it is not so obvious that I can be mistaken about what color it *looks to me*. More generally, in perception I have sensory experiences, and these sensory experiences lead me to have beliefs about my physical surroundings. I can be wrong about those surroundings, but can I be wrong about the character of my sensory experiences? If not, we might reasonably regard beliefs about the latter as basic, and take beliefs about physical objects to be supported only indirectly, by reasoning from beliefs about our sensory experiences.

It is useful to have some convenient terminology for describing the character of our sensory experiences. An artificial terminology that has acquired some currency in contemporary epistemology is the "appeared to" terminology. If, associated with a state of affairs P, there is a kind of sensory experience one standardly has when one is in that state of affairs, we can refer to that sensory experience as *being appeared to as if P*. Thus I can talk about being appeared to as if there is something red before me. Sometimes there will be a convenient adverbial locution that will allow us to shorten the description and say things like, "I am appeared to redly". A few philosophers have advanced complicated theoretical rationales for adopting this way of describing the character of sensory experience,[2] but I do not mean to endorse any such rationale here. For me, it is just a convenient way of talking.

The suggestion is that basic beliefs are beliefs about ways of being appeared to—"appearance beliefs" for short. This is motivated by the observation that the only other candidates for epistemologically basic beliefs—perceptual beliefs about physical objects—can be mistaken and thus seem to stand in need of justification themselves and cannot be epistemologically basic. This motivation needs to be examined more carefully. It involves the presumption that if a belief can be mistaken then it is not a basic belief, and also the presumption that appearance beliefs cannot be mistaken. Either of these presumptions could be denied. For a foundations theory to work, the class of basic beliefs must satisfy two conditions: (1) there must be enough basic beliefs to provide a foundation for all other justified beliefs, and (2) the basic beliefs must have a secure status that does not require them to be justified by appeal to further justified beliefs. This second condition might be formulated by saying that basic beliefs must be *self-justifying* in the sense that one can be justified in holding such a belief merely by virtue of the fact that one does hold it—one does not need an independent reason for holding a basic belief. The concept of a self-justifying belief can be made more precise in either of two ways. The simplest concept of self-justification is that of an "incorrigibly justified" belief:

2. See Roderick Chisholm [1957] and Michael Tye [1984].

DEFINITION:

A belief is *incorrigibly justified* for a person S if and only if it is impossible for S to hold the belief but be unjustified in doing so.

Few beliefs are incorrigibly justified. It is quite possible to believe, for no reason at all, and in the face of considerable evidence to the contrary, that there is a book before me. It would be unusual to hold that belief under those circumstances, but it would not be impossible, and if I were perverse enough to do so then the belief would not be justified. Thus the belief that there is a book before me is not incorrigibly justified. Similar reasoning will establish that most beliefs fail to be incorrigibly justified, but perhaps a few will slip through the net of the argument. Among these might be appearance beliefs. We will return to this question shortly.

If basic beliefs are incorrigibly justified then they provide the firmest possible foundation for the justification of other beliefs. That is the attraction of the concept of incorrigible justification. But incorrigible justification is more than is needed for basic beliefs. Basic beliefs are beliefs from which justification starts, and thus it must be *possible* to be justified in holding a basic belief without having a reason for it, but it need not be the case that one is *always* justified in holding such a belief. There must be a presumption in favor of justification, so that in the face of no counter-evidence one is justified in holding a basic belief, but this does not preclude the possibility that one's justification can be defeated by appropriate counter-evidence. In other words, one must be able to hold basic beliefs justifiably without having reasons for them, but reasons could still be relevant in a negative way by making one unjustified in holding such a belief when he has a reason for thinking it false. This is captured by the following definition:

DEFINITION:

A belief is *prima facie justified* for a person S if and only if it is only possible for S to hold the belief unjustifiedly if he has reason for thinking he should not hold the belief (equivalently, it is necessarily true that if S holds the belief and has no reason for thinking he should not then he is justified in holding the belief).[3]

When we have a belief, there is something that we believe. Objects of belief are called "propositions". The nature of propositions is a

3. This definition must be supplemented with an explanation of what counts as a reason for thinking S should not hold a belief P. At the very least, anything that is a reason for S to believe ~P despite the fact that he currently believes P is such a reason. More generally, I would suggest that something is a reason for S to think he should not believe P just in case, when conjoined with the fact that S does believe P, it yields a reason for doubting that S would not believe P unless P were true.

matter of philosophical dispute, and for that reason I tried to avoid talking about them in writing this book. But I found that very awkward stylistically, so I have capitulated and will make reference to propositions in talking about beliefs. As I use the term, propositions are just possible objects of belief. I make no substantive assumptions about the nature of propositions here, and I believe that at considerable stylistic expense, all reference to propositions in this book could be replaced by talk of "possible beliefs". Having said that, I will now allow myself free use of propositions. I will call the object of an epistemologically basic belief "an epistemologically basic proposition", and I will say that a proposition is incorrigibly justified or prima facie justified just in case belief in that proposition would be incorrigibly justified or prima facie justified.

I have made the abstract point that if basic beliefs are to provide a foundation for knowledge then they must be self-justifying, in the sense either of being incorrigibly justified or prima facie justified. But is there any reason to expect some beliefs to have such a status? What could make a belief self-justifying? The most common answer has been that some beliefs *cannot be mistaken*—if you hold such a belief then it follows logically that the belief is true. Such beliefs are said to be "incorrigible". The most common definition of incorrigibility is as follows:

PROVISIONAL DEFINITION:
A belief is *incorrigible* for a person S if and only if it is impossible for S to hold the belief and be wrong.

Ordinary beliefs are not incorrigible. Just as I can be unjustified in believing that there is a book before me, it is quite possible for me to believe that there is a book before me when there is none, so my belief that there is a book before me is neither incorrigibly justified nor incorrigible. It has seemed to many philosophers, however, that appearance beliefs are incorrigible. It has been urged that such beliefs cannot be mistaken. The simple motivation for this claim lies in the difficulty of imagining what could possibly show that one is wrong in thinking, for instance, that he is appeared to redly. It seems that other people can have various kinds of evidence for thinking that I am or am not appeared to redly, but that evidence cannot be relevant for me. *I* can tell, just by reflecting on the matter, whether I am appeared to redly.

People are persuaded by this kind of reasoning, but it does not constitute an argument. It really amounts to no more than an assertion that such beliefs are incorrigible. Nevertheless, it illustrates the intuitive appeal that that idea has. Regardless of whether we ultimately decide that appearance beliefs are incorrigible, one must acknowledge and be prepared to explain the intuitive pull of that idea.

The methodological attractiveness of incorrigibility is that it seems to offer an explanation for how basic beliefs could be self-justifying. If a belief cannot possibly be false, then it is apt to seem that you have the best possible justification for holding it. What more could you want? But this is misleading. It is now generally recognized that the above definition of incorrigibility includes beliefs that we do not want to regard as self-justifying. Consider any necessary truth P. For instance, P might be some complicated theorem of mathematics. Now consider a student who is trying to solve a problem on an exam. He has never seen this theorem, has no reason to believe it, and in fact the theorem is counter-intuitive. But it occurs to him that if the theorem were true then he could solve his problem, so wishful thinking leads him to believe it. Clearly, he is not justified in this belief. A person is not automatically justified in believing a mathematical truth if he believes it for no reason. We need reasons for believing principles of mathematics just as much as we do for believing contingent truths. But it is impossible to believe a mathematical truth and be wrong. Because mathematical truths are necessarily true, it is also necessarily true that if one believes a mathematical truth then one is right. So by the provisional definition, belief in any mathematical truth is incorrigible.

Incorrigibility, defined as above, does not guarantee that a belief is self-justifying. The difficulty is that the definition does not capture the idea of it being impossible for us to be mistaken about P. We want it to be impossible for us to be mistaken about *whether* P is true. In other words, believing P should guarantee that P is true, and believing ~P should guarantee that P is false. Thus I propose to redefine incorrigibility as follows:

DEFINITION:
A proposition P is *incorrigible* for a person S if and only if (1) it is necessarily true that if S believes P then P is true, and (2) it is necessarily true that if S believes ~P then P is false.

This defines incorrigibility for propositions. I will say that a belief is incorrigible just in case it is belief in an incorrigible proposition. This definition captures the idea that belief about whether P is true is a conclusive arbiter of whether P is true. Mathematical truths are not incorrigible in this sense. It remains at least somewhat plausible that appearance beliefs are incorrigible, and it seems reasonable that incorrigibility in this strong sense is sufficient to guarantee incorrigible justification.

If appearance beliefs are incorrigible, that suits them for service as epistemologically basic beliefs, but are they incorrigible? There is no consensus on this issue. There is something intuitively appealing about the thesis of incorrigibility, but there is also something perplexing about the idea that *any* belief could be incorrigible. What could make a belief incorrigible? That requires there to be some kind of strong logical relationship between having the belief and what the belief is about. For ordinary beliefs, holding the belief provides no logical guarantee that it is true, but there might be such a relationship in the case of appearance beliefs. It has occasionally been suggested that the requisite connection is a simple one—there is no difference between the state of being appeared to in a certain way and the state of thinking you are appeared to in that way. According to this view, these are two ways of describing one and the same mental state. We might call this *the identity thesis*. But note that if it is to explain both parts of the definition of incorrigibility, the identity thesis might include a second identity alleging that the state of not being appeared to in a certain way is the same state as that of thinking you are not appeared to in that way. Unfortunately, this putative identity is totally implausible. When, for example, you are not appeared to redly, you rarely have any thoughts about the matter, and so you can be in the state of not being appeared to redly without thinking that you are, and hence these must be two different states.

The identity thesis is false, but its failure suggests a more conservative hypothesis about the origin of incorrigibility. It would suffice for incorrigibility if the state of thinking that one is appeared to in a certain way merely *contained* the state of being appeared to in that way as part of it, and similarly for thinking that one is not appeared to in that way. Then one could not think one was appeared to in a certain way without being appeared to in that way. This *containment thesis* is not implausible. One way of defending the containment thesis is to urge that in order for one to think he is appeared to in a certain way he must focus his attention mentally on that way of being appeared to, and when he does that he *is* appeared to in that way. In other words, in the kind of appearance belief that is incorrigible one is appeared to in a way that involves a kind of mental demonstrative reference wherein he focuses his attention on some feature of his sensory experience and then thinks to himself, "I am appeared to *that* way". A necessary condition for one to be able to have the latter belief is that his sensory experience exhibits the feature to which he is attending, so it seems his belief cannot be mistaken. He cannot think he is appeared to in that way without being appeared to in that way, and hence the belief is incorrigible.

At one time I found this reasoning convincing,[4] but now it seems to me to be wrong. One difficulty is that the most it establishes is incorrigibility in the sense of the original, provisional, definition. It purports to show that you are appeared to in a certain way if you think you are, but it is of no help in showing that you are *not* appeared to in that way if you think you are not, and both of these are required for incorrigibility.[5]

I doubt that the argument is even successful in showing that you cannot be wrong in thinking you are appeared to in a certain way. The argument appeals to what I have called "mental demonstrative reference". In ordinary demonstrative reference, you can purport to refer to something that is not there, for example, Macbeth can purport to refer demonstratively to the putative dagger. Why should the fact that you purport to refer demonstratively to a way of being appeared to guarantee that, unlike the ordinary case of demonstrative reference, you really are appeared to in that way? There is an answer to this question, but I think it is mistaken. The answer is that your purporting to refer demonstratively to a way of being appeared to does guarantee something—namely, that you have a mental representation of that way of being appeared to. And it is apt to seem that the mental representation of the way of being appeared to is the same thing as the way of being appeared to—the way of being appeared to is self-representing. This, it may be claimed, is why you cannot be wrong in thinking you are appeared to in that way. But are ways of being appeared to self-representing? That is, can you think of a way of being appeared to simply by *being* appeared to in that way? It seems not, for the simple reason that you are normally unaware of being appeared to in a particular way when you are appeared to in that way. In such a case you are appeared to in that way without having the thought that you are, so being appeared to in that way cannot constitute thinking about that way of being appeared to. What this shows is that in ordinary perception you do not think about the way of being appeared to just by being appeared to in that way—you do it by being appeared to in that way and *thinking about it* in the way you can introspectively think about ways of being appeared to when you are appeared to in those ways. But this is now trivial. There is nothing self-representing here.

I have surveyed the major arguments that have actually been deployed in an attempt to show appearance beliefs to be incorrigible.

---

4. I argued in this way in Pollock [1974]. Moritz Schlick [1959] made remarks that at least suggest this argument.
5. I owe this point to James van Cleve, in conversation.

The arguments do not withstand scrutiny, but the lack of good arguments does not establish that such beliefs are not incorrigible. They might be incorrigible anyway. Most philosophers who have claimed that appearance beliefs are incorrigible have done so without argument, on the grounds that it just seems right that appearance beliefs cannot be mistaken.

Despite its popularity, the incorrigibility of appearance beliefs has also been denied rather frequently. There are two arguments that are sometimes given against incorrigibility. The first is the "super-electroencephalograph argument".[6] Suppose brain physiologists located that part of the brain whose neural activation constitutes a person's being appeared to redly, and they created a super-electroencephalograph that monitored that region of the brain. Suppose then that one of these brain physiologists thought he was being appeared to redly, but his colleagues were monitoring his brain and assured him that he was not. Assuming that the evidence for the reliability of the super-electroencephalograph was good enough, would it not be unreasonable for him to insist that he really was being appeared to redly and the super-electroencephalograph was wrong? This is intended to show that the belief that one is appeared to redly is not incorrigibly justified and hence not incorrigible. But the argument is question-begging. It would only be unreasonable for the scientist to continue to insist that he was appeared to redly if such beliefs were not incorrigibly justified, and that is the very question at issue. *Perhaps* such insistence would be unreasonable, but we need more of an argument to establish this.

The second argument against incorrigibility can be traced to Wilfrid Sellars [1963]. According to Sellars, to say that a person is appeared to redly is to say that he is appeared to in the way one is normally appeared to in the presence of red objects. But how red objects appear to a person is a contingent matter that can only be discovered inductively. Thus, rather than being incorrigible, the belief that one is appeared to redly is based upon induction and prior knowledge of physical objects. The standard response to this argument is due to Roderick Chisholm [1957], and consists of distinguishing between *comparative* and *noncomparative* appearance judgments. Comparative appearance judgments classify the way one is appeared to as being the way one is normally appeared to under some objectively describable circumstances. It is clear that many appearance judgments are comparative, but it seems that the very possibility of comparative appearance judgments presupposes our ability to make noncomparative appearance judgments. In order to know that I am appeared to in the way I am normally appeared to when I see

6. This argument is, apparently, due to David Armstrong.

something red, I must be able to tell how I am appeared to, I must know (inductively) how I am normally appeared to when I see something red, and then I must judge that these are the same. Being able to tell how I am appeared to, in this sense, is to be able to make a noncomparative judgment. (If it were to make a comparative judgment, then each comparative judgment would presuppose a prior comparative judgment, and we would have an infinite regress.) Sellars' argument against incorrigibility only applies to comparative appearance judgments, and the obvious response is that the foundationalist only means to be claiming that noncomparative appearance judgments are epistemologically basic.

Attacks on foundationalism have tended to focus on incorrigibility,[7] but foundationalism does not require incorrigibility. What foundationalism requires is self-justification, which is weaker than incorrigibility. The attraction of incorrigibility is that it offers an explanation for why certain kinds of beliefs might be self-justifying. But even if we were to decide that epistemologically basic beliefs are not incorrigible, it might still be possible to hold that they are self-justifying for some other reason.

It can be argued that a proposition and its negation could not both be incorrigibly justified without the proposition being incorrigible: suppose P is not incorrigible for S. This means that it is either possible for S to believe P and be wrong or possible for S to believe ~P and be wrong. Suppose it is the former (the latter case being analogous). S could then discover inductively that there are certain kinds of circumstances under which he has a propensity to believe P and be wrong (just as we discover that under certain kinds of circumstances objects tend not to be the colors they look to us). Then if S believes P but knows he is in such circumstances, it seems he is unjustified in believing P, and hence that belief is not incorrigibly justified. Note, however, that the belief might still be prima facie justified. What makes justification fail in this example is that S has a reason for thinking he should not believe P, and it was precisely to accommodate such "defeaters" that we were led to the concept of prima facie justification.

If we make the assumptions that the negation of an epistemologically basic proposition is itself epistemologically basic, and all epistemologically basic propositions have the same fundamental epistemic status, then it follows that if epistemologically basic beliefs are not incorrigible then they must be only prima facie justified. Thus a possible, and somewhat attractive, version of foundationalism posits

7. Such attacks have been pressed by both Keith Lehrer [1974] and Richard Rorty [1979].

the existence of prima facie justified epistemologically basic beliefs. Such a theory should be more appealing to those who are suspicious of incorrigibility. The theory does have a weakness, however, that is not present in more traditional incorrigibility theories. Incorrigibility provides an *explanation* for why epistemologically basic beliefs are self-justifying, but if we take epistemologically basic beliefs to be merely prima facie justified then we are just positing self-justification without any explanation. Furthermore, prima facie justification can seem puzzling. How could any belief be prima facie justified? What could confer such a status on a belief? That seems mysterious and in need of explanation.

Foundationalism requires that there be self-justifying epistemologically basic beliefs. We have not resolved the question whether there are any beliefs of that nature, but we have clarified the logical geography of the concept of self-justification and prepared the way for a more definitive discussion that will occur in section five. Before undertaking that discussion, however, it is convenient to investigate the matter of epistemic ascent.

3. Epistemic Ascent

Even if there were no difficulty regarding epistemologically basic beliefs, the problem would remain of getting from them to other justified beliefs. Nonbasic beliefs are justified by reasoning from basic beliefs. Reasoning proceeds in terms of reasons. We can define:

DEFINITION:
A belief P is a *reason* for a person S to believe Q if and only if it is logically possible for S to become justified in believing Q by believing it on the basis of P.

This definition appeals to the psychological relation of holding one belief on the basis of another. This is called *the basing relation*. The basing relation is important in epistemology. To be justified in believing something it is not sufficient merely to *have* a good reason for believing it. One could have a good reason at one's disposal but never make the connection. Suppose, for instance, that you are giving a mathematical proof. At a certain point you get stuck. You want to derive a particular intermediate conclusion, but you cannot see how to do it. In despair, you just write it down and think to yourself, "That's got to be true." In fact, the conclusion follows from two earlier lines by *modus ponens*, but you have overlooked that. Surely, you are not justified in believing the conclusion, despite the fact that you have impeccable reasons for it at your disposal. What is lacking is that you do not believe the conclusion *on the basis of* those reasons.

Although the basing relation is of manifest importance to epistemology, it is difficult to say much about it in an a priori way. It is in some loose sense a causal relation, but the mere fact that holding one belief causes a person to hold another is not sufficient to guarantee that he holds the second belief on the basis of the first. Our beliefs can be tied together by all sorts of aberrant causal chains. I might believe that I am going to be late to my class, and that might cause me to run on a slippery sidewalk, lose my footing, and fall down, whereupon I find myself flat on my back looking up at the birds in the tree above me. My belief that I was going to be late to class caused me to have the belief that there were birds in that tree, but I do not believe the latter on the basis of the former. Giving an informative philosophical analysis of the basing relation is what has come to be called *the problem of the basing relation*. At this point it is hard to say anything helpful about it, but when we return to this problem in chapter five we will be able to make some progress with it.

3.1 *Defeasible Reasons*

In chapter one, when we discussed Hume's skeptical argument regarding induction, we encountered the assumption that a reason can only be a good reason for believing its conclusion if it logically entails that conclusion. That has been a common assumption in the history of epistemology. A frequently encountered variant of it has been that reasons must be either entailments or inductive reasons. To my mind one of the most important advances of contemporary epistemology has been the rejection of both of these assumptions and the recognition of reasons that are neither inductive reasons nor logical entailments.[8]

8. The two contemporary epistemologists who have made the most of this are Roderick Chisholm ([1966], [1977], and [1981]), and myself (originally in my Ph.D. dissertation at Berkeley in 1965, then in [1967], [1970], and [1974]). Chisholm and I arrived at this view of reasons independently. I was primarily influenced by the rather sketchy remarks about "criteria" in Wittgenstein [1953]. Chisholm has never acknowledged the existence of undercutting defeaters (see below). It is interesting that defeasible reasoning was discovered independently a few years later by researchers working on artificial intelligence, and has been the subject of a lot of research in that field. They use the terms "default reasoning" and "non-monotonic reasoning" for defeasible reasoning. The original papers were those of Doyle [1979], Reiter [1978] and [1980], and McDermott and Doyle [1980]. A general overview of AI work on non-monotonic reasoning can be found in Winograd [1980] and Doyle [1982]. The AI work is inadequate in the same way that much philosophical work has been inadequate, namely, it cannot accommodate undercutting defeaters.

A reason that does entail its conclusion is a *conclusive* reason. Inductive reasons are nonconclusive reasons, and it will be argued below that there are many other kinds of nonconclusive reasons as well. Let us begin by exploring the logical characteristics of nonconclusive reasons, taking induction to be a paradigm of such a reason. The most important characteristic of nonconclusive reasons is that they are *defeasible*. For instance, inductive evidence creates a rational presumption in favor of a generalization, and in the absence of any other relevant information it can justify belief in the generalization, but the presumption can be *defeated* by various kinds of considerations. Most simply, if we know of lots of A's and they are all B, that can justify us in believing that all A's are B, but if we subsequently encounter even a single A that is not B, all of the previous evidence counts for nothing. We are still justified in believing the evidence that constituted our original reason, but now we have further information that constitutes a *defeater*. Precisely:

DEFINITION:
If P is a reason for S to believe Q, R is a *defeater* for this reason if and only if R is logically consistent with P and (P&R) is not a reason for S to believe Q.

Defeasible reasons are reasons for which there can be defeaters. Such a reason is called a *prima facie reason*.

There are two kinds of defeaters for prima facie reasons. The simplest is a reason for denying the conclusion:

DEFINITION:
If P is a prima facie reason for S to believe Q, R is a *rebutting defeater* for this reason if and only if R is a defeater (for P as a reason for S to believe Q) and R is a reason for S to believe ~Q.

A counterexample to an inductive generalization is a rebutting defeater for the inductive evidence.

It has often been overlooked that there is a second kind of defeater for prima facie reasons. These are defeaters that attack the connection between the reason and the conclusion rather than attacking the conclusion itself. In chapter one I gave the example of a pollster attempting to predict what proportion of residents of Indianapolis will vote for the Republican gubernatorial candidate in the next election. He randomly selects a sample of voters and determines that 87 percent of those polled intend to vote Republican. This gives him a prima facie reason for thinking that approximately 87 percent of all Indianapolis voters will vote Republican. But then it is discovered that purely by chance, his randomly chosen sample turned out to consist exclusively of voters in their twenties. This constitutes a defeater for the inductive reasoning, but it is not a reason for thinking it false that approximately 87 percent of the voters will vote Republican. The discovery is neutral to that question. Instead, it is a reason for denying that we would not have the inductive evidence unless the conclusion were true. The defeater attacks the connection between the evidence and the conclusion rather than attacking the conclusion itself. More generally:

DEFINITION:

If P is a prima facie reason for S to believe Q, R is an *undercutting defeater* for this reason if and only if R is a defeater (for P as a reason for S to believe Q) and R is a reason for S to deny that P would not be true unless Q were true.[9]

The exact connection between defeaters and justified belief is complicated. It might seem, for example, that a necessary condition for a person to believe Q on the basis of a prima facie reason P is that he not believe any defeater for that prima facie reason. But notice that defeaters acquire their status as defeaters by being reasons for other propositions (i.e., for ~Q or for denying that P would not be true unless Q were true), and they might be merely prima facie reasons for those other propositions. If they are merely prima facie reasons and they are defeated, that defeats their action as defeaters. So in other words, there can be defeater defeaters, and defeater defeater defeaters, and so on. Putting this all together is complicated. I will not pursue it here, but I will say a bit more about it in section four.

3.2   *The Problem of Perception*

Thus far I have argued that there are nonconclusive reasons, but the only examples I have given are inductive reasons. I want next to argue that there are other nonconclusive reasons as well. I will do this by focusing on the problem of perception. This is the problem of explaining how we can acquire knowledge of our physical surroundings through sense perception. For instance, we might judge that an object is red because it looks red to us. What justifies our reasoning in this way?

Although I have rejected the idea that the only reasons are conclusive reasons, that supposition played an important historical role in

9. The distinction between rebutting defeaters and undercutting defeaters origi-nates in my [1970] and was explored further in Pollock [1974], where they were called "Type I" and "Type II" defeaters, respectively. Using 'A > B' to symbolize the subjunctive conditional 'B would be true if A were true', an undercutting defeater is a reason for denying (~Q > ~P).

the problem of perception. On that supposition, we could only explain perceptual knowledge by finding logical entailments between the way things look and the way they are. To get from an object's looking red to its being red we would have to find some further premise which, when conjoined with the fact that the object looks red to us, entails that the object is red. Epistemologists in the first half of the twentieth century supposed that the only way such an entailment could arise is from a logical analysis of what it is for an object to be red, where that analysis proceeds in terms of appearances.[10] They believed this because they adopted a particular view of concepts according to which concepts are characterized by definitions stating necessary and sufficient conditions for something to exemplify them. Such definitions state the *truth conditions* of the concepts. It was supposed that, with the exception of some "logically simple" concepts that do not have definitions, the logical nature of a concept is completely given by its definition and all logical properties of a concept must emerge from its definition. In particular, entailments between concepts must arise from the definitions of those concepts. Thus, if there is to be an entailment between something's looking red under some circumstances C and its being red, this must result from the definition of either the concept of something being red or the concept of its looking red. The latter was generally accepted as one of the logically simple concepts in terms of which definitions must ultimately be framed, so it was assumed that the requisite entailments must arise from a correct analysis of the concept of something being red.

The proposal was to solve the problem of perception by finding entailments of the form:

x's looking red to S under circumstances of type C entails that x is red.

If circumstances of type C involve reference to the states of material objects, then this will not solve the problem of perception because it will presuppose some perceptual knowledge in order to obtain other perceptual knowledge. Consequently, circumstances of type C can only involve reference to appearances. As such an entailment was supposed to arise out of the definition of 'red', it followed that there had to be a definition of 'red' that proceeded entirely in terms of appearances. The view that the problem of perception can be solved by finding such definitions is called *phenomenalism*. Phenomenalism was once the predominant theory in epistemology, not because phi-

---

10. See, for example, Rudolf Carnap [1967], C. I. Lewis [1946], and Nelson Goodman [1951].

losophers had concrete phenomenalist analyses to actually propose, but because reasoning like the above convinced them that phenomenalism was the only possible solution to the problem of perception.

Phenomenalism is apt to seem antecedently preposterous. What kind of analysis of material object concepts could possibly be proposed in terms of ways of being appeared to? But phenomenalists had some ingenious proposals to make in this connection. The most sophisticated phenomenalist analysis was that proposed by C. I. Lewis [1946]. His suggestion was that 'x is red' can be analyzed as a conjunction of possibly infinitely many conditionals of the form 'if I were to do A in circumstances C then I would be appeared to R'ly', where R describes some way of being appeared to. For example, such a conditional might tell us that if we look at x under normal lighting conditions then it will look red to us.

There are a number of problems with such a phenomenalist analysis. The most serious difficulty concerns the circumstances C to which the conditionals appeal. The example was 'lighting conditions are normal', but that will not do because these conditionals must be formulated entirely in terms of appearances without making appeal to the states of material objects. The circumstances must be "phenomenal" circumstances in the sense that they are formulated entirely in terms of appearances. If we look seriously for phenomenal circumstances that might do the job, no plausible candidates come to mind. Furthermore, there is a simple argument that seems to show that there can be no phenomenal circumstances that can play the requisite role in a phenomenalist analysis. This is due to Roderick Firth [1950], and it is called *the argument from perceptual relativity*. The argument proceeds by noting that being in circumstances of type C must logically entail that if x is red and I look at it then it will appear red to me. But there can be no phenomenal circumstances that have this entailment. No matter what we propose for C, we can always imagine elaborate conditions under which the putative entailment will be falsified. For example, a person might be wired into a computer that interferes with his perceptual inputs selectively, so that it does not prevent normal perception in most cases, but it does regulate his perceptual experience to the extent of making phenomenal circumstances C hold no matter what is going on around him. If we then place him in a standard sort of situation in which red things fail to look red (e.g., illumination by green light), he may see a red object and it may fail to look red to him. Thus it seems that no such phenomenalist entailments can hold, and hence a phenomenalist analysis is impossible.

The main attraction of phenomenalism was that it offered the prospect of explaining perceptual knowledge within a framework that recognized only conclusive reasons. But once it is acknowledged that at least inductive reasons are nonconclusive reasons, there is little reason for wanting to confine ourselves to such a framework. This suggests that perceptual knowledge might be accommodated by various kinds of inductive reasoning. The simplest kind of inductive reasoning would involve discovering that objects that look red usually are, or perhaps that objects that look red under specifiable circumstances are always red. Then noting that something looks red (under the appropriate circumstances) would give us a reason for thinking it is red. But this kind of reasoning cannot legitimate perceptual knowledge because we could only make such discoveries if we had independent access to the colors of objects and the colors they look to us and could then compare them. We have no ultimate access to the colors of things except via how they appear to us, and it is the legitimation of that inference that is in question in the problem of perception. Thus we would have to already solve the problem of perception before we could confirm such inductive generalizations.

There is, however, another form of inductive reasoning that has seemed to hold out more hope. A kind of induction that is common in everyday life and, in some form, underlies much of science, is what has come to be called 'inference to the best explanation'.[11] Given a set of observations, we often take a hypothesis to be confirmed because it is the best explanation of those observations. For example, if I see dust in the air and the limbs of the trees swaying about outside the window I may infer that it is windy because that is the best explanation for what I see. Similarly, a physicist may infer that most elementary particles are composed of quarks on the grounds that that best explains the interrelationships that have been observed between elementary particles. The confirmation of scientific theories is probably best viewed in terms of inference to the best explanation. There are lots of problems concerning how this form of induction is to be analyzed and made precise, but let us waive those problems for now. It cannot reasonably be denied that they have solutions even if we are not yet in a position to give them.

It looks at first as though it is very easy to reconstruct perceptual knowledge in terms of inference to the best explanation. Under ordinary circumstances, surely the best explanation for why something looks red to us is that it is red! But before we endorse this account too hastily, recall the distinction between comparative and noncomparative appearance judgments. If "looks red" is being used comparatively, then it seems right that the best explanation for an object's looking red is ordinarily that it is red. But comparative

11. See, particularly, Gilbert Harman [1973] and [1980].

judgments about how things look are not epistemologically basic, so this does not secure epistemic ascent from basic beliefs. We must instead focus on noncomparative appearance judgments. If "looks red" is being used noncomparatively, then there is no obvious connection between the concept of looking red and the concept of being red. "That looks red to me" seems to amount to thinking about a particular way things can look and then thinking, "This looks *that way* to me". But why should something's being red count as an explanation for its looking that way to me? Its being green would be just as much of an explanation, which is to say that neither is any explanation at all. More accurately, the object's being red only explains its looking the way it does to me if I already know that that is the way red things ordinarily look to me, but of course, I cannot know that without first acquiring some perceptual knowledge. So despite initial appearances, perceptual knowledge cannot be modeled on this sort of use of inference to the best explanation.

There is another way to approach the problem of perception by using inference to the best explanation. According to what is sometimes called *scientific realism*, we posit the existence of the physical world as the best explanation for why things appear to us as they do.[12] This differs from the previous use of inference to the best explanation by taking perception to involve inference to a global theory of the world rather than just local inferences to, for instance, the color of a particular object. By thus changing the scope of the theory it avoids the earlier logical difficulties. For example, rather than inferring that something is red because it looks red, this account would have us infer much more generally that there is a way things tend to be when they look red to us, and we call that way 'being red'. But the cost of avoiding the logical difficulties is to make the account subject to overwhelming psychological difficulties. The perception of objects is a largely automatic process that does not involve anything like deliberate postulation for the sake of explanation. The main place this makes a difference is to the amount of evidence that is required for a reasonable perceptual judgment. According to scientific realism we are at each point confirming a global theory of the physical world, so before we can even get started reasoning this way we must acquire a great deal of information about how things appear to us on various occasions and what regularities there are in how things appear to us. In fact, however, we rarely take note of how things appear to us, and we almost never remember enough about how things appeared to us on other occasions to formulate generalizations about appearances. Instead, we just automatically make judgments about physical objects

12. Such a view was advocated by Bertrand Russell [1912], pp. 21–4.

as a result of being appeared to in various ways. Nor, it seems, are we doing anything epistemically objectionable by making perceptual judgments in this way. Thus scientific realism imposes unreasonable burdens on rational perceivers.[13]

We turned to induction as a way of accommodating the fact that perceptual knowledge cannot proceed entirely in terms of conclusive reasons. Inductive reasons are the only nonconclusive reasons that are considered uncontroversial in contemporary philosophy, so they provided the obvious candidate for the nonconclusive reasons involved in perceptual knowledge. But it now seems that perceptual knowledge cannot be reconstructed in terms of inductive reasons. If perceptual knowledge requires nonconclusive reasons, and those reasons are not inductive reasons, then it is inescapable that there must be noninductive nonconclusive reasons. And once we have made this admission, an obvious hypothesis is that what justifies our ordinary inference from 'x looks red to me' to 'x is red' is the simple fact that the former is a prima facie reason for the latter. Upon reflection, this seems rather obvious. Normally, we do not hesitate to judge that something is the way it looks to us. We only desist from that inference when we have information that constitutes a defeater. For example, if I see a book and it looks red to me then I will normally judge that it is red. But if I am assured by its author that it is not red, this may give me pause and make me reconsider my judgment. We can account for this by noting that the report of the author constitutes a rebutting defeater for the prima facie reason. Alternatively, if I learn that I am viewing the book under red lights, and I know that red lights can make things look red when they are not, that may also make me withhold judgment about the color of the book. This is because it gives me a reason to doubt that it would not look red to me unless it were, and that is an undercutting defeater for the prima facie reason.

I propose that this is the only way a foundations theory can handle the problem of perception. The epistemic ascent involved in perceptual knowledge must proceed in terms of noninductive prima facie reason. This constitutes more of a "resolution" of the problem of perception than a solution. It does not solve the problem by reducing it to something deeper, but rather eliminates the problem by claiming

13. An objection to scientific realism that may be logically more conclusive emerges from the realization that there is a problem about memory that is analogous to the problem of perception. This problem is discussed at length in section four. As will become apparent then, if we were to attempt to apply scientific realism to the combination of perceptual and memory knowledge, we would not be able to do so because the "data" available to us at any given time would be severely impoverished, never consisting of more than about seven items.

that there is nothing deeper and the inferences involved in perceptual knowledge are primitive constituents of our epistemic framework. This contrasts with traditional attempts, which tried to solve the problem by justifying the inferences on the basis of more complicated arguments proceeding in terms of allegedly simpler kinds of reasons.

Once we have acknowledged the existence of a few noninductive prima facie reasons, other candidates will occur quite naturally. This will be illustrated in section four when we consider the role of memory in reasoning.

3.3 The Possibility of Prima Facie Reasons

I have argued that prima facie reasons play an indispensable role in our ratiocinative framework. Without them, knowledge of the world would be impossible. At the very least, both perception and induction proceed in terms of prima facie reasons, and it is arguable that the same thing is true of memory, a priori knowledge, and moral knowledge.[14] The importance of prima facie reasons is also illustrated by another phenomenon. Gilbert Harman [1973] has called attention to the fact that reasoning can lead not only to the adoption of new beliefs but also to the rejection of old beliefs. If all reasoning proceeded exclusively in terms of conclusive reasons, that would be inexplicable. Conclusive reasons are nondefeasible, so if we are justified in believing P and P gives us a conclusive reason for Q and we come to believe Q on that basis, there is nothing that could rationally make us retract our endorsement of Q except by making us retract our endorsement of P. And if P is also held on the basis of conclusive reasons, the same thing goes for it. Thus if all reasoning were conclusive, nothing could ever rationally commit us to taking anything back (except by retracting some of our initial appearance judgments, which we never or virtually never do). It is the fact that we reason in terms of prima facie reasons, and the latter are defeasible, that explains how reasoning can lead to the rejection of previously held beliefs. Reasoning accomplishes this by producing defeaters for the reasons for which we hold the beliefs. For example, I may justifiably believe that something is red because it looks red to me. I have a justified belief here. But if I then acquire a further belief, namely, that the lighting is peculiar in certain ways, that may justify me in believing a defeater for the original prima facie reason and may have the result that I am no longer justified in believing that the object in question is red. If I am rational, I will then reject that belief.

As important as prima facie reasons are for understanding the

14. For further discussion of this, see my [1974] and [1986].

nature of reasoning and the possibility of knowledge, there is also a major problem concerning prima facie reasons, and this problem makes some philosophers suspicious of their existence despite their seeming indispensability. The problem is to explain how there can be such things as prima facie reasons. This is related to the theory of concepts discussed earlier according to which concepts are individuated by their *truth conditions*. What makes a concept the concept it is are the conditions that must be satisfied for something to exemplify that concept. These conditions comprise its truth conditions. For example, what distinguishes *red* from *blue* is that different conditions must be satisfied for an object to be red than for an object to be blue. This theory of concepts has become almost a dogma of contemporary philosophical logic. The truth condition account of concept individuation is often either identified with or taken to support the claim that concepts have definitions—statements of necessary and sufficient conditions for objects to exemplify those concepts. It is this latter thesis that makes prima facie reasons seem mysterious and has led some philosophers to doubt their existence. If concepts have definitions then it seems that the logical character of a concept must follow from its definition. What makes something a good reason for ascribing a concept to an object must be a function of the logical character of the concept. Thus it seems that an account of our epistemic norms governing the use of a concept must be derivable from the definition of the concept. But there appears to be no way to derive prima facie reasons from a definition. How then can there be such things as prima facie reasons? This is a serious problem that must be faced by the proponent of prima facie reasons. As it seems that any viable form of foundationalism must proceed in terms of prima facie reasons, this problem must be addressed by the defender of foundationalism. Furthermore, we will find as we proceed that prima facie reasons play an indispensable role in some nonfoundationalist theories as well. The problem of explaining how prima facie reasons are possible does not have a simple solution. I will return to it in chapter five where I will propose that the ultimate solution lies in adopting a different theory of the individuation of concepts.

4. Reasoning and Memory

Epistemic ascent proceeds by reasoning, and reasons are the atomic links in reasoning. But it is problematic just how reasons are combined in reasoning to support new beliefs. We need not work out all the details here, but we should explore the matter enough to see what general kind of account a foundationalist might adopt.

Reasoning proceeds by stringing reasons together into arguments. We can think of an argument as a finite sequence of propositions ordered in such a way that for each proposition P in the sequence, either (1) P is epistemologically basic or (2) there is a proposition (or set of propositions) earlier in the sequence that is a reason for P.[15] A person *instantiates* an argument if and only if he believes the propositions comprising the argument and he believes each nonbasic proposition in it on the basis of reasons for it that occur earlier in the argument. Let us say that an argument *supports* a proposition if and only if that proposition is the final proposition in the argument.

What is the connection between arguments and justified belief? It might be supposed that a foundationalist should take belief in P to be justified for a person S if and only if S instantiates an argument supporting P.[16] But this simple proposal fails because it overlooks defeasibility. To illustrate, suppose a person S simultaneously instantiates arguments of each of the forms shown in Figure 2.2, where P_1 and Q_1 are epistemologically basic. The conclusion of the second argument is an undercutting defeater for the second step of the first argument. Under the circumstances, it seems that S is not justified in believing P_3. Of course, that could change if S also instantiates an argument supporting a defeater for some step of the second argument. That would reinstate the first argument.

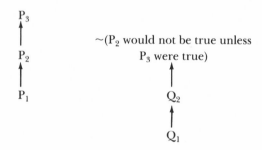

Figure 2.2

To handle defeasibility in a general way, we must recognize that arguments can defeat one another and that a defeated argument can

15. This is probably simplistic in at least one respect. It seems likely that we should allow arguments to contain subsidiary arguments. For example, an argument might contain a subsidiary argument supporting a conditional by conditional proof, or a subsidiary argument supporting a negation by *reductio ad absurdum*. The additional sophistications that this requires are not relevant to the present discussion, so I will ignore them for now.

16. To accommodate belief in epistemologically basic propositions, we can think of such a proposition in isolation as comprising a one-line argument and take this as the limiting case of an argument supporting a proposition.

be reinstated if the arguments defeating it are defeated in turn. We can think of arguments as provisional vehicles of justification, and then give rules for when these provisional vehicles succeed in conferring justification and when they do not. This can be captured by talking about arguments being "undefeated" at different "levels". We can say that every instantiated argument is undefeated at level 0. Among these arguments, some will support defeaters for others. An argument is undefeated at level 1 if and only if it is not defeated by any other arguments. Thus some arguments undefeated at level 0 may be defeated at level 1. Among these may be some of the arguments that defeated other arguments. We can regard the latter as reinstated at level 2. This is captured by saying that an argument is undefeated at level 2 if and only if it is not defeated by any argument undefeated at level 1. In general, an argument is undefeated at a level $n + 1$ if and only if it is not defeated by any argument undefeated at level n. As defeating arguments are themselves defeated or reinstated, an argument may fluctuate between being undefeated at some levels and defeated at others. Only if all the defeating arguments eventually get defeated and stay defeated does an argument justify belief in its conclusion. This can be captured by saying that an argument is *ultimately undefeated* if and only if there is a level beyond which it stays undefeated. The foundationalist can then propose:

S is justified in believing P if and only if S instantiates an ultimately undefeated argument supporting P.[17]

Next I want to discuss a complication that has generally gone unnoticed. Recognition of this complication will fundamentally alter our entire picture of reasoning. We have thus far implicitly adopted a kind of "mental blackboard" picture of reasoning according to which (1) we have an array of interconnected beliefs all available for simultaneous inspection and evaluation and (2) arguments are built out of these beliefs and are evaluated by such inspection. That is the picture normally adopted, but it is unrealistic. To see this, let us begin by distinguishing between thoughts and beliefs. At any given time, we are not thinking about most of the things we believe at that time. We all believe that $2 + 2 = 4$, but this is not something that is likely to have "occurred to" the reader in the past five minutes. It is not something that he has actually *thought*. Thoughts, on the other hand, are what we are occurrently thinking. At any given time we are apt to have many beliefs but few thoughts. It is difficult to hold very many thoughts in mind at one time. In particular, we rarely hold an entire argument

17. We still require an account of when one argument defeats another. That turns out to be more complicated than one might expect, but I will not pursue it here.

(even a simple one) in mind at one time. Psychological evidence indicates that people can hold about seven items in mind at one time. There is some evidence that the number may be even smaller for complex items like complicated propositions.[18]

The term "thought" is normally used to refer to either occurrent beliefs or to a more general class of mental events that includes our entertaining ideas without mentally endorsing them. In the latter sense thoughts may include hypotheses, fears, musings, daydreams, and so on. However, I will restrict my use of the term to occurrent beliefs. So thoughts are beliefs, but most beliefs are not thoughts. Given this distinction, which are involved in arguments and in the determination of justification—beliefs in general or just thoughts? Reasoning is an occurrent process, so it might seem that insofar as justification emerges from reasoning it can only be thoughts that enter into considerations of justification. The trouble with this is that we have too few occurrent thoughts at any one time to be able to construct arguments out of them. Although reasoning is an occurrent process, that does not mean that we occurrently hold an entire argument in mind. Rather, we progress through the argument one step at a time, occurrently holding each step in mind as we come to it but not holding the entire argument in mind. Memory plays an indispensable role in such reasoning, in at least two ways. On the one hand, we employ memory to supply us with premises for arguments. These premises will typically be the conclusions of earlier arguments, but we do not have to rehearse those arguments in order to make new use of their conclusions. We also keep track of the course of an argument by relying upon memory to ensure that the first part (which we are no longer holding in mind) went all right and to alert us when there is a step in the argument for which we subsequently acquire a defeater.

How do these observations about the role of memory in reasoning fit into the foundationalist picture of epistemic justification? I think that the foundationalist must say different things about the different roles played by memory in reasoning. Let us begin with what might be called 'premise memory'. Most of the information at our disposal at any given time is stored in memory and recalled when we need it. What are we to say about the justifiedness of beliefs held on the basis of memory? Reasoning is an occurrent process. It can proceed only in terms of what we occurrently hold in mind. We do not have to hold the entire argument in mind in order for it to justify its conclusion, but we do have to hold each step in mind as we go through it. Thus memory can only contribute premises to an argument insofar as we

18. See W. Kintsch and J. M. Keenan [1973], and W. Kintsch [1974].

occurrently remember those premises. Furthermore, we can have varying degrees of difficulty in recalling beliefs that are stored in memory. If we remember something (hold it in memory) but are unable to occurrently recall it just now, then it can play no role in justifying new beliefs. In other words, only occurrent memory can supply premises for arguments.

Granted that only occurrent memory can supply premises, what are we to say about the justification of those premises and the justification of conclusions inferred from those premises? A common view has been that when we hold a belief on the basis of remembering it, what determines whether the latter belief is justified is the argument we instantiated when we first acquired it.[19] On this picture we have an evolving network of arguments that grows longer and more complex over time. Old arguments are extended as we continue to reason from their conclusions, and new arguments are added as we acquire new basic beliefs and reason from them, but the old arguments do not drop out of the picture just because we are no longer thinking about them. They continue to represent the justificatory structure underlying our beliefs.

Critics of foundationalism commonly associate this picture with foundationalism,[20] but foundationalists need not adopt such a picture and they would be well advised not to. The difficulty with the picture is that it overlooks some important facts about memory. It has already been noted that we can have varying degrees of difficulty recalling things, and our memory is not infallible. Sometimes we "remember" incorrectly. When that happens, what are we to say about the justified-ness of beliefs inferred from the incorrect memories? We do not automatically regard a person as unjustified in holding a belief just because that belief is inferred from false memories. If he has no reason to suspect that his memory is faulty, we regard his behavior as epistemically beyond reproach. This is true even if he is misremembering. For example, consider a person who has all of his memories altered artificially without his knowing it. Is he then unjustified in everything he believes? Surely not. Recall that when we talk about justification we have in mind the reason-guiding sense of justification. If a person has no reason to be suspicious of his apparent memories, then he is doing the best he can if he simply accepts them. Consequently, he is justified. But if he is misremembering, the belief in question is not one that he previously held or for which he previously

19. See Norman Malcolm [1963], pp. 229–30, and Robert Squires [1969]. Of course, we can also come to instantiate new arguments for old beliefs, in which case the source of justification may change, but the view is that that is not what is involved in memory.

20. See Gilbert Harman [1984].

had reasons. This seems to indicate that it is the process of remembering itself that confers justification on the use of a memory in a present argument, and not whatever reasons one may or may not have had for that belief originally.

The only way the foundationalist can allow that the process of remembering can confer justification on a belief is by supposing that memory provides us with epistemologically basic beliefs. *What* is remembered can be a proposition of any sort at all. By definition, epistemologically basic beliefs comprise a privileged subclass of the set of all possible beliefs, so it cannot be true that the proposition remembered is always epistemologically basic. Rather, memory must operate on analogy with sense perception. Sense perception provides us with beliefs about material objects, but according to foundationalism it does so only indirectly by providing us with beliefs about appearances from which we can infer beliefs about material objects. Similarly, if we are to accommodate memory within foundationalism, memory must provide us with beliefs about what we "seem to remember" and then we infer the truth of what are ordinarily regarded as memory beliefs from these apparent memories. The viability of such an account turns in part on whether there is such a psychological state of "seeming to remember" that is analogous to being appeared to in some way or other. Some philosophers have denied that there is any such state,[21] but it is not too hard to see that they are wrong. It is possible to hold the same belief on the basis of memory, or perception, or for no reason at all, and when we hold the belief we can tell introspectively which is the case. In other words, we can discriminate between memory beliefs and other beliefs.[22] But to say this is just to say that memory has an introspectively distinguishable mental characteristic. The mental state so characterized is the state of "seeming to remember". This can be made clearer by considering an example. Imagine that you are trying to quote the first line of a poem. It is on the tip of your tongue, but you cannot quite get it. Finally, a friend tires of watching you squirm and tells you the line. This can have two possible effects. It may jog your memory so that the line comes flooding back and you now remember it clearly. Alternatively, it may fail to jog your memory. You believe your friend when he tells you how the lines goes, but you still do not remember it. In either case you come to have the same occurrent belief about the line, but there is a clear introspectible difference between the two cases. The difference is precisely that in the first case you come to be in the state of seeming

21. Norman Malcolm [1963], pp. 229–30, and Robert Squires [1969].
22. Of course, by 'memory beliefs' I mean 'putative memory beliefs'. I do not mean that we can tell introspectively whether we are correctly remembering what we take ourselves to be remembering.

to remember that the line goes that way, whereas in the second case you have no such recollection. Cases like this show that there is such a psychological state as that of seeming to remember.

Given that there is such a state as seeming to remember, the natural move for the foundationalist is to treat memory as a source of knowledge parallel to sense perception and posit the following "mnemonic" prima facie reason:

'S seems to remember P' is a prima facie reason for S to believe P.

This becomes the foundationalist's explanation for how memory can supply premises for arguments that confer justification on new beliefs. Furthermore, it seems to be the only possible way to integrate premise memory into a foundationalist theory.

What about the other aspects of memory as it is used in reasoning? We were led to the topic of memory by the observation that the mental blackboard picture of reasoning is wrong. We do not hold an entire argument in mind at one time. Rather, we step through it sequentially, holding no more than a few lines at a time in occurrent thought. Insofar as we have to know that the earlier parts of the argument were all right, we must rely upon memory. It is tempting to try to assimilate this use of memory to premise memory in the following way. Suppose we reason through the complicated argument in Figure 2.3 and on that basis come to believe P_n.

As we occurrently step through the ith line of the argument we may occurrently recall nothing earlier than the $i-1$st line. At that point, only memory can certify that the earlier parts of the argument were all right. This suggests that the basis upon which we actually come to believe P_i is not argument (1) at all, but rather a much shorter argument whose first premise is supplied by memory; see argument (2), Figure 2.4. Having inferred P_{i-1}, in order to proceed to P_i all we have to do is remember P_{i-1}. Premise memory certifies P_{i-1}, and then we infer P_i from P_{i-1}. This is what justifies us in coming to believe P_i.

But this is puzzling. It seems to indicate that argument (1) is not doing any work. It is not on the basis of that argument that we become justified in holding the individual beliefs comprising it. That argument represents the historical genesis of the beliefs, but in an important sense it does not represent the dynamics of their justification. The latter is represented by lots of little arguments of the form of argument (2). An apparent problem for this view is that we do not regard argument (1) as irrelevant to our justification. If we discover inadequacies in early stages of argument (1) (e.g., if we acquire a defeater for a prima facie reason used early in argument (1)), we take that to make us unjustified in holding the later beliefs in the argu-

Argument (1)

Figure 2.3

ment. How can it do that if we do not hold those beliefs on the basis of argument (1)?

Argument (1) and argument (2) are both important in understanding the justification of P_i. I will distinguish between them by calling them the *genetic argument* and the *dynamic argument*, respectively. Note that as I am using the term, dynamic arguments do not always begin with apparent memories. They might begin instead, for instance, with an appearance belief and infer a physical-object belief. The important thing about dynamic arguments is that they represent what we are currently thinking. To use a computer metaphor, the dynamic argument is short and fits into "working memory". We can regard the mental blackboard picture as true of dynamic arguments.

The genetic argument and the dynamic argument are both rele-

Argument (2)

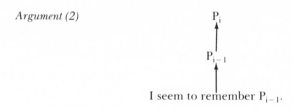

I seem to remember P_{i-1}.

Figure 2.4

vant to justification, but in different ways. The dynamic argument is "positively relevant" in that it tells us what makes us currently justified in believing P_i. The genetic argument is not positively relevant in the same way. If we are no longer able to recall the earlier steps of the genetic argument, it can play no positive role in the justification of our occurrent belief in P_i. On the other hand, the genetic argument is "negatively relevant" to the justification for our occurrently believing P_i, because if (a) we know that the genetic argument does underlies our having come to believe P_i and (b) we acquire a defeater for some step of the genetic argument, we regard that as defeating our justification for P_i.

How can we put these observations together into a coherent account of the relationship between reasoning and justification? Earlier it was suggested that justification can be identified with holding a belief on the basis of an ultimately undefeated argument. But justification *cannot* be identified with holding a belief on the basis of an ultimately undefeated genetic argument. The genetic argument for a belief may stretch back over a period of years as you slowly accumulate the diverse premises. If you can no longer recall the arguments for some of those premises (which is quite likely), then if you presently acquire a defeater for one of those early steps in the argument but do not realize that it is a defeater or do not in any way appreciate its relevance to P_i, we would not regard the acquisition of that defeater as making it unreasonable for you to believe P_i. (Intuitively, this is because you currently believe P_i on the basis of the dynamic argument rather than the genetic argument.) Consequently, it is not a necessary condition for justified belief in P_i that your genetic argument for P_i be ultimately undefeated.

Can we instead identify justification with holding a belief on the basis of an ultimately undefeated dynamic argument? We can once we recognize that genetic arguments play a role in determining whether a dynamic argument based on memory is undefeated. Such a dynamic argument proceeds in terms of the following mnemonic prima facie reason:

'I seem to remember P' is a prima facie reason for me to believe P.

It is obvious upon reflection that one kind of defeater for this prima facie reason is any reason for thinking that I do not actually remember P. A necessary condition for remembering P is that one originally knew P. If, for instance, my original belief in P was unjustified, but was retained in memory, then even though I now *seem* to remember P, it would be incorrect to describe me now as remembering P. Thus, any reason for thinking that I did not originally know P is also a reason for thinking that I do not remember P now. I did not originally know P if there is a true undefeated defeater for some step of the reasoning (i.e., the genetic argument) underlying my belief in P. Thus the following is a defeater for the mnemonic prima facie reason:

Q is true, and Q is a defeater for some step of my genetic argument for P.[23]

I will call this "the genetic defeater". The concepts of a defeater and a genetic argument seem like technical philosophical concepts not shared by the man in the street. On this ground, it might be doubted that ordinary people actually have beliefs of the form of the genetic defeater. But I think that they do. They could not formulate them using this technical terminology, but they could formulate them less clearly by saying things like, "In coming to believe P in the first place I assumed A and concluded B, but because Q is true, I should not have done that." I do not think there is anything psychologically unrealistic about supposing that people often have thoughts they could formulate in such a way as this, and these are the thoughts expressed more precisely by the above formulation of the genetic defeater.

My proposal is that, on a foundationalist picture, justification should be identified with holding a belief on the basis of an ultimately undefeated dynamic argument. What I mean by this is that the arguments to which we appeal in determining whether a dynamic argument is ultimately undefeated must all be in working memory at the same time as the dynamic argument. This makes the requirement of being ultimately undefeated a rather minimal one, because we cannot get much into working memory at one time. From one point of view, formulating the requirement in this way seems obviously correct—if we do not occurrently remember an argument for a defeater, we *cannot* take it into account in deciding what to believe,

23. Of course, there are other kinds of defeaters as well. The kind of defeater operative in cases where we discover that we are misremembering is 'I did not originally believe P'.

and so we should be deemed epistemically beyond reproach if we ignore it. On the other hand, this makes the requirement that the dynamic argument be ultimately undefeated seem so weak as to be virtually useless. It seems we will almost never have any defeating arguments in working memory at the same time as the argument to be defeated, and so a dynamic argument will almost always be ultimately undefeated in this sense. I think, however, that this objection is wrong. As a matter of psychological fact, when we acquire a new belief that constitutes a defeater for the genetic argument, we often remember that it does, and thus we add the dynamic argument in Figure 2.5 to working memory.

Argument (3)

Q is true, and Q is a defeater for some step of my genetic argument for P.

$\uparrow$

Q is true, and Q is a defeater for the inference from A to B.

$\uparrow$

I inferred B from A in the genetic argument for P.

$\uparrow$

I seem to remember that I inferred B from A in the genetic argument for P.

Figure 2.5

Thus my working memory comes to contain both argument (2) and argument (3), and the latter is a defeating argument for the former. Hence argument (2) is not ultimately undefeated.

According to this account, if we have a defeater for the inference from A to B but we do not remember inferring B from A in the genetic argument for P, then our present belief in P is justified. That seems to be correct. The reason this does not trivialize the requirement that the dynamic argument be ultimately undefeated is that we frequently have the requisite memories. Memory allows us to monitor the course of our arguments and alerts us when we subsequently encounter a defeater for an earlier stage of an argument. This is how memory supplies us with genetic defeaters. This aspect of memory is intriguing, partly because it does not fit into naive models of memory that would attempt to reduce all memory to premise memory. In this connection, it might be tempting to suppose that we acquire genetic defeaters by occurrently recalling the earlier parts of the genetic argument and inspecting them to see whether each newly drawn conclusion constitutes a defeater for any of the earlier steps. This would reduce the monitoring function of memory to premise memory. But obviously, we do not really do it that way. To suppose we must is to adopt a simplistic view of memory. This is best illustrated by considering memory searches. When we search our memory for something, we do not have to proceed sequentially through all the beliefs held in memory, calling each to consciousness, inspecting it to see if it is what we are looking for, and if it is not, then rejecting it and going on to the next item. For example, in trying to remember someone's name, despite the fact that this is something that we can voluntarily undertake to do, the process whereby we do it is not a conscious process. We set ourselves to do it, and then we wait a moment and see whether anything emerges into occurrent thought. If we are able to remember the name, the only thing that occurs at a conscious level is the recollection of the name. If we are unable to remember the name, we may feel frustrated and we may continue to "try" to remember it, but nothing happens at the conscious level. The point is that, to use computer jargon, human recollection involves built-in search procedures. If asked to name a famous composer, my memory can find one. It does it by searching my unconscious memory for someone remembered as a famous composer, and because it is searching unconscious memory, this search is not something I do consciously.

Human recollection also involves a somewhat more complicated operation that we might call 'primed search.' Consider a birdwatcher who has a mental list of rare birds he would like to observe. This need not be a fixed list. Each month he may add new birds to the list when he reads about them in his birdwatcher's magazine, and he strikes items off the list when he observes them. Furthermore, the way in which the list evolves need not consist of his recalling the entire list to mind and then altering it. He can alter such a mental list by adding or deleting items without ever thinking about the list as a whole. Given such a list, when our birdwatcher sees a bird on the list, he immediately recalls that it is one of the listed birds and he may get very excited. The point is that one can prime oneself to be on the lookout for things on such a nonoccurrent mental list. This is an unconscious mental function that humans are capable of performing, and it involves memory in accessing the list itself, but the memory processes involved cannot be reduced to any kind of simple memory of individual facts.

Primed search is what is involved in monitoring our reasoning and being on the lookout for newly inferred defeaters for previous steps of reasoning. We remember what those earlier steps were, although we do not do so occurrently, and we remain on the lookout for defeaters for those earlier steps, and when we encounter such a defeater we then occurrently remember the earlier step and note that we have a defeater. The only conscious output of this primed search consists of occurrently remembering that a certain step occurred in the argument, and we combine that with the observation that a particular newly acquired belief is a defeater for that step. This is how we acquire a genetic defeater for a dynamic argument.

To recapitulate, reflections on the role of memory in reasoning have led us to a radically different picture of the relationship between reasoning and epistemic justification. We have been led to distinguish between the genetic argument for a belief and the dynamic argument, concluding that it is only the latter that is directly relevant to the assessment of the belief as justified or unjustified. The genetic argument is indirectly relevant because genetic defeaters for the dynamic argument appeal to the genetic argument and are supplied by some of the more sophisticated operations of memory.

5. Reconsideration of Epistemologically Basic Beliefs

My purpose thus far has been to sketch as plausible a foundations theory as possible. A foundations theory has two parts: (1) an account of epistemologically basic beliefs, and (2) an account of epistemic ascent. With regard to (1), I have argued that although epistemologically basic beliefs might be incorrigible, that is not a strict requirement of foundations theories. All that is really required is that they be self-justifying, and the weakest kind of self-justification is prima facie justification. With regard to (2), I have maintained that epistemic ascent is a matter of reasoning and must proceed in terms of a combination of prima facie and conclusive reasons. I have also urged that memory plays a much more involved role in reasoning than has generally been recognized.

I believe that the picture I have drawn of reasoning is basically correct, but I think that there are fundamental problems for the foundationalist claims about epistemologically basic beliefs and their role in knowledge. In fact, I believe that all foundations theories are false, and that where they go wrong is in their claims about epistemologically basic beliefs. Recall that foundations theories are doxastic theories. Doxastic theories assume that the justifiability of a belief is a function of one's overall doxastic state. The motivation for this assumption is the idea that in deciding what to believe you can only take account of something insofar as you have beliefs about it. Thus only beliefs can contribute to the determination of what you can be justified in believing. There are two kinds of doxastic theories— foundations theories and coherence theories. What distinguishes a foundations theory from a coherence theory is that according to a foundations theory there is a privileged subclass of beliefs (the epistemologically basic beliefs) that have two properties: (1) they are self-justifying; and (2) all other beliefs are justified ultimately by appeal to epistemologically basic beliefs. This was originally motivated by the observation that all justified belief derives ultimately from the evidence of our senses, and the doxastic assumption that that evidence must come to us in the form of beliefs. If this is right and if we are ever to be able to get started in the acquisition of such sensory beliefs, it cannot be required that the justification of the sensory beliefs involves justificatory appeal to other beliefs, so the sensory beliefs must be self-justifying. Further substance was lent to this picture by the observation that we seem to treat sensory beliefs as incorrigibly justified, and that requires them to be incorrigible.

I think, however, that this picture is wrong on all counts. I will begin by arguing that sensory beliefs are not incorrigible. In order to argue this, note first that it seems we are not always aware of how we are appeared to. This can result from the simple fact that we do not always attend to how we are appeared to. Suppose, for example, that you are driving on a icy road and your car begins to skid. While you are fighting to regain control of your careening automobile you pass a bright red billboard. Because you are concentrating on controlling the car you may not notice the billboard, and if you do not then it seems that you form no beliefs about how you are appeared to relative to the billboard. Later, when you have brought your car safely to rest at the side of the road you may "relive" your frightening experience. The whole series of events may pass before your mind again, and this time you may notice the billboard. It seems that this sort of thing really does happen. But in order for it to happen, it seems clear that you must have perceived the billboard when you passed it. Thus you can have perceptual experiences without being aware of them.

Although I find the preceding example persuasive, we need not actually endorse the conclusion that we can have perceptual experiences without being aware of them. All we need assume at this point is that a person could *believe* that that is possible. For example, he might believe it on the basis of the argument I have just given. Suppose then that you are a person who believes that he can have perceptual experiences without being aware of them. Then it becomes possible for you to have inductive reasons for believing that you have perceptual experiences of various kinds. For example, suppose you have a clock that, upon the hour, both strikes and flashes a red light. Suppose the clock and its light are situated in the lower left corner of your visual field while you are attending closely to something in the center of your visual field (e.g., a wasp buzzing around your nose). If you hear the clock strike you may form the belief that the red light is flashing and hence that you are appeared to redly in the lower left corner of your visual field, but you may not attend to that part of your visual field because you are much too intent upon what the wasp is doing. In effect, you believe yourself to currently be in a situation analogous to the driver in the preceding example. You believe that you are being appeared to redly without being "directly" aware of it. Notice that this example in no way turns upon whether it is actually possible to be appeared to redly without being directly aware of it. All that is required is that one could *believe* that to be possible. This sort of example appears to make perfectly good sense and to describe a situation one could actually be in. Furthermore, it is apparent that in a case like this you could be wrong about how you are appeared to. If the clock is broken and the light not flashing, then you may not be appeared to redly at all. It follows that the belief that you are appeared to redly is not incorrigible.[24]

It was pointed out above that epistemologically basic beliefs might be merely prima facie justified rather than incorrigible. The preceding example can also be used to argue that the belief that you are appeared to redly is not epistemologically basic by virtue of being prima facie justified. Suppose you have all the beliefs described in the previous paragraph, but your inductive evidence is faulty and you are unjustified in believing that the light flashes whenever the clock strikes. Then you are unjustified in believing that you are appeared to redly. If the belief is prima facie justified, you can only be unjustified in holding it if you have some reason for thinking you should not hold it. Do you have any reason for thinking that you should not believe that you are appeared to redly? The answer to this question is a bit complicated. There is some temptation to claim that you automatically have such a reason with regard to any belief that you hold for bad reasons. This is an epistemic principle that will be explored below in more detail. It has the consequence that this example does not show that appearance beliefs are not prima facie justified, but this is only because it makes *all* beliefs prima facie justified. To see this, consider any belief P and suppose you are unjustified in believing P. Then you do not believe P for a good reason, and so by the proposed principle it follows that you have a reason for thinking you should not believe P. Thus you can only be unjustified in believing P if you have a reason for thinking you should not believe P, and hence belief in P is prima facie justified. And this argument works for *any* P. Thus, although this epistemic principle would make the belief that you are

appeared to redly prima facie justified, it would not make it epistemologically basic. There would be no epistemologically basic beliefs if
this principle were true. The result would be a coherence theory
rather than a foundations theory, because an essential claim of a
foundations theory is that the epistemologically basic beliefs form a
privileged *subset* of beliefs on the basis of which other beliefs are
justified. So a foundations theorist cannot defend his theory against
the clock example by endorsing this epistemic principle. It seems to
follow that the belief that you are appeared to redly cannot be prima
facie justified.

A common reaction to the clock example is that all it shows is that
we have not properly described the beliefs that are incorrigible. The
example correctly demonstrates that the belief that you are appeared
to redly is not incorrigible, but it also suggests that the correct
candidate for incorrigibility is a belief you can only have by being
"directly aware" of being appeared to redly. The problem with the
belief that you are appeared to redly is that you can hold it for
"indirect" inductive reasons. The direct/indirect distinction does correctly diagnose what is going on here, but I doubt that it can be
reflected by a distinction in the *contents* of beliefs. The direct/indirect
distinction is a distinction between two different kinds of reasons or
grounds one can have for thinking one is appeared to redly. If the
belief that one is appeared to redly is to have an incorrigible (or prima
facie justified) sibling, that sibling must be a belief that can only be
held on "direct" grounds, but it does not seem that there is any such
belief. It must be concluded that beliefs about appearances are
neither incorrigible nor prima facie justified, and hence they are not
epistemologically basic.

Foundations theories are subject to a different kind of objection
that is ultimately more illuminating. Foundations theories are motivated by the idea that all justified belief derives ultimately from the
evidence of our senses, and that evidence comes to us in the form of
beliefs. We cannot fault the first part of this motivation, but I think it
is a mistake to suppose that the evidence of our senses comes to us in
the form of beliefs. We rarely have any beliefs at all about how things
appear to us. In perception, the beliefs we form are almost invariably
beliefs about the objective properties of physical objects—not about
how things appear to us. If only the latter are candidates for being
epistemologically basic, then it follows that perception does not usually provide us with epistemologically basic beliefs and hence perceptual knowledge does not derive from epistemologically basic beliefs in
the way envisaged by foundations theories. This objection to foundations theories seems to me to be decisive, but let us examine its details
a bit more closely. I am urging (1) that we rarely have beliefs about

how things appear to us, but (2) only beliefs about how things appear to us are plausible candidates for being the epistemologically basic beliefs underlying perceptual knowledge, so (3) perceptual knowledge is not based upon epistemologically basic beliefs and hence foundationalism is wrong. The foundationalist must deny either (1) or (2).

It is undeniable that we are rarely *aware* of having thoughts about how things appear to us. When I walk into a room I think things like 'That is Jones standing over there' and 'The couch has been reupholstered in a bright red fabric'. I am not aware of thinking things like 'A bright red trapezoidal shape appears in the upper right-hand corner of my visual field'. I *can* think things like the latter, but that normally involves a conscious shift of attention and a reorientation in my thinking. It does not seem that such thoughts normally occur of their own accord. The only way to deny this is to insist that we have such thoughts but do not normally attend to them and hence are unaware of having them.

If it is granted that we are normally unaware of having thoughts about how things appear to us, I see no reason to believe that we normally have such thoughts. I should think the burden of proof is on the foundations theorist to establish the existence of these thoughts. But we can go further and produce a reason for thinking that people do not ordinarily have such thoughts. If we were only unaware of having such thoughts because we do not attend to them, then all we would have to do to become aware of them is to direct our attention to them. But that seems wrong. It is not that easy to become aware of how things appear to you. It *is* fairly easy to turn your attention inwards and focus it on your sensory experience, but that does not automatically either generate or reveal beliefs about that sensory experience. To explain what I mean, consider the distinction between sensing something and forming beliefs about it. Suppose, for example, that I happen upon an abstract painting that I find very attractive. I may spend some time gazing at it, "drinking it in" perceptually. I am sensing the patterns in the painting, but if they are quite abstract and irregular so that they are not easily categorized, I may not be forming any beliefs about those patterns. This illustrates that consciously sensing something does not *automatically* involve forming beliefs about it (although I should think that in *most* cases of consciously sensing something we do form beliefs about it). Applying this to our ability to turn our attention inward and focus on our sensory experience, what that amounts to is the ability to introspectively sense our sensory experience, but that does not automatically involve our having beliefs about that sensory experience. Psychologically, our perceptual beliefs about the objects in our immediate environment are caused by our having sensory experiences of certain types, and by introspection we can readily become aware of having the sensory experiences, but that does not mean that we also have the beliefs that the sensory experiences are *of* the requisite types. Very often we are not even aware of what the requisite types are. For instance, when face to face with a friend I form the belief that he is before me and I form that belief because I have a certain type of sensory experience, but I have no idea precisely what type of sensory experience it is that leads me to have the belief that my friend is before me. There is a very complicated abstract pattern whose exemplification by my sensory experience causes me to have the belief, but I have no clear idea what that abstract pattern is and accordingly it seems I have no belief to the effect that my sensory experience exemplifies that pattern. Face recognition is an obvious case in which we do not know what patterns are responsible for recognition, but it takes little reflection to realize that the same phenomenon occurs in recognizing something as a vase or a tree or just about anything else. With considerable training one can become aware of some of these patterns. Acquiring such awareness is an important part of becoming a painter, but it is a difficult process. Think what a discovery it was of the pointillists that the appearance of an object can be reproduced with discontinuous dots of color. A discovery made fairly early by every landscape painter is that snow looks blue (particularly the shadows). Most people think snow looks white to them, but they are wrong.

I take all of this to indicate that we do not have the beliefs about appearances that foundations theories would require us to have. We are not ordinarily aware of even *having* sensory experiences. By shifting our attention we can make ourselves aware of our sensory experiences, but that need not involve having beliefs about them and hence it gives us no reason to think that in more ordinary cases we have such beliefs but they are unconscious. Furthermore, the painter examples show that insofar as we do have beliefs about our sensory experience they are often wrong. This is related to the earlier argument I gave to show that such beliefs are not incorrigible. When looking at a snowcovered field I may think that the shadows in the snow look grey to me when they actually look blue to me. This is made possible by the fact that I have the mistaken general belief that snow looks white and shadows in snow look grey, and so without really attending to my current sensory experiences I jump to the conclusion that the shadows look grey in this case.

It must be concluded that beliefs about how things appear to us are illsuited to play the role demanded of them by foundations theories. We rarely have *any* such beliefs. We most definitely do not have *enough* beliefs of this sort to base all our other beliefs upon them. Further-more, such beliefs would not provide a firm foundation because they are not self-justifying. More accurately, they are not incorrigible, and although we have not ruled out the possibility that they might be prima facie justified, they can only be prima facie justified if *all* beliefs are prima facie justified. In the latter case all beliefs have the same epistemological status, and hence there is no privileged class of epistemologically basic beliefs and so foundations theories fail any-way.

A related point must be made about memory. I have urged that memory plays a very important role in reasoning, and I attempted to reconstruct this within a foundations theory by endorsing the follow-ing mnemonic prima facie reason:

'I seem to remember P' is a prima facie reason for me to believe P.

The trouble is, we do not have beliefs about seeming to remember ("memory experiences") any more often than we have beliefs about sensory experiences. In normal cases of remembering, where we have no reason to doubt our memory, we just remember. The only thought involved in such remembering is what is remembered. We have no thoughts *about* remembering. We usually only have thoughts about seeming to remember when doubt is cast upon the veridicality of our memory. It follows that we cannot account for the justifiedness of memory beliefs by appealing to the mnemonic prima facie reason. It also follows that we cannot accurately reconstruct the role of memory in reasoning by appealing to that prima facie reason. The founda-tionalist account of memory is no more defensible than the founda-tionalist account of perception.

I conclude that foundations theories cannot successfully claim that we have the beliefs about appearances and memory experiences that we would be required to have in order to base all knowledge upon epistemologically basic beliefs of these sorts. A foundations theory can only be defended by adopting a different view of what beliefs are epistemologically basic. Recall again that the basic idea behind foun-dations theories is that all justified belief derives ultimately from the evidence of our senses, and that evidence comes to us in the form of beliefs. We must either reject this basic idea or adopt a different view of what beliefs formulate the evidence of our senses. In ordinary perception the only beliefs we seem to have are beliefs directly about the objective properties of physical objects. These are beliefs about how things are—not about how things appear to us. Perhaps then we should take these physical-object beliefs to be epistemologically basic. The problem with this proposal is that epistemologically basic beliefs must be self-justifying if they are to provide a foundation for the justification of other beliefs. Physical-object beliefs are clearly not incorrigible, so the only way for them to be self-justifying is for them to be prima facie justified. Consider an ordinary physical-object belief, for example, the belief that my daughter is wearing a coat. I frequently hold such a belief on the basis of perception, and in that case it is usually justified. But suppose now that my daughter has gone to a football game, the evening has turned cold, and I am worried about whether she took a coat. I may think to myself, "Oh, I am sure she is wearing a coat". But then on reflection I may decide that I have no reason to believe that—my initial belief was just a matter of wishful thinking. Prior to deciding that I held the belief on the basis of wishful thinking, was the belief justified? It certainly does not seem so. Even though I had not yet decided that I held the belief on the basis of wishful thinking, that was my basis, and that seems sufficient to make the belief unjustified. Furthermore, not yet having decided that I held the belief on the basis of wishful thinking, it does not seem that I had any reason for thinking I should not hold the belief. So it is apparently possible to hold such a belief unjustifiably without having any reason for thinking that one should not hold the belief, and hence it is not prima facie justified. Consequently, such physical-object beliefs cannot be epistemologically basic.

The above argument is predicated on the assumption that if we hold a belief for bad reasons but have not yet decided that we hold the belief for bad reasons, then we do not have a reason for thinking we should not hold the belief. Suppose that is denied and it is insisted instead that whenever we hold a belief for no reason or for bad reasons then we automatically have a reason for thinking we should not hold the belief. This is the epistemic principle discussed above. Endorsing this principle would vitiate the above argument and make my belief that my daughter is wearing a coat prima facie justified. But as I argued above, this is only because it would make all beliefs prima facie justified. Thus, once again, what is generated is not a foundations theory, but a coherence theory. So this is not a way of defending foundations theories.

This argument against foundations theories is quite general. What we are finding is that all beliefs (even beliefs about appearances) can be held for bad reasons. Depending upon what we say about what counts as a reason for thinking we should not hold a belief, this either has the consequence that no belief is prima facie justified or that all beliefs are prima facie justified. In either case, foundationalism fails, because foundationalism requires there to be a privileged subclass of beliefs that are prima facie justified and on the basis of which all other beliefs are justified. I regard this as a decisive refutation of foundationalism.

If foundationalism fails, what should we erect in its place? We have two options. We can retain the doxastic assumption and adopt a coherence theory, or we can reject the doxastic assumption and adopt a nondoxastic theory. My ultimate proposal will be that we follow the latter course, but because the doxastic assumption has so much intuitive appeal I will first explore the possibility of adopting a coherence theory. That is the topic of the next chapter.

3

COHERENCE THEORIES

1. Motivation

DOXASTIC THEORIES begin by assuming that all that can enter into the determination of whether a belief is justifiable is what other beliefs one holds. Foundations theories give a subclass of beliefs—the epistemologically basic beliefs—a privileged role in this determination. A coherence theory is any doxastic theory denying that there is such an epistemologically privileged subclass of beliefs. Coherence theories insist that all beliefs have the same fundamental epistemic status, and the justifiability of a belief is determined jointly by all of one's beliefs taken together. This has typically been expressed by saying that what determines whether a belief is justified is how it "coheres" with the set of all your beliefs. To generate an actual theory of this sort, we must give a precise account of the coherence relation. There is a broad array of possible coherence theories resulting from different ways of analyzing the coherence relation. But they all turn upon the fundamental idea that it is a belief's relationship to all other beliefs, and not just to a privileged subclass of beliefs, that determines whether it is justified.

Coherence theories as a group can be motivated by several different kinds of considerations. The most straightforward is that some coherence theory must be true because all foundations theories are false. This turns upon the doxastic assumption, which we will eventually reconsider, but most philosophers have been inclined to grant the doxastic assumption.

There is a second motivation that has been equally prominent in persuading people of the correctness of coherence theories. This motivation is quite separate from the technical failure of foundations theories, and is well expressed by the Neurath metaphor cited in chapter one: "We are like sailors who must rebuild their ship upon the open sea." At any given time we have a large stock of beliefs—our "doxastic system"—and among these are beliefs telling us how to go about modifying this very stock of beliefs, adding new ones and rejecting old ones. We cannot forsake all of our beliefs and start over again, because then we would not know how to start. To proceed rationally, we must have beliefs that direct our way of proceeding. But these procedural beliefs are not sacrosanct either, because if our beliefs about how to proceed conflict too drastically with the bulk of the rest of our beliefs, we will take that to refute the procedural beliefs. As was emphasized in chapter one, the validity of an argument does not determine whether the conclusion should be accepted or the premises rejected. All the validity of the argument determines is that we should not simultaneously accept the premises and the denial of the conclusion. Which of these we reject must be determined by our relative confidence in them. We should reject that of which we are least confident. To this we can add that another option is to reject the validity of the argument. The apparent conflict between premises of which we are confident and a conclusion we are convinced to be false may persuade us that our beliefs about valid inference are in error. The latter are just further beliefs in our stock of beliefs. Our general strategy must be to attempt to render the entire set of beliefs internally consistent by using the procedural beliefs in the set to guide us, the latter also being subject to revision. So we start with the set of beliefs we already have and use its members to guide its own overhaul.

The Neurath picture has played a prominent role in motivating coherence theories,[1] but I think that the philosophical credentials of coherence theories are best disengaged from it. If we had not already rejected foundations theories on the grounds that there are no epistemologically basic beliefs, the Neurath picture would not provide differential support for coherence theories. There are two things wrong with it. Part of the picture turns on a mistake, and the part of the picture that is correct can be accommodated by a foundations theory. The part that is mistaken is the supposition that belief change is always guided by beliefs. It is not. For example, if I infer Q from P and $(P \supset Q)$, this is not because I have the *belief* that Q follows from P and $(P \supset Q)$. Of course, having been trained in logic I do have that belief, but there was a time when I had no such beliefs (I had not even thought about the matter), and most nonphilosophers probably have very few such beliefs. We reason in accordance with rules like *modus ponens*, but to reason in accordance with them and to be guided by them does not require that we be self-reflective about our reasoning to the extent of having beliefs about what rules we use. Furthermore, complicated kinds of reasoning often proceed in terms of rules that even philosophers cannot articulate. A clear example of this is induction. The "new riddle of induction" is the problem of giving a precise

1. See for example, W. V. Quine and Joseph Ullian [1978], Keith Lehrer [1974], and Gilbert Harman [1973] and [1984].

account of rules of inductive inference, and it was illustrated in chapter one just how difficult a problem that is. We all reason inductively, but not even experts have been able to formulate rules of inductive inference that systematize our reasoning in all respects. Obviously, we do not guide our inductive reasoning by *beliefs* about correct rules of inductive reasoning. Consequently, it is a mistake to suppose that in modifying our total stock of beliefs we appeal to beliefs in that stock pertaining to how to reason. That may go on to some extent, when we employ learned patterns of reasoning, but most native reasoning is mediated by rules we cannot easily articulate and regarding which we may have no beliefs at all.

Perhaps it should be regarded as an inessential part of the Neurath picture that we have beliefs about how to change our beliefs. A coherence theory could still be defended merely by insisting that in changing our beliefs we reason from the beliefs we already have, and when beliefs conflict all we can do is weigh the conflicting beliefs against one another in terms of our relative confidence in them. This is partly right, but it constitutes an incomplete account of belief change. We do often acquire new beliefs and reject old beliefs by making inferences from the beliefs we already hold. But a source of new beliefs that is at least equally important is perception. We acquire beliefs about our physical environment by perceiving it. Such beliefs are not inferred from other beliefs. Perception is not inference from previously held beliefs, and it is not mediated by beliefs about how to acquire perceptual beliefs. Perception and inference are alike in that both processes go on "under the surface", unmediated by procedural beliefs concerning how to do it. Consequently, no correct account of belief change can appeal exclusively to the beliefs we already have. It must also allow for the introduction into our doxastic system of new perceptual beliefs.

The accommodation of perception is a major problem for any doxastic theory. The most natural view of epistemic justification is the doxastic assumption according to which the justifiability of a belief is a function exclusively of what one believes. Foundations theories try to accommodate the doxastic assumption by supposing that perception issues in beliefs about sensory experience. By supposing that those beliefs are self-justifying, the foundations theorist avoids the question of how they are to be justified, and then tries to reconstruct perceptual knowledge of physical objects in terms of perfectly ordinary belief-to-belief reasoning from the basic beliefs about sensory experience. The difficulty, of course, is that perception does not usually issue in beliefs about sensory experience, and hence perceptual knowledge cannot be regarded as the result of reasoning from basic beliefs. The difficulty for coherence theories, on the other hand, is that it is not clear what alternatives exist that are compatible with the doxastic assumption. How else can we get perceptual beliefs into our doxastic system? We know that foundationalism is false, but that does not help us very much in determining the true account of perceptual knowledge.

Leaving aside the problems of inference and perception, there is a residual core in the Neurath picture that seems unmistakably correct, and it is really this core that made the whole picture seem right in the first place. The core idea is that beliefs are innocent until proven guilty. When we start with a stock of beliefs, they tend to become disengaged from the reasons for which we originally came to hold them. We tend not to remember our reasons—just our conclusions. If we no longer remember our reasons for a belief, then it seems that the credentials of the belief no longer depend upon those reasons. Finding something wrong with the reasons cannot discredit the belief if we have no idea that the belief was originally derived from those reasons. This might seem perplexing. It might seem that we *should* keep track of our reasons. But it is an undeniable matter of fact that we do not. For example, we all believe that Columbus landed in America in 1492, but how many of us have any idea what our original reason was for believing that? We can guess that we learned it from our parents or from a teacher, but we do not really know and we certainly do not know the details. Furthermore, there is a simple explanation for why human beings are not built in such a way that they do habitually remember their reasons. We are information processors with a limited capacity for storage. If we had to remember our reasons in addition to our conclusions, that would clutter up our memory and overstress our limited storage capacity.[2]

The observation that beliefs become disengaged from their reasons and acquire a presumptive epistemic status of their own lends substance to the picture of a web of interrelated and interacting beliefs with epistemic justification consisting of a belief's having a secure niche in this web. We still have to get perception into the picture somehow, and we have to explain how reasoning works in playing some parts of the web off against other parts, but the general result is a structure of the sort that coherence theorists find intuitively appealing. What is often overlooked, however, is that this structure is entirely compatible with a foundations theory. When beliefs become disengaged from their reasons they are remembered. That is what memory is. And any foundations theory is going to contain an account of memory. The theory I sketched in chapter two treats memory as analogous to sense perception and takes seeming-to-

2. Gilbert Harman [1984] makes this point.

remember as providing a prima facie reason for what is remembered. When beliefs become disengaged from their reasons and enshrined in memory we become able to recall them, and when we recall them we believe them on the basis of seeming to remember them. Thus memory itself gives the beliefs an evidential status independent of their original reasons, and we should automatically continue to hold such beliefs unless we acquire a defeater for the mnemonic prima facie reason. When several such memory beliefs come in conflict with each other, they constitute rebutting defeaters for each other, and in deciding which to reject we have to weigh the strengths of our various mnemonic reasons. That is the same thing as asking how confident we are of the various beliefs. So the correct part of the Neurath picture is readily accommodated by a foundations theory and constitutes no argument for a coherence theory. Of course, the foundations theory that accommodates it has already been discredited on the grounds that in remembering something we do not usually have beliefs about seeming to remember, but this is just an instance of the general objection that we rarely have beliefs of the sort styled as epistemologically basic. So it is not the Neurath picture that should lead us to reject foundations theories, but rather the lack of epistemologically basic beliefs. This observation is important because it shows where the real disagreement between coherence theories and foundations theories lies. They do not disagree about the defensible parts of the Neurath picture. What they disagree about is whether we have epistemologically basic beliefs, and in this I think we must side with the coherence theories.

Because we do not have appropriate epistemologically basic beliefs, all foundations theories are false, but this is not yet to say which theory is true. If the doxastic assumption can be maintained then it will follow that some coherence theory is true. But another option is to deny the doxastic assumption, thus rejecting both foundations theories and coherence theories. Because it is their inability to handle perceptual input in terms of beliefs that leads to the downfall of foundations theories, one might suspect that the real culprit is the doxastic assumption, and that will eventually be my conclusion. But first, let us survey the various possible kinds of coherence theories to see if they can solve the problem.

2. A Taxonomy of Coherence Theories

The essential feature of a coherence theory is that it is a doxastic theory that assigns the same inherent epistemic status to all beliefs. Insofar as we can demand reasons for holding one belief, we can demand reasons for holding any belief; and insofar as we can be justified in holding one belief without having a reason for doing so, we can be justified in holding any belief without having a reason for doing so.

We can classify coherence theories in two different ways—in terms of the nature of the reasons they embrace, and in terms of the role they assign to those reasons.

2.1   *Positive and Negative Coherence Theories*

Some coherence theories take all beliefs to be prima facie justified. According to these theories, if one holds a belief, one is automatically justified in doing so unless he has a reason for thinking he should not. All beliefs are "innocent until proven guilty". This is the view expressed by the Neurath metaphor. According to theories of this sort, reasons function in a negative way, leading us to reject beliefs but not being required for the justified acquisition of belief. I call these *negative coherence theories. Positive coherence theories*, on the other hand, demand positive support for all beliefs. Positive coherence theories require the believer to actually have reasons for holding each of his beliefs. Different positive coherence theories are generated by giving different accounts of reasons.

The motivations for positive and negative coherence theories are different. Negative coherence theories are motivated by something like the Neurath metaphor. Positive coherence theories are motivated more directly by the failure of foundations theories to find epistemologically basic beliefs. Defenders of positive coherence theories share the intuition of the foundations theorist that justified belief requires reasons, but go on to conclude that because there are no epistemologically basic beliefs, when we trace out the reasons for a belief (and the reasons for the reasons, etc.), the tracing can never terminate with epistemologically basic beliefs requiring no further reasons. Either the tracing of reasons must be allowed to go on indefinitely, or else the nature of reasons must be radically different from what the foundations theorist envisages. These two options are reflected by a second distinction yielding a different classification of coherence theories.

2.2   *Linear and Holistic Coherence Theories*

I have talked about the role of reasons in coherence theories, but for some coherence theories that is a somewhat misleading way of talking. Consider positive coherence theories. Some positive coherence theories embrace essentially the same view of reasons and reasoning as a foundations theory. On this view, P is a reason for S to believe Q by virtue of some relation holding specifically between P and Q. A reason for a belief is either another individual belief or a small set of beliefs,[3] and is not automatically the set of *all* one's beliefs. On this view of reasons it always makes sense to inquire about our reasons for our reasons, and so on. A positive coherence theory adopting this view of reasons will be called *linear*. On a linear theory, if we trace the reasons for a belief, and the reasons for the reasons, and so on, we can never reach a stopping point. If there were a stopping point, it would have to consist of epistemologically basic beliefs, and coherence theories deny that there are epistemologically basic beliefs. There are just two ways in which the tracing of reasons can go on forever—either there is an infinite regress of reasons, or eventually the reasons go around in a circle. Thus a linear positive coherence theory must acknowledge that justified belief can result from either an infinite regress of reasons, or from circular reasoning.

Both of these possibilities seem a bit puzzling, and foreign to the classical view of reasoning that appears to underlie linear theories.[4] Hence it is tempting to reject linear positive theories and instead adopt a holistic view of reasons. According to a *holistic* positive coherence theory, in order for S to have reason for believing P, there must be a relationship between P and the set of *all* of his beliefs (where this relationship cannot be decomposed into simple reason relationships holding between individual beliefs).[5] Note that on a holistic theory it is more natural to talk about "having reason" for holding a belief rather than "having *a* reason". In particular, it makes no sense to inquire about the reasons for one's reason for a belief. On this theory, one does not have *a* reason in the sense of a particular belief—rather, one has reason for a belief by virtue of his belief being appropriately related to his entire doxastic system.

The holistic/linear distinction can also be applied to negative coherence theories. A linear negative coherence theory is one taking all beliefs to be prima facie justified and adopting a "classical" view of the reasons and reasoning that can lead to the defeat of such prima facie justified beliefs. Alternatively, a holistic negative coherence theory will also take all beliefs to be prima facie justified but will insist that

3. For example, {P,(P ⊃ Q)} is a reason for Q.

4. I do not know of anyone who has endorsed a linear positive coherence theory in print, although I have heard such theories endorsed tentatively in discussions. Lawrence Bonjour [1985] constructs a theory that looks initially like a linear coherence theory (see pp. 117ff.), but closer inspection reveals that he takes beliefs to the effect that one has a certain belief to be prima facie justified (this is what he calls 'the doxastic presumption'), and hence in the taxonomy of this book his theory is a foundations theory.

5. Examples of holistic positive coherence theories are provided by Lawrence Bonjour [1976], Gilbert Harman [1970], and Keith Lehrer [1974].

what defeats a person's justification for a belief is the relationship between that belief and the set of all the person's beliefs (where, again, this relationship cannot be decomposed into relationships between individual beliefs).

It is worth emphasizing that even linear theories can be more holistic than one might initially suppose. Linear theories are linear in the sense that the reason for one proposition is another proposition or a small set of propositions, but if reasons are defeasible then in an important sense what justifies a belief is not the individual proposition that is the reason but rather that proposition together with the absence of defeaters, and the latter appeals to all one's beliefs.

Holistic theories adopt a novel view of reasons according to which one's having reason for a belief is determined by the relationship of that belief to the whole amorphous structure of beliefs comprising his total doxastic system. Such a view of reasons contrasts with the more traditional view of reasons adopted by foundations theories and linear coherence theories, and although the vague picture of holistic reasons has intuitive appeal, it is a bit difficult to imagine just what they might be like. A concrete example of such a theory will be discussed in section three.

2.3   *The Regress Argument*

There are two familiar arguments that have been deployed repeatedly against coherence theories as a group. The first of these is the *regress argument*, which objects that coherence theories lead to an infinite regress of reasons and such a regress cannot provide justification. This objection has often been regarded as fatal to all coherence theories, but in fact it is telling against only a few. It is simply false that all coherence theories lead to an infinite regress of reasons. This argument has no apparent strength against negative coherence theories, because they do not require reasons for beliefs. The regress argument really only bears upon some of the least plausible linear positive coherence theories. A linear positive coherence theory that identifies *having P as a reason for believing Q* with *having explicitly inferred Q from P* would run afoul of the regress argument, because it would require one to have performed infinitely many explicit inferences before one could be justified in believing anything, and that is presumably impossible. However, weaker understandings of what it is to have P as a reason for believing Q make the regress argument problematic, and holistic positive coherence theories would seem to avoid the regress argument altogether.

Although the regress argument fails to dispose of more than a few varieties of coherence theories, it is related to a more concrete objection that can be leveled against all linear positive coherence theories and seems to me to be fatal to them. Linear positive coherence theories look much like foundations theories as long as we focus our attention on beliefs not directly based upon perception. But the two types of theories diverge radically when we consider perceptual beliefs. According to foundations theories justification terminates at that point on epistemologically basic beliefs, but according to a linear positive coherence theory justification must instead loop back up to other "high level" beliefs. Foundations theories fail at this juncture because of their inability to handle perception, and linear positive coherence theories seem to fail for the same reason. The failure of foundations theories results from their attempt to base perceptual belief on epistemologically basic appearance beliefs, because we do not usually have such beliefs. Linear positive coherence theories seek to avoid this failure by taking perceptual beliefs to be based upon more ordinary physical-object beliefs, whose justification in turn rests upon other ordinary beliefs, and so on. This would indeed avoid the problem of not having appropriate epistemologically basic beliefs, but the difficulty with the proposed solution is that perceptual beliefs do not seem to be based, in the way envisioned, on physical-object beliefs either. For instance, suppose I see a book on my desk and judge perceptually that it is red. A typical foundations theory would allege that my reason for thinking that the book is red is my epistemologically basic belief that it looks red to me. But I normally have no such belief. A linear positive coherence theory proposes instead that my reason for thinking the book is red is some more ordinary physical-object belief. The trouble with this proposal is that there are no plausible candidates for such a reason. What could such a reason be? One suggestion I have heard is that our reason is the second-order belief that we believe the book to be red, but the claim that we ordinarily have such second-order beliefs is no more plausible than the foundationalist claim that we ordinarily have appearance beliefs. Furthermore, what could our reason be for the second-order belief? Certainly not that we believe that we believe the book is red. Nor do there seem to be any other candidates with greater plausibility. The general difficulty is that perception is not inference. When I believe on the basis of perception that the book is red, I do not infer that belief from something else that I believe. Perception is a causal process that inputs beliefs into our doxastic system without their being inferred from or justified on the basis of other beliefs we already have. This seems undeniable, and it appears to constitute a conclusive objection to all linear positive coherence theories.

2.4   *The Isolation Argument*

There is a second familiar argument that has often been leveled against coherence theories as a group. This is the *isolation argument*, which objects that coherence theories cut justification off from the world. According to coherence theories, justification is ultimately a matter of relations between the propositions one believes, and has nothing to do with the way the world is. But our objective in seeking knowledge is to find out the way the world is. Thus coherence theories are inadequate.[6]

I think that there is a good point concealed in the isolation argument, but as stated, the argument is not compelling. The difficulty for the argument emerges when we ask for a clearer statement of the way in which coherence theories are supposed to cut justification off from the world. As with any doxastic theory, they make justification a function of what one believes, but what one believes is causally influenced by the way the world is. That is precisely what perception is all about. Perception is a causal process by virtue of which physical states of the world influence our beliefs. It might be objected that a merely causal relationship between our beliefs and the world is inadequate—what is required is some sort of *rational* relationship. But it is not at all clear how that would be possible. Rationality only seems to pertain to relations between beliefs. (This is the doxastic assumption.) Notice, in particular, that foundations theories do not differ from coherence theories with respect to the relationship between our beliefs and the world. The only way the world can influence our beliefs on either a foundations theory or a coherence theory is causally. Foundations theories and coherence theories differ only with regard to which beliefs are the causal progeny of our environment. Foundations theories suppose they are epistemologically basic appearance beliefs, while coherence theories suppose they are more ordinary physical-object beliefs having no privileged epistemic status. As far as I can see, the isolation argument provides no basis for preferring foundations theories to coherence theories.

Although, as stated, the isolation argument does not succeed in refuting coherence theories, I believe that there is a good point lurking beneath it. The point concerns doxastic theories in general, not just coherence theories, and it consists of a general difficulty in accommodating perception within any such theory. On a doxastic theory, the connection between our beliefs and the world can only be a causal one. But as difficult as this is to make clear, it seems that there

---

6. I believe that the isolation argument was first formulated in my [1974]. As should be apparent from the text, I have subsequently abandoned it.

should also be a rational connection of some sort. The reason for saying this is that we do distinguish between reasonable and unreasonable (justified and unjustified) perceptual beliefs. For instance, if a person sees a book, it looks red to him, and he judges that it is red, we will normally regard his belief that the book is red to be reasonable. But if he also knows that he is in a room bathed in red light and he knows the effect red light can have on apparent colors, then even if he is caused to believe that the book is red, we will not regard that belief as reasonable. Under the circumstances, given what he knows, he *should not* have come to believe that.

Doxastic theories can attempt to accommodate this intuition in various ways. In the end, I think that they are all unsuccessful. I will return to this objection at the end of the chapter where I will make it more precise and use it to motivate the adoption of a nondoxastic theory.

3. Holistic Positive Coherence Theories

I have argued that linear positive coherence theories all fail because of their inability to produce plausible candidates for reasons for beliefs that result directly from perception. This failure turns specifically on the assumption that reasoning proceeds in terms of relations between individual beliefs. If we turn to holistic positive coherence theories, this objection no longer has any force. If the justifiedness of a belief is determined by its relationship to *all* other beliefs in a way that cannot be decomposed into linear reasons, then it is no longer clear whether we can be said to have reason for perceptual beliefs. Holistic positive coherence theories require further exploration. There is only one such theory that has been carefully worked out, and that is due to Keith Lehrer [1974]. Thus I will begin by giving a brief sketch of Lehrer's theory in order to give the reader some feeling for what holistic positive coherence theories are like. Then I will go on to make some more general remarks about holistic positive coherence theories as a group.

3.1 *Lehrer's Theory*

As a first approximation, Lehrer's proposal is that a belief P is justified for a person S if and only if for each belief with which P "competes", S believes that P is more probable than that competitor. To make the theory precise, we must make this notion of competition precise. We obviously want a proposition to compete with any proposition with which it is incompatible, but Lehrer argues that we must also allow propositions to compete with propositions with which they are logically consistent. He bases this on consideration of a lottery. Suppose S holds one ticket in a fair lottery consisting of 1000 tickets, each ticket having the same probability of being drawn, and S has true beliefs about all the relevant probabilities. The probability of any given ticket being drawn is thus one in a thousand. On this basis S may be tempted to conclude that his ticket will not be drawn. But note that S has equally good reason to draw the same conclusion about each ticket in the lottery. If he draws all those conclusions, the result is incompatible with something he already knows—namely, that some ticket will be drawn. Lehrer assumes that it cannot be reasonable to hold such an explicitly contradictory set of beliefs, but there is nothing to favor one of the tickets over any of the others, so he concludes that it cannot be reasonable to infer of *any* ticket that it will not be drawn. Consequently, Lehrer seeks to tailor his definition of competition so that his account of justification yields the result that in this example S is not justified in believing, of any ticket, that it will not be drawn.

Before examining Lehrer's definition of competition, we should take note of the assumption on which his argument is based. This is the assumption that one cannot be justified in holding an explicitly contradictory set of beliefs. Perhaps most epistemologists will endorse some principle such as this, but a few have explicitly rejected this principle. I propose to simply grant Lehrer this assumption without further discussion so that we can give his theory a fair hearing.[7]

In order for his criterion of justification to yield the result that S is not justified in believing that any particular ticket will not be drawn, Lehrer wants to define competition in such a way that the proposition that a given ticket will lose competes with the proposition that any other ticket will lose. If these propositions are all in competition with each other, then because they are believed by S to be equally probable, S does not believe any of them to be more probable than each of its competitors. It follows by Lehrer's criterion that S is not justified in believing any of these propositions. This suggested to Lehrer that we should say that P competes with Q if and only if S believes Q to be "negatively relevant" to P. To say that Q is negatively relevant to P is to say that the probability of P *on the assumption that Q is true* is less than the probability of P without that assumption, that is, $prob(P/Q) < prob(P)$. This definition of competition will handle the lottery example, because any given ticket's not being drawn will slightly raise the

---

7. I do not want to give the impression that Lehrer is unaware of the contentiousness of the consistency assumption. He explicitly defends it in his [1975].

probability of any other ticket being drawn and hence is negatively relevant to that other ticket's not being drawn.

Lehrer illustrates his analysis by considering the perceptual judgment that he sees a red apple. He observes that he not only believes that he sees an apple, but he also believes that the proposition that he sees a red apple is more probable than the proposition that he sees a wax imitation, or a painting of an apple, or that he is hallucinating, and so forth. All of the latter are negatively relevant to his actually seeing a red apple and hence are in competition with that proposition, but in each case he believes them to be less probable.

This is only a crude sketch of Lehrer's theory. He goes on to argue that a number of complicated amendations are required in order to make the theory work, but I will not pursue them here. This at least gives the flavor of the theory. It is an ingenious theory, and it is the only attempt to actually construct a precise holistic positive coherence theory that can be found in the contemporary literature. Lehrer's theory illustrates how the justifiedness of a belief might be a function of one's total doxastic system without being determined by relations between individual beliefs of the sort envisioned by "classical" theories of reasons and reasoning.[8]

3.2   Problems for Holistic Positive Coherence Theories

Holistic positive coherence theories constitute an interesting, although largely unexplored, category of epistemological theory. But despite their intuitive appeal, there are some general difficulties that infect them as a group. One kind of problem is analogous to a problem we encountered in trying to construct a plausible foundations theory. The picture underlying coherence theories is of a vast web of interrelated beliefs, but this picture becomes dubious when we reflect upon the distinction between occurrent and non-occurrent beliefs. The picture may give an accurate portrayal of our total doxastic system if we construe it as consisting of occurrent and non-occurrent beliefs alike, but it is quite inaccurate as a portrayal of our occurrent beliefs alone. What must be asked is whether non-occurrent beliefs can play a direct role in justification. It certainly *seems* that beliefs should be relevant to justification only insofar as one recalls them. Non-occurrent beliefs can be recalled with varying degrees of difficulty, and if one is at the moment unable to recall a particular non-occurrent belief then it does not seem that that belief should play

8. For more recent incarnations of Lehrer's views, see his [1981] and [1982].

any role in determining whether some other occurrent belief is justified.

In deciding whether this objection has any real strength, we must give some thought to the concept of epistemic justification. Epistemic justification is supposed to be "regulatory" in some sense. It is concerned with which beliefs we should hold and which we should not. Considerations of epistemic justification are supposed to guide us, somehow, in deciding what to believe. It seems that a consideration can guide us in this way only if we have access to it. This is the same intuition that underlies the doxastic assumption. It seems that we do not have access, in the requisite sense, to non-occurrent beliefs, and so they cannot be relevant to justification.

It is hard to assess this objection. For one thing, it seems to turn upon an illegitimate kind of "doxastic voluntarism"—we do not literally *decide* what to believe. We do not have voluntary control over our beliefs. We cannot just decide to believe that $2 + 2 = 5$ and thereby do it. We have at most indirect control over what we believe. We can try to get ourselves to believe something by repeatedly rehearsing the evidence for it, or putting countervailing evidence out of our minds, or by deliberately seeking new evidence for it, but we cannot voluntarily make ourselves believe something in the same sense that we can voluntarily clench our fists. This makes it hard to understand how epistemic norms and considerations of epistemic justification can play a regulatory role in belief. If we cannot directly control what we believe, how can we regulate it in accordance with epistemic norms? On the other hand, epistemic justification is definitely a normative notion, and we do raise questions about whether we *should* hold various beliefs. Some kind of regulation seems to be involved, but it is hard to see what it amounts to.

The way in which epistemic norms regulate belief will become clearer in chapter five. In the meantime it is hard to evaluate the objection that, because we only have access to those of our beliefs that are occurrent, non-occurrent beliefs can play no direct role in epistemic justification. There is something intuitively persuasive about this; if it is correct then it seems to create difficulties for holistic coherence theories (positive or negative) because there will not be enough material available for a coherence relation to appeal to. Taking Lehrer's theory as an example, suppose S believes P, which competes with $Q_1, \ldots, Q_n$. S may non-occurrently believe that P is more probable than each Q_i (even this is dubious—do people normally have such beliefs?), but it is quite unlikely that in a normal situation S will have any occurrent probability beliefs of this sort. Thus if we are only allowed to appeal to occurrent beliefs, it will result from Lehrer's theory that we are hardly ever justified in believing anything.

This objection has a certain amount of intuitive force, but it is hard to be sure whether it should be regarded as fatal to Lehrer's theory. What this underscores is a problem that will become central when we turn to nondoxastic theories. This is the problem of understanding what epistemic justification is all about. Thus far we have taken the notion as given, we have assumed that we have a rough understanding of it, and we have formulated epistemological theories in terms of it. But what we are finding is that our grasp of the concept of epistemic justification is unclear in important respects, and that makes it difficult to adjudicate disputes between rival epistemological theories. Furthermore, it is not satisfactory to leave the central concept of epistemology unanalyzed. Only by providing some sort of analysis or clarification of the concept can we ultimately resolve these disputes. Unfortunately, providing such an analysis has proven to be a very hard problem. Most epistemologists have remained mute on the subject, not because they have no interest in it but because they have no answers to propose. The only epistemologists to propose analyses have been the externalists, and we will examine their accounts in chapter four. I will proffer my own analysis in chapter five.

The preceding objection is tempting but inconclusive. We can raise a different sort of objection to holistic positive coherence theories that seems more conclusive. This concerns the problem of the basing relation, which was discussed briefly in chapter one. There is a distinction between having good reason for believing something (perhaps without appreciating the reason) and believing something *for* a good reason. This is, roughly, the distinction between a justif*ied* belief and a justif*iable* belief. A justifiable belief is one the believer could become justified in believing if he just put together in the right way what he already believes. To illustrate, a man might have adequate evidence for believing that his wife is unfaithful to him, he might systematically ignore that evidence. However, when his mother, whom he knows to be totally unreliable in such matters and biased against his wife, tells him that his wife is unfaithful to him, but he believes it on that basis. Then his belief that his wife is unfaithful is unjustified but justifiable.

Any correct epistemological theory must allow this distinction. The problem with holistic positive coherence theories is that they seem to be incompatible with the distinction. The basing relation is at least partly a causal relation.[9] Being justified in holding a belief on a certain basis consists of your belief "arising out of" that basis in some appropriate way. But this does not seem to be possible on a holistic

---

9. Lehrer [1971] has argued against this, but I do not find his counterexample persuasive.

positive coherence theory. In order for the notion of a justified (as opposed to a merely justifiable) belief to make sense within such a theory, the coherence relation (whatever it is) must be such that the belief's cohering with one's overall doxastic system *can* cause one (in an appropriate way) to hold the belief. The coherence relation must be "appropriately causally efficacious" in the formation of belief. There are just two possibilities for the nature of the causal chains leading from coherence to belief. On the one hand, they might be "doxastic", whereby the believer first comes to believe that P coheres with his other beliefs and then comes to believe P on that basis. The simple objection to such a doxastic reconstruction of the basing relation is that we do not ordinarily have any such beliefs about coherence. A second objection is that it seems to lead to an infinite regress—would we not have to be justified in believing that P coheres, and if so would that not require our first coming to believe that the belief that P coheres with our other beliefs coheres with our other beliefs? I think it is clear that a holistic positive coherence theory cannot adopt such a doxastic account of the basing relation. Consequently, it must be possible for the kind of causal connection involved in the basing relation to cause belief in P without the believer having any beliefs about whether P coheres with his other beliefs. But is it at all plausible to suppose that the coherence relation is such that P's cohering with the believer's other beliefs can cause belief in a nondoxastic way? This must depend upon the nature of the proposed coherence relation, but it is hard to see how any plausible coherence relation could be appropriately causally efficacious. Consider, for example, Lehrer's proposed coherence relation. If coherence consists of S's believing P to be more probable than each of its competitors (individually, not collectively), how *could* this cause S to believe P except via S's first coming to believe that P coheres in this way? The same thing would seem to be true for any plausible coherence relation. Without concrete candidates to examine it is hard to be absolutely sure, but it seems that coherence relations will always involve elaborate logical relationships between beliefs, and the holding of such relationships can only be causally efficacious by virtue of one's coming to *believe* that the relationships hold. As a matter of psychological fact, such elaborate relationships cannot be nondoxastically causally efficacious. It seems quite unlikely that there could be any holistic coherence relation that can be appropriately causally efficacious in belief formation in such a way as to allow us to distinguish between justified and merely justifiable belief. This argument is not conclusive, because we cannot examine all possible putative coherence relations, but it provides a strong reason for being suspicious of holistic positive coherence theories as a group, and it seems to provide a conclusive reason for rejecting concrete examples of such theories.

The preceding arguments at least *suggest* the rejection of all positive coherence theories. If any coherence theory is to be defensible, it must be a negative coherence theory, so I turn to those theories next.

4. Negative Coherence Theories

Negative coherence theories accord all beliefs the status of prima facie justification. A negative coherence theory tells us that we are automatically justified in holding any belief we do hold unless we have some positive reason for thinking we should not hold it.[10] Something like the Neurath metaphor provides the principal motivation for such a theory. The idea is that we must start with the stock of beliefs we already have and then amend those beliefs in light of themselves.

Negative coherence theories differ in their account of what can defeat the justification of a belief. Perhaps the most natural account is one adopting the "classical" picture of reasons embodied in the foundations theory described in chapter two. However, Gilbert Harman ([1973], [1980], [1984], and [1986]) is the only author to argue vigorously for a negative coherence theory, and he adopts a nonclassical view of defeaters. Harman [1984] writes:

> Reasoning is a process of change in overall view. One's conclusion is in a sense one's whole modified view and not any single statement. . . . Reasoning involves two factors—conservatism and coherence. One seeks in reasoning to minimize change in one's overall view, modifying it only to explain more and leave less unexplained [p. 154].

According to Harman, coherence is *explanatory coherence*. We modify our overall doxastic system only in response to explanatory considerations. We may add a belief because it explains other things we believe, and we may delete a belief because we cannot explain how it could be true or because it is incompatible with something else we believe on explanatory grounds.

Harman's theory illustrates something interesting about negative coherence theories. By definition, negative coherence theories hold that reasons are not required for the justification of a belief—beliefs are automatically justified unless you have a reason for rejecting them. This gives reasons a negative role in belief change. On the surface, this is compatible with their also playing a positive role. It

---

10. This is what Gilbert Harman [1984] and [1986] calls "the principle of positive undermining".

may be that reasons also function to justify the acquisition of new beliefs on the basis of beliefs already held. Harman's theory seems to incorporate both sorts of elements, telling us that we should add beliefs under some circumstances and delete beliefs under others. According to Harman, we need reasons to accept beliefs but we do not need reasons to retain them. Harman's theory is subject to criticism on this ground. A negative coherence theory should never assign reasons more than a negative role. The difficulty is that epistemic norms never tell us that it is *epistemically obligatory* to believe something—only that it is *epistemically permissible* to do so. It is not true, for example, that if I believe both P and (P ⊃ Q) then, in the absence of conflicting reasons, I ought to believe Q. This is because I may not care about Q. Harman himself ([1984] and [1986]) has repeatedly made the point that we have a limited capacity for information-processing. We do not want to clutter up our minds drawing conclusions willy-nilly. We only draw conclusions in which, for some reason, we are interested. Thus epistemic rules governing the acquisition of new beliefs must always be permission rules. There can be epistemic rules telling us that it is obligatory to *reject* certain beliefs already held, but it can never be obligatory to *acquire* a belief not already held.

It may seem that a negative coherence theory can accommodate this observation by taking the positive role of reasoning to be one of making it permissible to acquire new beliefs under various circumstances. After all, this would be the positive role accorded to reasoning by either a foundations theory or a positive coherence theory. But a negative coherence theory cannot adopt this line. That is because according to a negative coherence theory it is *always* permissible to adopt a new belief—*any* new belief. Because beliefs are prima facie justified you do not need a reason for adopting a new belief. Of course, having adopted a new belief it may immediately become obligatory to reject it (because it is incoherent with your other beliefs). But having positive reasons for the new belief could only ensure that it is not obligatory to reject it if the positive reasons are constructed so as to automatically ensure that there are no negative reasons legislating the rejection. In that case (assuming a negative coherence theory), the positive reason is really playing no role other than the negative one of ruling out reasons for rejecting the new belief. In other words, it is still just a defeater. So within a negative coherence theory, a positive role cannot be assigned to reasons in any way that is consistent with the observation that epistemic norms governing belief acquisition can only be permission rules.

This suggests modifying Harman's theory a bit by assigning only negative roles to explanatory coherence, taking a belief to be unjustified if either (1) we cannot (within the context of our overall doxastic system) explain how it could be true, or (2) the best explanation for other features of our beliefs is incompatible with this particular belief. Harman defends these principles of belief revision by arguing that as a matter of psychological fact people do not stop believing things whenever they cease to have reasons for believing them. On the contrary, a principle of conservativeness operates in belief revision, leading us to reject beliefs only when we acquire positive reasons for doing so. His argument for this is, roughly, that we do not usually remember our reasons for very long, and when we forget them we persist in holding the belief anyway. Furthermore, that is the only reasonable way for a creature with limited memory storage to function. We do not have the capacity to remember all our reasons. Normally, what is important is the conclusions—not the reasons. All of this seems right, but as I pointed out in the introduction to this chapter, such considerations do not constitute a defense of negative coherence theories. This is because they can be accommodated just as well by according memory a positive role in epistemic justification, supposing that one's seeming to remember something constitutes a positive reason for believing it. Harman is certainly right that a principle of conservativeness operates in our system of belief revision, but this can be accommodated *either* by adopting a negative coherence theory *or* by adopting a positive view of reasons and taking apparent memory to supply positive reasons. To decide between these two accounts we must examine them more closely.

I have always found negative coherence theories appealing, and have repeatedly returned to the task of trying to construct a defensible theory of this sort. But despite their intuitive appeal, I am convinced that such theories cannot be successfully defended. There are two related sorts of considerations that lead me to this conclusion. The first is analogous to one of the objections I raised to holistic positive coherence theories. Any reasonable theory must make it possible to draw the distinction between justified and merely justifiable beliefs. But that distinction seems to be incompatible with a negative coherence theory. The distinction has to do with the basing relation and the basis upon which one holds a belief. But if reasons do not play some positive role in belief formation, there can be no such thing as holding a belief for a particular reason or on a particular basis. If reasons play only a negative role, then they are only relevant as defeaters for beliefs already held. According to a negative coherence theory, how one comes to hold a belief is irrelevant to its justification. But this seems clearly false. The examples used earlier to illustrate the distinction appear to demonstrate conclusively that reasons do play a positive role in the justification of belief. For instance, recall the example in chapter two of the person who is constructing a mathematical proof, who wants to draw a particular conclusion at a certain point, who has earlier lines in his proof from which that conclusion follows immediately, but who overlooks that connection and in despair simply writes down the desired conclusion thinking to himself, "Oh, that's got to be true." That person is not justified in believing the conclusion, and the reason he is not justified is that he does not believe it on the basis of the earlier lines from which it follows. Those earlier lines would give him a good reason if he just saw the connection, but he does not and so he is unjustified in believing the new conclusion.

When one believes something by remembering it, positive and negative accounts of reasoning give the same result. The above objection amounts to a defense of the principle that if one holds a non-memory belief for a bad reason or for no reason at all, that belief is not justified. This is precisely what a positive account of reasons would predict. As I remarked in chapter two, there seems to be just one way that a negative account can accommodate this, and that is by supposing that when one holds a belief for a bad reason or for no reason at all, that automatically gives him a reason for thinking he should not hold the belief. In point of fact, the negative coherence theorist cannot formulate the supposition in this way because he does not accord reasons a positive role, but he might instead formulate the supposition as follows:

If one believes P unjustifiably then he automatically has a belief that is a defeater for believing P.

But does one automatically have such a belief? Thus far I have avoided simply rejecting this epistemic principle, but my only reason for doing so was to make doxastic theories more plausible for the sake of the discussion. In fact, this epistemic principle seems obviously wrong. This is because one need not be aware of why one holds a belief. Upon reflecting on a belief I may decide that I have no good reason for holding it and that it is just a manifestation of wishful thinking or some other epistemically proscribed cognitive process. Once I have decided that, it seems I have a reason for thinking I should not hold the belief, but prior to deciding that it does not seem that I have any such reason. Nevertheless, if I hold the belief on the basis of wishful thinking, then my belief is unjustified. But then it follows that the belief can be unjustified without my having a defeating belief (or more intuitively, without my having a reason for thinking I should not hold the belief). In other words, not all beliefs are prima facie justified, and hence negative coherence theories are false

These two objections seem to me to be conclusive. Reasons must be accorded some sort of positive role in justification. The intuition to the contrary turns upon confusing memory belief with believing something for no reason. These are two quite different phenomena. In light of the preceding discussion, it seems inescapable that memory itself plays a certifying role in memory beliefs. The belief is justified *because* we seem to remember it. On the other hand, the certifying role of memory is no more easily accommodated by foundations theories than it is by coherence theories. This is because, as we noted in chapter two, when we remember something we do not usually have a belief to the effect that we seem to remember it, and hence the memory belief cannot be regarded as being held on the basis of an epistemologically basic belief about seeming to remember. This difficulty is a very general one. I regard it as symptomatic of the failure of all doxastic theories. Doxastic theories are based on the doxastic assumption according to which the only things relevant to the justifiedness of a belief are one's beliefs. Neither perception nor memory can be accommodated within a doxastic theory. Arguing that will be the burden of the next section.

5. Nondoxastic Theories and Direct Realism

Perception is a causal process that injects beliefs about physical objects into our doxastic system. Given the doxastic assumption, the only belief changes that are subject to rational epistemic evaluation are those made exclusively in response to your other beliefs. Facts about the perceptual situation, such as how you are appeared to, can only be relevant to the epistemic evaluation of your perceptual belief insofar as you believe those facts. In a normal case you have no beliefs about how you are appeared to, and the beliefs you do have prior to acquiring the perceptual belief are not sufficient to uniquely determine what perceptual belief you should acquire. For example, the beliefs you have antecedently will not normally determine whether, upon examining a new object, you should believe it to be red or green. You normally have to look at an object to determine what color you should believe it to be. In other words, perception is not inference from antecedently held beliefs. Because perceptual beliefs cannot be inferred from other beliefs, there is no way to "consider a potential perceptual belief" before we acquire it and make a rational decision whether to adopt it. We can, of course, consider counterfactually whether a certain belief would cohere if we were to adopt it, but that cannot be what transpires in perception because we do not know which potential perceptual belief to evaluate until we actually have the belief. "There is a red book before me" and "There is a green book before me" may both cohere with the rest of my beliefs. It is not coherence that determines which to evaluate—it is the causal processes of perception that inject one of these beliefs rather than the other into my doxastic system. It would only be possible to evaluate a potential perceptual belief "before the fact" if I had appearance beliefs and were deciding whether to adopt the perceptual belief in response to them. In other words, it is only possible to evaluate potential perceptual beliefs about physical objects prior to acquiring them if we can reduce perception to inference from epistemologically basic beliefs, and we have seen that that cannot be done.

Although it follows from the doxastic assumption that the perceptual acquisition of beliefs about physical objects cannot be subject to epistemic evaluation, the beliefs themselves can be subject to epistemic evaluation in terms of how they are related to other beliefs. But this can only happen *after* they become beliefs. Thus if we accept the doxastic assumption, we must view the perceptual acquisition of beliefs as automatically epistemically permissible and hence the beliefs themselves are automatically justified *unless* they conflict somehow with other beliefs. That is, they must be prima facie justified.

Apparently, any doxastic theory must regard the beliefs issuing most directly from perception as prima facie justified. (The same point can be made about memory beliefs.) Doxastic theories can differ with regard to which beliefs are the ones issuing most directly from perception, and how generally the property of prima facie justification is shared by other beliefs, but they must accord this status to whichever beliefs they identify as perceptual beliefs. Stereotypical foundations theories assume that the beliefs issuing most directly from perception are appearance beliefs (and they typically assign them an even stronger status than prima facie justification), but that seems to be psychologically inaccurate. The normal doxastic progeny of perception are perfectly ordinary beliefs about physical objects. A psychologically realistic foundations theory must maintain that physical-object beliefs are prima facie justified while most other beliefs are not. I argued at the end of chapter two, however, that such a position is untenable. The difficulty was that one can believe the very same thing either perceptually or for a variety of non-perceptual reasons, and if one holds the belief for a non-perceptual reason and it is a bad reason then one is not justified in holding the belief. The only way around this, and hence the only way to assign prima facie justification to physical-object beliefs, is to embrace the epistemic principle that when one holds a belief for no reason or for a bad reason one automatically has a reason for thinking he should not hold the belief. This has the consequence that *all* beliefs are prima facie justified. Thus we are forced to trade a foundations theory for a negative coherence theory. The conclusion to be drawn is that the only way to accommodate perception within a doxastic theory is to adopt a negative coherence theory. The difficulty with this way of accommodating perception is that it turns upon the epistemic principle that when one holds a belief for no reason or for a bad reason one automatically has a reason for thinking he should not hold it. As I urged at the end of the last section, that principle seems to be false. It follows that the doxastic assumption must be false as well.

This argument against the doxastic assumption is of vital importance, so let me briefly repeat it stripped of explanatory remarks:

1. Suppose the doxastic assumption holds. Then the justifiedness of a perceptual belief can only depend upon your other beliefs and cannot depend upon any features of perception not encoded in belief. In particular, it cannot depend upon your being appeared to in appropriate ways if (as is usually the case) you do not have beliefs to the effect that you are appeared to in those ways.

2. In a normal case, your other beliefs cannot determine that just one possible perceptual belief could be justified. You cannot, for example, tell what color you should believe something to be without looking at it. Therefore, perceptual beliefs cannot be evaluated before being acquired, because it is the very fact of acquiring the perceptual belief that determines which possible belief (e.g., 'That is red' rather than 'That is green') to evaluate.

3. It follows that the acquisition of a perceptual belief is automatically justified, and its relationship to other beliefs can only be relevant negatively. In other words, perceptual beliefs must be prima facie justified.

4. Perceptual beliefs are ordinary physical-object beliefs, and such beliefs can also be held for non-perceptual reasons. If such reasons are bad reasons, the beliefs are not justified. But then it follows that they are not prima facie justified.

5. (4) conflicts with (3), so the assumption from which (3) followed, namely the doxastic assumption, must be false.

The falsity of the doxastic assumption can also be argued more straightforwardly by looking at physical-object beliefs held directly on the basis of perception. The doxastic assumption implies that the acquisition of such beliefs is not subject to epistemic evaluation—the only thing we can evaluate epistemically is one's continuing to hold such a belief after it is acquired. On the doxastic assumption we must adopt the belief first and then decide whether to discard it rather than deciding whether to adopt it in the first place. But this is manifestly false. For example, suppose you know you are in a room bathed in red light (e.g., this is done in military maneuvers to enhance night vision), and you know the effect this has on the colors things look. Under these circumstances, if you see a piece of paper before you and it looks red, you would be unjustified in making the perceptual judgment that it is red. It is not just that you would be unjustified in retaining that belief once you acquire it—you should not acquire it in the first place. You "know better". This is a normative epistemic judgment. The possibility of such a judgment indicates that epistemic norms apply to the perceptual acquisition of beliefs, and hence must be able to appeal to nondoxastic states. What makes a normal perceptual belief epistemically permissible (i.e., justified) is that one *is in* an appropriate perceptual state (i.e., is appeared to in appropriate ways) and has no defeating beliefs. The latter is a matter of beliefs, but the former is not. One does not have to *believe* that he is in the perceptual state. So the justifiedness of a belief is a function of more than just one's beliefs. At the very least, how one is appeared to is also relevant. The same point can be made about memory. The *fact that* one seems to remember can make one justified in holding a belief—one does not have to believe that he seems to remember. It follows that the doxastic assumption is false.

To recapitulate, foundations theories and coherence theories fail for basically the same reason—epistemic rationality is not just a function of one's beliefs. Both beliefs and nondoxastic perceptual and memory states are relevant to the justifiedness of a belief. Foundations theories try to take account of perceptual states and memory states by supposing we always have beliefs about them, but in this they are mistaken. Coherence theories rightly reject such epistemologically basic beliefs, but they throw out the baby with the bathwater. By rejecting appearance and apparent-memory beliefs but refusing to allow nondoxastic appeal to perceptual states and memory states they make it impossible to accommodate perception and memory. The right response is to reject appearance beliefs, in the sense of admitting that the justifiedness of perceptual and memory beliefs does not depend upon our having appearance and apparent-memory beliefs, but to acknowledge that our epistemic norms must be able to appeal to perceptual and memory states directly and without doxastic mediation. It is *the fact that* I am appeared to redly that justifies me in thinking there is something red before me, and it is *the fact that* I seem to remember that Columbus landed in America in 1492 that justifies me in believing that. It is not my *believing* that I am appeared to redly or my *believing* that I seem to remember that Columbus landed in 1492 that is required for justification.

The true epistemological theory must be nondoxastic. This still leaves us with a wide variety of possibilities. In particular, there are both internalist and externalist nondoxastic theories. Internalist theories insist that although the justifiedness of a belief is not a function exclusively of one's other beliefs, it is a function exclusively of one's internal states, where the latter include both beliefs and nondoxastic states. Internal states are, roughly, those to which we have "direct access". Externalist theories insist, on the other hand, that the justifiedness of a belief may also be determined by entirely external considerations like the reliability (in the actual world) of the cognitive processes producing the belief.

Externalist theories depart radically from traditional doxastic theories, and they will be the subject of the next chapter. Nondoxastic internalist theories, however, may have structures very similar to classical foundations theories. For instance, *direct realism* is the view that perceptual states can license perceptual judgments about physical objects directly and without mediation by beliefs about the perceptual states. Direct realism can have a structure very much like a foundations theory. My own view is that the foundations theory sketched in chapter two gets things almost right. Where it goes wrong is in adopting the doxastic assumption and thereby assuming that perceptual input must be mediated by epistemologically basic beliefs. It now seems clear that epistemic norms can appeal directly to our being in perceptual states and need not appeal to our having beliefs to that effect. In other words, there can be "half-doxastic" epistemic connections between beliefs and nondoxastic states that are analogous to the "fully doxastic" connections between beliefs and beliefs that we call 'reasons'. I propose to call the half-doxastic connections 'reasons' as well, but it must be acknowledged that this is stretching our ordinary use of the term 'reason'. The motivation for this terminology is that the logical structure of such connections is analogous to the logical structure of ordinary prima facie reasons. That is, the halfdoxastic connections convey justification defeasibly, and the defeaters are completely analogous to the defeaters proposed by the foundations theory formulated in chapter two.

Direct realism retains the attractive intuitions about the connection between justification and reasoning that are part and parcel of classical foundations theories, while avoiding the shortcomings of such theories by giving up the doxastic assumption. I am inclined to regard some form of direct realism as true. I have not yet argued for this conclusion, however. The basic argument so far has been against the doxastic assumption, and nondoxastic theories other than direct realism are possible. In particular, there are externalist nondoxastic theories. I will turn to the consideration of externalist theories in the next chapter. Finally, in chapter five, I will argue that a correct understanding of the nature of epistemic norms requires that a true epistemological theory be internalist. As it must also be nondoxastic, I will take that to be a defense of direct realism, and I will give a somewhat more detailed sketch of how direct realism should be formulated.

4

EXTERNALISM

1. Motivation

ALL OF THE THEORIES discussed so far have been internalist theories. Doxastic theories take the justifiability of a belief to be a function exclusively of what else one believes. Internalist theories in general loosen that requirement, taking justifiability to be determined more generally by one's internal states. Beliefs are internal states, but so are perceptual states, memory states, and so on. Internal states have been only vaguely characterized as those to which we have "direct access". This vagueness must eventually be remedied, but further clarification will have to await chapter five. Externalist theories loosen the requirement for justifiability still further, insisting that more than the believer's internal states is relevant to the justifiability of a belief. For instance, reliabilism takes the reliability of the cognitive process generating the belief to be relevant to its justifiability.

The primary motivation for externalism proceeds in two stages. The first consists of the rejection of all doxastic theories. That rejection was defended above on the grounds that doxastic theories cannot handle perceptual input, which is basically a nondoxastic process that is nevertheless subject to rational evaluation. Thus we must select an epistemological theory from among nondoxastic theories. The externalist proposes that this selection be driven by a particular intuition. This is the intuition that we want our beliefs to be probable—we should not hold a belief unless it is probable. Probability, however exactly it is brought to bear on the selection of beliefs, is an external consideration. The probability of one's belief, or the reliability of the cognitive process producing it, is not something to which one has direct access. Thus we are led to an externalist theory that evaluates the justification of a belief at least partly on the basis of external considerations of probability.

There is also a secondary motivation for the particular kinds of externalist theories that have been proposed in the literature. The doxastic theories discussed above propose very elaborate criteria for the justification of a belief. For instance, both the foundations theory of chapter two and the version of direct realism sketched at the end of the last chapter proceed by laying down a complex array of epistemic rules governing the justification of various kinds of judgments. A linear coherence theory proceeds similarly, adopting a structure of reasons similar to those involved in foundations theories (although in the case of negative coherence theories the rules only concern defeaters). And a similar point can be made about extant holistic coherence theories. For example, although Lehrer's theory does not proceed in terms of linear reasons, he too proposes a very complicated criterion for justification. (The full complexity of his criterion is not indicated by the brief sketch of his theory given in chapter three.) All of these theories proceed by initially taking the concept of epistemic justification for granted, and then using our intuitions about epistemic justification to guide us in the construction of a criterion that accords with those intuitions. A telling objection can be raised against all of these internalist theories—they are simultaneously ad hoc and incomplete. They are ad hoc in that they propose arrays of epistemic rules without giving any systematic account of why those should be the right rules, and they are incomplete in that they propose no illuminating analysis of epistemic justification.[1] The methodology of internalism has been to describe our reasoning rather than to justify it or explain it. These two points are connected. As long as we take the concept of epistemic justification to be primitive and unanalyzed, there is no way to *prove* that a particular epistemic rule is a correct rule. All we can do is collect rules that seem intuitively right, but we are left without any way of justifying or supporting our intuitions.

It might be responded that internalist theories do not leave the concept of epistemic justification unanalyzed. The criteria of justifiedness that they propose could be regarded as analyses of justification.[2] But even if one of these criteria correctly described which beliefs are justified, it would not explain what epistemic justification is all about. The criterion would not provide an *illuminating* analysis. Because of its very complexity we would be left wondering why we should employ such a concept of epistemic justification. Its use would be unmotivated. What we would have is basically an ad hoc theory that is contrived to give the right answer but is unable to explain in any deep way why that is the right answer. What we really want is an analysis of epistemic justification that makes it manifest why we should be interested in the notion. The analysis could then be used to generate a principled account of epistemic norms. An account of this sort would not proceed by simply listing the epistemic rules that seem to be required to license those beliefs we regard as actually being justified.

1. Ernest Sosa [1980] raises this objection.
2. For example, Lehrer casts his theory as an analysis of epistemic justification.

Instead, it would *derive* the rules from the concept of epistemic justification. No epistemological theory yet discussed in this book has that character.

Most doxastic theorists have had remarkably little to say about the analysis of epistemic justification. This is not due to lack of interest—it is due to lack of ideas. Within the context of an internalist theory, the analysis of epistemic justification has proven to be an extremely difficult problem. Here is a respect in which externalist theories appear to have a marked advantage. If it is granted that the justifiedness of a belief can be determined partly by external considerations, then it becomes feasible to try to analyze justification in terms of probability. That seems like a very hopeful approach. Lehrer [1974] expresses this idea succinctly in his critical discussion of foundationalism:

> What I object to is postulation without justification when it is perfectly clear that an unstated justification motivates the postulation. The justification is that people are so constructed that the beliefs in question, whether perceptual beliefs, memory beliefs, or whatnot, have a reasonable probability of being true. [p. 77]

It is worth noting, however, that Lehrer's own theory diverges from this basic idea and thereby becomes subject to the same sort of criticism. This is because technical considerations lead him to an analysis no less complex than other internalist analyses. The simple intuition that justified beliefs must be probable provides no explanation at all for this complicated structure. Lehrer has merely replaced the complicated structure of foundations theories by another complicated structure, without any explanation for why justification should have either structure. He is as guilty of postulating epistemic rules as the foundations theorist.[3]

The hope that some simple analysis can be given of epistemic justification in terms of probability has had a powerful influence on epistemologists and has made externalist theories seem attractive. But it must be emphasized that such an analysis has to be simple. If the externalist is led to a complicated analysis, he will have been no more successful than the internalist in explaining why epistemic justification is a notion of interest to us. His theory will be no less ad hoc. The only virtue of the externalist theory will be the same one claimed (perhaps falsely) by all other theories, namely, that they correctly pick out the right beliefs as justified. Of course, that itself would be no mean feat.

---

3. Lehrer's theory diverges from his basic intuition in another respect as well. His theory is formulated in terms of *beliefs about* probabilities rather than in terms of the probabilities themselves. Otherwise, his theory would not be a doxastic theory.

To summarize, there are two sources for the appeal externalism has exercised on recent epistemologists. On the one hand, externalist theories seek to capture the common intuition that there is an intimate connection between epistemic justification and probability. On the other hand, there is the hope that an externalist analysis can explain what justification is all about rather than merely providing a correct criterion for justifiedness.

Externalist theories promise dividends not provided by any of the theories thus far discussed. But to evaluate these promisory notes, we must look more carefully at actual externalist theories. Two kinds of externalist theories can be found in the literature—probabilism and reliabilism. Probabilism attempts to characterize the justifiedness of a belief in terms of its probability and the probability of related beliefs. Reliabilism seeks instead to characterize the justifiedness of a belief in terms of more general probabilities pertaining not just to the belief in question but to the cognitive processes responsible for the belief. Probabilism and reliabilism will be the subjects of sections three and four, respectively. Before we can discuss them, however, we must lay some groundwork.

2. Varieties of Probability

Philosophers tend to make too facile a use of probability. They throw the word around with great abandon and often just assume that there is some way of making sense of their varied pronouncements, when frequently there is not. The main difficulty is that there is more than one kind of probability and philosophers tend to conflate them. A reasoned assessment of externalist theories requires us to make some careful distinctions between different kinds of probability. One important distinction is that between physical probability and epistemic probability. *Physical probability* pertains to the structure of the physical world and is independent of knowledge or opinion. For instance, the laws of quantum mechanics state physical probabilities. Physical probabilities are discovered by observing relative frequencies, and they are the subject matter of much of statistics. Physical probability provides the stereotype in terms of which most philosophers think of probability. But another important use of the word 'probable' in ordinary speech is to talk about degree of justification. For instance, after looking at the clues the detective may decide that it is probable that "the butler did it". Probability in this sense is directly concerned with knowledge and opinion and has no direct connection to the physical structure of the world. The *epistemic probability* of a proposition is a measure of its degree of justification. Epistemic

probability is relative to a person and a time. It is an open question
whether numerical values can be assigned to epistemic probabilities,
and even if they can it is not a foregone conclusion that they will
conform to the same mathematical principles (the probability calculus) as physical probabilities.

In addition to physical and epistemic probabilities, it is arguable
that there are *mixed physical/epistemic probabilities* that are required for
decision theory, weather forecasting, and so on. These probabilities
appeal both to general physical facts about the world and to our
knowledge of the present circumstances and how they relate to those
general physical facts.[4] I will say more about these mixed probabilities
below.

There is a second distinction that is related to but not identical with
the distinction between physical and epistemic probabilities. We can
distinguish between *definite probabilities* and *indefinite probabilities*. Definite probabilities are the probabilities that particular propositions are
true or that particular states of affairs obtain. Indefinite probabilities,
on the other hand, concern concepts or classes or properties rather
than propositions. We can talk about the indefinite probability of a
smoker contracting lung cancer. This is not about any particular
smoker—it is about the class of all smokers, or about the property of
being a smoker and its relationship to the property of contracting
lung cancer. Some theories of probability take definite probabilities to
be basic, and others begin with indefinite probabilities. Epistemic
probabilities are always definite probabilities. Physical probabilities
might be either. Theories taking physical probabilities to be closely
related to relative frequencies make them indefinite probabilities.
This is because relative frequencies concern classes or properties
rather than single individuals. But there is also an important class of
theories—"propensity theories"—that take the basic physical probabilities to pertain to individual objects. For example, we can talk about
the probability that a particular coin will land heads on the next toss.
Such "propensities" are definite probabilities.

There are three broad categories of probability theories to be
found in the current literature, and externalists could in principle
appeal to any of them, so I turn now to a brief sketch of each kind of
theory.

2.1 *Subjective Probability*

Theories of subjective probability begin with the platitude that
belief comes in degrees, in the sense that I may hold one belief more

4. For more on the interrelationships between these various kinds of probability,
see my [1984a], and for a complete account see my [198?c].

firmly than another, or that I can have varying degrees of confidence in different beliefs. The subjectivist is quick to explain, however, that he is using 'degree of belief' in a technical way. What he *means* by 'degree of belief' is something measured by betting behavior.[5] Officially, to say that a person has a degree of belief 2/3 in a proposition P is to say that he would accept a bet with 2:1 odds that P is true but would not accept a bet with less favorable odds. Given this technical construal of degrees of belief, the subjective probability of a proposition (relative to a person and a time) is identified with either (a) the person's degree of belief in that proposition, or (b) the degree of belief he rationally should have in the proposition given his overall situation. We can distinguish between these two conceptions of subjective probability as *actual degree of belief* and *rational degree of belief*.[6] It is generally claimed that subjective probability is a variety of epistemic probability.

There are problems for both conceptions of subjective probability. The principal difficulty for subjective probability as actual degree of belief is that the degrees of belief of real people will not satisfy the probability calculus. According to the probability calculus, probabilities satisfy the following three conditions:

THE PROBABILITY CALCULUS:

(1) $0 \leq \text{prob}(P) \leq 1$.

(2) if P and Q are logically incompatible with each other then $\text{prob}(P \lor Q) = \text{prob}(P) + \text{prob}(Q)$.

(3) If P is a tautology then $\text{prob}(P) = 1$.[7]

A person's degrees of belief are said to be *coherent* (in a sense unrelated to coherence theories of knowledge) if and only if they conform to the probability calculus. It is generally granted by all concerned that real people cannot be expected to have coherent degrees of belief. If there was ever any doubt about this, contemporary psychologists have delighted in establishing this experimentally. For some purposes the lack of coherence would not be a difficulty, but for the uses to which probability is put in epistemology it is generally essential that probability satisfy the probability calculus. Recall, for example, its use in Lehrer's theory. To carry out the kinds of calcula-

---

5. See, for example, Rudolf Carnap [1962].

6. Leonard Savage [1954] proposed to distinguish between these by calling them 'subjective probability' and 'personalist probability', but this terminology is used only infrequently.

7. It is customary to add a fourth axiom, to the effect that logically equivalent propositions have the same probability. This axiom implies that necessary truths have probability 1. I will not assume this axiom in the current discussion because it only exacerbates the problem of making fruitful use of probability within epistemology.

tions required by his theory, he must assume that probabilities conform to the probability calculus. It follows that subjective probability as actual degree of belief is of little use in epistemology.

Mainly because of the failure of actual degrees of belief to satisfy the probability calculus, most subjectivists adopt the 'rational degree of belief' construal of subjective probability. But this construal is beset with its own problems. The first concerns whether rational degrees of belief satisfy the probability calculus any more than do actual degrees of belief. There is a standard argument that is supposed to show that they do. This is the Dutch book argument. In betting parlance, a "Dutch book" is a combination of bets on which a person will suffer a collective loss no matter what happens. For instance, suppose you are betting on a coin toss and are willing to accept odds of 2:1 that the coin will land heads and are also willing to accept odds of 2:1 that the coin will land tails. I could then place two bets with you, betting 50 cents against the coin landing heads and also betting 50 cents against the coin landing tails, with the result that no matter what happens I will have to pay you 50 cents on one bet but you will have to pay me one dollar on the other. In other words, you have a guaranteed loss— Dutch book can be made against you. The Dutch book argument consists of a mathematical proof that if your degrees of belief (which, remember, are betting quotients) do not conform to the probability calculus then Dutch book can be made against you.[8] It is alleged that it is clearly irrational to put yourself in such a position, so it cannot be rational to have incoherent degrees of belief.

A number of objections can be raised to this argument. First, recall the distinction between epistemic rationality and prudential rationality. As we saw in chapter one, these are distinct concepts. The Dutch book argument seems to be concerned with prudential rationality— not epistemic rationality. It may be prudentially irrational to put yourself in a situation in which you are guaranteed to lose, but what has that to do with the epistemic rationality of belief? This is connected with the definition of subjective probability. Subjective probability is defined to be the degree of belief it is rational to have in a proposition, but this overlooks the distinction between prudential and epistemic rationality. Which should be employed in the definition of subjective probability? The degree of belief it is epistemically rational to have in a proposition looks initially like what was defined above as epistemic probability, but this does not fit well with the technical notion of 'degree of belief' defined in terms of betting behavior. It does not seem to make any sense to say that certain betting behavior is or is not epistemically rational. Only prudential rationality is applica-

---

8. This was first proven by Bruno de Finetti [1937].

ble to betting behavior, and it seems that subjective probability must be understood in this way.

Two stances are now possible. It could be that the subjectivist has simply confused these two kinds of rationality and that the confusion pervades his entire theory. A more charitable reading of subjective probability theory would take it as an explicit attempt to reduce epistemic rationality to prudential rationality. On this understanding, subjective probability is defined as the degree of belief it is prudentially rational to have, and so understood it may be used to explicate epistemic rationality. Subjective probability might be used in different ways to explicate epistemic rationality. The simplest proposal would be to identify the epistemic probability of a proposition with its (prudential) subjective probability, but other more complicated alternatives are also possible and I will say more about them in the next section.

Adopting the charitable construal of subjective probability, does the Dutch book argument establish that subjective probabilities must conform to the probability calculus? I do not think that it does. Contrary to the argument, it is not automatically irrational to accept odds allowing Dutch book to be made against you. If you are considering a very complicated set of bets (as you would be if you were betting on all your beliefs at once), it may be far from obvious whether the odds you accept satisfy the probability calculus. If you have no reason to suspect that they do not, and could not be expected to recognize that they do not without undertaking an extensive mathematical investigation of the situation, then surely you are not being *irrational* in accepting incoherent odds. You may be making a mistake of some sort, but you are not automatically irrational just because you make a mistake.

The Dutch book argument will not do it, but perhaps there is some other way of arguing that the degrees of belief it is prudentially rational to have must conform to the probability calculus. Let us just pretend for the moment that this is the case. Thus one constraint on rational degrees of belief becomes satisfaction of the probability calculus. Are there any other constraints? Some probability theorists write as if this were the only constraint. But others acknowledge that there must be further constraints. For example, so-called "Bayesian epistemologists" (discussed below) adopt constraints regarding how our degrees of belief should change as we acquire new evidence. But these are still rather minimal constraints.

The question I want to raise now is whether subjective probability as *the* degree of belief one should rationally have in a proposition is well defined. Specifically, is there any reason to think that, in each specific case, there is a *unique* degree of belief it is rationally permissible to have? Consider someone who has actual degrees of belief that do not satisfy the probability calculus (as we all have). If rational degrees of belief must be unique then there must be a unique way of transforming his actual degrees of belief into ideally rational degrees of belief. Whether this is so will depend upon what constraints there are. If the only constraint is that rational degrees of belief satisfy the probability calculus, there will be infinitely many ways of changing our actual degrees of belief so that the resulting degrees of belief are rational. The coherence constraint gives us no way to choose between them, because it tells us nothing at all about how our rationally changed degrees of belief should be related to our initial degrees of belief. The coherence constraint only concerns the product of changing our degrees of belief to make them rational; it does not concern how those resulting degrees of belief are gotten from the original incoherent degrees of belief. In fact, no constraints that have ever been proposed are of any help here. Some, like the Bayesian constraints, *sound* as if they should be helpful because they concern how degrees of belief should change under various circumstances, but they are of no actual help because they assume that the degrees of belief with which we begin satisfy the probability calculus.

The possible confusion between epistemic and prudential rationality is relevant here. If we are allowed to bring all the resources of epistemology to bear, it seems likely that there will be a unique degree of belief (in the sense of degree of confidence) that we should have in any particular proposition in any fixed epistemic setting. However, characterizing subjective probability in this way involves giving up its characterization in terms of prudential rationality. If we proceed in this way, then it will obviously be circular to turn around and use subjective probability to analyze epistemic justification, and the latter is the avowed purpose of the externalist endeavor.

If subjective probability is to be useful to the externalist, it must be defined in terms of prudential rationality rather than epistemic rationality, so we cannot appeal to epistemic constraints to guarantee that there is a unique degree of belief we rationally ought to have in each proposition. The constraints can only be prudential. It might be supposed that although no one has been able to enumerate them, there are some prudential constraints on rational degrees of belief that will enable us to get from incoherent actual degrees of belief to unique rational degrees of belief satisfying the probability calculus. Is this at all plausible? I think not, because I think that unlike epistemically rational degrees of confidence, rational betting quotients are not always uniquely determined by the epistemic situation. For example, suppose I hold one ticket from each of two lotteries—lottery A and lottery B. One of the lotteries is a 100–ticket lottery, and the other is a

1000–ticket lottery, but I do not know which is which. I am now required to bet on whether I will win lottery A and whether I will win lottery B. Is there a unique rational bet that I should make? It does not seem so. I know that *either* my chances of winning A are .01 and my chances of winning B are .001, *or* vice versa, but I have no way of choosing between these two alternatives. Perhaps it is irrational for me to bet in accordance with any combination of odds other than one of these two, but there can be no rational constraint favoring one of them over the other. Alternatively it might be insisted that I should regard it as equally likely that (a) lottery A has 100 tickets and lottery B has 1000, and (b) lottery A has 1000 tickets and lottery B has 100, and so I should weigh these possibilities equally and arrive at a degree of belief of $.01 \times .5 + .001 \times .5 = .0055$ for winning either lottery. But this seems wrong. Intuitively, there would be nothing irrational about betting at odds of 1:99 and 1:999 instead.[9] It certainly seems as though there is no unique rational bet in this case, and it follows that the subjective probability does not exist. Furthermore, although this is a contrived case, reflection indicates that it is not atypical of most of the situations in which we actually find ourselves. So it must be concluded that unique prudentially rational degrees of belief rarely, if ever, exist.

To summarize, I regard the entire theory of subjective probability as being pervasively confused, turning upon a conflation of epistemic and prudential rationality. If we define subjective probability in terms of prudential rationality, subjective probabilities do not exist. If instead we define subjective probability in terms of epistemic rationality and forgo the characterization of degrees of belief in terms of betting behavior, then the notion makes sense but it becomes identical with epistemic probability defined as 'degree of justification'. In the latter case, none of the technical apparatus of subjective probability theory can be brought to bear any longer. The Dutch book argument becomes inapplicable, and there is no reason to attribute any particular mathematical structure to epistemic probabilities. In fact, reasons will be given shortly for denying that epistemic probabilities satisfy the probability calculus.

This conclusion will be unpopular among externalists, because subjective probability has been the favored kind of probability for use in probabilist theories. I stand by the negative conclusions I have drawn regarding subjective probability, but a number of philosophers are too firmly wedded to subjective probability to be dissuaded by

9. A further difficulty with the weighting strategy is that it seems to presuppose something like the Laplacian principle of insufficient reason, but as intuitive as that principle is it is also well known that it is inconsistent. In this connection, see Wesley Salmon [1966], p. 66ff.

such arguments, and accordingly I will occasionally pretend that the notion makes sense in order to discuss popular versions of probabilist theories of knowledge.

2.2 *Indefinite Physical Probabilities*

The most popular theories of physical probability relate physical probabilities to relative frequencies. Where A and B are properties, the relative frequency, freq[A/B], is the proportion of all actual B's that are A's. For example, given a coin that is tossed four times and then destroyed, if it lands heads just twice then the relative frequency of heads in tosses of that coin is 1/2. Some theories identify the physical probability, prob(A/B), with the relative frequency freq[A/B]. Others take the prob(A/B) to be the limit to which freq[A/B] would go if the set of all actual B's were hypothetically extended to an infinite set. Another alternative is to take prob(A/B) to be a measure of the proportion of B's that are A's in all physically possible worlds (rather than just in the actual world). On the latter theory, the connection between freq[A/B] and prob(A/B) is only epistemic—observation of relative frequencies in the actual world gives us evidence for the value of the probability.[10] The physical probabilities described by all of these theories are indefinite probabilities. They relate properties rather than attaching to propositions or states of affairs.

There is something quite commonsensical about the idea that the most fundamental kind of physical probability is an indefinite probability. At the very least our epistemological access to physical probabilities is by way of observed relative frequencies, and these always concern general properties. But it cannot be denied that for many purposes we require definite probabilities rather than indefinite probabilities. This is particularly true for decision theoretic purposes. For example, if I am betting on whether Blindsight will win the third race, my bet should be based on an assessment of the probability of Blindsight winning the third race. The latter is a definite probability. It is incumbent upon any theory of physical probability to tell us how such definite probabilities are related to the more fundamental indefinite probabilities. The traditional answer has been that definite probabilities are inferred from indefinite probabilities by what is called "direct inference". The details of direct inference are problematic, and there are competing theories about how it should go, but in broad outline it is fairly simple. The basic idea is due to Hans Reichenbach [1949] who proposed that the definite probability, PROB(A*a*), should

10. My own theory is of the latter sort. It is sketched in my [1984a], and worked out in detail in my [1984d] and [198?c].

be identified with the indefinite probability prob(A/B) where B includes as much information as possible about a, subject to the constraint that we have statistical information enabling us to evaluate prob(A/B). To illustrate, suppose we want to know the probability that Blindsight will win the third race. We know that he wins 1/5 of all the races in which he participates. We know many other things about him, for instance, that he is brown and his owner's name is 'Anne', but if we have no information about how these are related to a horse's winning races then we will ignore them in estimating the probability of his winning this race, and we will take the latter probability to be 1/5. On the other hand, if we do have more detailed information about Blindsight for which we have statistical information, then we will base our estimate of the definite probability on that more detailed information. For example, I might know that he is injured and know that he wins only 1/100 of all races in which he participates when he is injured. In that case I will estimate the definite probability to be 1/100 rather than 1/5.

Perhaps the best way to understand what is going on in direct inference is to take the definite probability PROB(Aa) to be the indefinite probability prob(Ax/x $= a$ & K), where K is the conjunction of all our justified beliefs. In direct inference we are estimating this indefinite probability on the basis of the known indefinite probability prob(Ax/Bx), where B includes all the things we are justified in believing about a and for which we know the relevant indefinite probabilities.[11]

For present purposes, the important thing to be emphasized about those definite probabilities at which we arrive by direct inference is that they are mixed physical/epistemic probabilities. We obtain definite probabilities by considering indefinite probabilities conditional on properties we are justified in believing the objects in question to possess. The epistemic element is essential here. In decision theoretic contexts we seek to take account both of the probabilistic structure of the world and of our justified beliefs about the circumstances in which we find ourselves.

It is worth noting that an analogous account of direct inference to non-epistemic definite probabilities cannot work. Such an account would have us estimating the definite probability of Aa by considering all *truths* about a rather than all justified beliefs about a. In other words, in direct inference we would be trying to ascertain the value of prob(Ax/x $= a$ & T) where T is the conjunction of all truths. But among the truths in T will be either Aa or $\sim$Aa, so prob(Ax/x $= a$ &

---

11. For a detailed account of direct inference based upon this idea, see my [1984d] and [198?c].

T) is always either 1 or 0 depending upon whether Aa is true or false. Direct inference to such non-epistemic probabilities could never lead to intermediate values. Such an account of definite probabilities and direct inference would be epistemologically useless.

2.3 Definite Propensities

An approach to physical probabilities that is less popular but by no means moribund takes the fundamental physical probabilities to be definite probabilities that pertain to specific individuals. These are propensities. We can, for example, talk about the propensity of a particular coin to land heads on the next toss. These are supposed to be purely physical probabilities, untinged by any epistemic element, and are supposed to reflect ineliminable chance relationships in the world.[12] The defenders of propensities usually agree that propensities would always be either 0 or 1 in a deterministic world.[13]

Propensity theories have not been developed to the same extent as subjective theories and frequency theories, and most philosophers remain suspicious of propensities, but it would be premature to reject them outright. We must at least keep them in the back of our minds in considering what kinds of probabilities to use in formulating externalist theories of knowledge.

3. Probabilism

The distinction between probabilism and reliabilism can now be made precise by saying that probabilism seeks to characterize epistemic justification in terms of the definite probabilities of one's beliefs, while reliabilism seeks to characterize epistemic justification in terms of more general indefinite probabilities pertaining to such things as the reliability of the cognitive processes that produce the beliefs. Probabilism represents the most straightforward way of trying to capture the intuition that in acquiring beliefs we should adopt only probable beliefs.

3.1 The Simple Rule and Bayesian Epistemology

The simplest form of probabilism endorses what I call *the simple rule*:

12. Propensity theories have been proposed by Ian Hacking [1965], Isaac Levi [1967], Ronald Giere [1973], [1973a], and [1976], James Fetzer [1971], [1977], and [1981], D. H. Mellor [1969] and [1971], and Patrick Suppes [1973]. A good general discussion of propensity theories can be found in Ellory Eells [1983].

13. Giere [1973], p. 475.

> A person is justified in believing P if and only if the probability of P is sufficiently high.

This rule seems intuitively quite compelling, and at various times it has been endorsed by a wide spectrum of philosophers.[14] The simple rule, if acceptable, admirably satisfies the requirement that an analysis of epistemic justification must explain why the notion should be of interest to us. What could be more intuitive than the claim that in deciding what to believe we should be trying to ensure that our beliefs are probably true?

The endorsement of the simple rule allows us to bring all of the mathematical power of the probability calculus to bear on epistemology, and the results have often seemed extremely fruitful. For example, the simple rule pertains most directly to what we believe in a fixed epistemic setting, but what happens when our epistemic situation changes through the acquisition of new data (e.g., in perception)? Probabilists typically appeal to what is known as *Bayes' Theorem*,[15] according to which

$$\mathrm{prob}(P/Q) = \mathrm{prob}(Q/P) \times \frac{\mathrm{prob}(P)}{\mathrm{prob}(Q)}.$$

Taking P to be the proposition whose epistemic status is to be evaluated and Q to be the new evidence, prob(P/Q) is interpreted as the probability of P given the new evidence; prob(P) is the prior probability of P (i.e., the probability prior to acquiring the evidence); prob(Q) is the prior probability of acquiring that evidence; and prob(Q/P) is the prior probability of acquiring the evidence given the specific assumption that P is true. This principle then tells us how to alter our probability assignments in the face of new evidence.

Epistemology based upon the simple rule and Bayes' Theorem is known as *Bayesian epistemology*.[16] It has exerted a strong influence on technically minded philosophers, partly because of the intuitiveness of its basic principles and partly because of its mathematical elegance and power. It has spawned an extensive literature and has seemed to be extremely fruitful when applied to problems like the problem of induction or the analysis of the confirmation of scientific theories. Unfortunately, Bayesian epistemologists have concentrated more on

14. It was endorsed, for example, by Roderick Chisholm [1957], p. 28, and Carl Hempel [1962], p. 155. Its most ardent recent defender is probably Henry Kyburg [1970] and [1974]. See also Richard Jeffrey [1970], Rudolf Carnap [1962] and [1971], David Lewis [1980], and Isaac Levi [1980].

15. After Thomas Bayes.

16. Sometimes the term 'Bayesian epistemology' is reserved for theories proceeding in terms of subjective probability.

the mathematical elaboration of the theory than on its foundations. There are major problems with the foundations. These concern the very idea of acquiring new data. Note that it follows from the proposed interpretation of Bayes' theorem that when we acquire new data Q, it will come to have probability 1. This is because $prob(Q/Q) = 1$. But what is it to acquire new data through, for instance, perception? This is just the old problem of accommodating perceptual input within an epistemological theory. The beliefs we acquire through perception are ordinary beliefs about physical objects, and it seems most unreasonable to regard them as having probability 1. Furthermore, it follows from the probability calculus that if $prob(Q) = 1$ then for any proposition R, $prob(Q/R) = 1$. Thus if perceptual beliefs are given probability 1, the acquisition of further data can never lower that probability. But this is totally unreasonable. We can discover later that some of our perceptual beliefs are wrong.[17]

The idea that "data" should receive probability 1 is reminiscent of the appeal to epistemologically basic beliefs. What is happening here is that although Bayesian epistemology is a nondoxastic theory, it is nondoxastic in the wrong way. Doxastic theories fail to handle perception correctly because the only internal states to which they can appeal are beliefs. Specifically, they do not appeal to perceptual states. But beliefs are also the only internal states to which Bayesian epistemology appeals. Bayesian epistemology is nondoxastic because it appeals to probability, not because it appeals to internal states other than beliefs. Consequently, Bayesian epistemology encounters precisely the same sort of problem as do doxastic theories in accommodating perception. Contrary to both doxastic theories and Bayesian epistemology, the justifiability of a perceptual belief is partly a function of nondoxastic internal states.

It should be emphasized that the use of Bayes' theorem in describing perception and belief change is not required by the simple rule. These are independent principles. Thus we can reject Bayesian epistemology without rejecting the simple rule. The simple rule might be combined with a more sophisticated account of perception and memory without robbing it of the power inherent in its use of probability. And the simple rule would still retain its intuitive appeal in capturing the idea that what we should be doing in the epistemological evaluation of beliefs is choosing beliefs that are probable. Unfortunately, this elegant rationale for the simple rule begins to crumble when we examine the rule more closely. In evaluating the simple rule we must decide what kind of probability is involved in it. It

17. Richard Jeffrey [1965] has proposed a variant of the Bayesian rule that avoids this problem by allowing new data to have probability less than 1, but it does not tell us how to assign probability to the new data.

is a definite probability, but we have taken note of the (at least putative) existence of four distinct kinds of definite probability: epistemic probability, subjective probability, mixed physical/epistemic probability, and propensities.

3.1.1   *Epistemic Probabilities*

The simple rule is a truism when interpreted in terms of epistemic probabilities. So understood it claims no more than that a belief is justified if and only if its degree of justification is sufficiently high. This claim cannot be faulted as long as it is understood that there is no presupposition either that epistemic probabilities are quantifiable or that if they are quantifiable then they satisfy the probability calculus. But, of course, understood in this way the simple rule is trivial and unilluminating. In particular, it does not constitute an analysis of epistemic justification, because epistemic probability is itself defined in terms of epistemic justification.

3.1.2   *Subjective Probabilities*

What is no doubt the favorite interpretation of the simple rule in contemporary philosophy is the one proceeding in terms of subjective probability. So construed, the simple rule becomes the claim that epistemic probabilities are the same as subjective probabilities. I have argued that no sense can be made of subjective probability, and I regard this as the most serious objection to the endorsement of the simple rule construed in terms of subjective probability. But suppose we waive this difficulty, pretending that there is always a unique betting quotient that one prudentially should accept for each given proposition. This construal of the simple rule then yields an analysis of epistemic justification that is not obviously circular, and an immense literature has grown up around it. Is this a plausible analysis?

The simple rule, construed in terms of subjective probabilities as actual degrees of belief, would tell us that a belief is justified if and only if it is firmly held. That obviously has nothing to recommend it, so let us confine our attention to subjective probabilities as rational degrees of belief. A simple objection to the use of such subjective probabilities in the simple rule consists of questioning whether prudential rationality can be understood without first understanding epistemic rationality. It certainly seems that what we prudentially should do is a function in part of what we (epistemically) reasonably believe. Whether I should bet that Blindsight will win the next race is going to be determined in part by what I am justified in believing about Blindsight. If it is correct that prudential rationality presupposes epistemic rationality, then it becomes circular to analyze epistemic rationality in terms of prudential rationality, and hence it becomes circular to analyze epistemic rationality in terms of subjective probabilities. This objection is inconclusive, because we do not really know how to analyze prudential rationality, but it is at least suggestive.

3.1.3 Mixed Physical/Epistemic Probabilities

We might interpret the simple rule in terms of the mixed physical/ epistemic probabilities that are obtained from indefinite physical probabilities by direct inference. This is the proposal of Henry Kyburg.[18] But any such proposal is subject to a simple objection—the resulting analysis of epistemic justification is circular. Recall that these physical/epistemic definite probabilities are obtained by direct inference from indefinite probabilities, and direct inference proceeds by considering indefinite probabilities conditional on *what we are justified in believing* about the objects in question. For example, what makes it true that the probability (for me) is 1/2 of Jamie having an accident while driving home this evening is that I am *justified in believing* that he is inebriated, driving on busy streets, and so on, and the indefinite probability of someone having an accident under those circumstances is 1/2. It is not the mere *fact* that Jamie is inebriated that makes the probability high. Only what I am justified in believing about Jamie can affect the mixed physical/epistemic probability. Thus mixed physical/ epistemic probabilities cannot be used non-circularly in the analysis of epistemic justification.

3.1.4 Propensities

An analysis of epistemic justification in terms of propensities would not be obviously circular. Can we take a proposition to be justified if and only if it has a sufficiently high propensity to be true? It is hard to evaluate this suggestion without a better understanding of propensities. Notice, however, that according to most propensity theorists, nontrivial propensities only exist in nondeterministic worlds. If the world were deterministic, all propensities would be either 0 or 1, depending upon whether the proposition in question were true or false. The simple rule would then reduce to the absurd principle that we are justified in believing something if and only if it is true. We might avoid this objection by insisting that nontrivial propensities exist even in deterministic worlds, but to defend this we need a better understanding of propensities than anyone has yet provided. It is

18. In Kyburg [1974], and elsewhere.

rather difficult to say much specifically about the propensity interpretation of the simple rule without a better theory of propensities.

3.1.5 General Difficulties

I have raised objections to each of the interpretations of the simple rule in terms of different kinds of definite probabilities. Some of those objections are more telling than others. I turn now to some more general objections that apply simultaneously to all versions of the simple rule. A reasonably familiar objection is that it follows from the probability calculus that every tautology has probability 1.[19] It would then follow from the simple rule that we are justified in believing every tautology. Such a conclusion is clearly wrong. If we consider some even moderately complicated tautology such as

$$[P \equiv (R \vee \sim P)] \supset R$$

it seems clear that *until we realize that it is a tautology*, we are not automatically justified in believing it. The only way to avoid this kind of counterexample to the simple rule is to reject the probability calculus, but that is a very fundamental feature of our concept of probability and rejecting it would largely emasculate probability. It is because probability has the nice mathematical structure captured by the probability calculus that it has proven so fruitful, and that mathematical structure has played an indispensable role in the employment of probability in epistemology.

The preceding difficulty illustrates one respect in which epistemic justification seems to have a more complicated structure than can be captured by the probability calculus. Supposing that epistemic probability satisfies the probability calculus forces us to regard different propositions (different tautologies) as equally justified when it seems clear that we want to make epistemic distinctions between them. The converse problem also arises. There are cases in which we want to regard propositions as equally justified when the probability calculus would preclude that. Consider a pair of unrelated propositions, P and Q, regarding which we know essentially nothing. Under the circumstances, we should neither believe these propositions nor disbelieve them—we should withhold belief. We can express this by saying that we should be *epistemically indifferent* with respect to P, and also with

19. I have avoided endorsing the standard axiom requiring logically equivalent propositions to have the same probability. In fact, I think that that axiom must be added for a reasonable axiomatization of probability, but I have not endorsed it here in order to avoid begging questions against probabilism. Probabilism would encounter even more severe difficulties in the face of that axiom and its consequence that all necessary truths (not just tautologies) have probability 1.

respect to Q. We are precisely as justified (or unjustified) in believing
P and in believing ~P, and similarly for Q. The simple rule and the
probability calculus would require that in this sort of case, prob(P) =
prob(~P) = 1/2, and prob(Q) = prob(~Q) = 1/2. But now consider
the disjunction (P $\lor$ Q). If we are completely ignorant regarding P
and Q and they are logically unrelated, then we are also completely
ignorant regarding (P $\lor$ Q). We should withhold belief with respect to
(P $\lor$ Q) just as we did with respect to P and with respect to Q. Thus we
should conclude, as above, that prob(P $\lor$ Q) = prob(~(P $\lor$ Q)) = 1/
2. The difficulty is that the probability calculus commits us to regarding (P $\lor$ Q) as more probable than either P or Q individually, so we
cannot assign probability 1/2 to all three of P, Q, and (P $\lor$ Q).[20] Thus
the simple rule precludes our being epistemically indifferent to all
three of P, Q, and (P $\lor$ Q), and yet intuition seems to indicate that
there are circumstances under which such indifference is epistemically prescribed. Once again, the structure of epistemic justification is
not properly reflected by the probability calculus.

I regard these "formal" objections to the simple rule as decisive.
The structure of epistemic justification is too complicated to be
captured by the probability calculus. Why then does the rule seem so
intuitive? I think that there is a twofold explanation for this. First, a
very common use of 'probable' in English is to express epistemic
probability, and the simple rule understood in terms of epistemic
probability is a truism.[21] Philosophers confuse this truism with more
substantive versions of the simple rule that proceed in terms of other
varieties of probability. Only those more substantive versions can
hope to provide a noncircular account of epistemic justification, but
those more substantive versions have fatal flaws and are not themselves directly supported by our intuitions.

The second part of the explanation amounts to observing that we
also have the intuition that we should not believe something if it is
improbable, where the kind of probability involved is the mixed
physical/epistemic probability involved in decision theory. This intuition is correct, but it lends no support to probablism. It is correct
because mixed physical/epistemic probabilities are conditional on the
conjunction of all justified beliefs, and hence the probability of any
justified belief will automatically be 1.[22] But this lends no support to

---

20. Technically, prob(P $\lor$ Q) = prob(P) + prob(Q) − prob(P & Q), and because P
and Q are unrelated, prob(P & Q) = prob(P) × prob(Q) = 1/4, with the result that
prob(P $\lor$ Q) = 3/4.

21. Note that it follows from this that if epistemic probabilities can be assigned
numerical values (which strikes me as dubious), they will not satisfy the probability
calculus.

22. It is a theorem of the probability calculus that prob(P/P & Q) = 1.

probabilism, because mixed physical/epistemic probabilities are defined in terms of justified belief and hence cannot be used noncircularly to analyze epistemic justification.

3.2   Other Forms of Probabilism

The simple rule is the most natural form of probabilism, but it fails due to the fact that the mathematical structure of epistemic justification cannot be captured by the probability calculus and hence degree of justification cannot be identified with any kind of probability conforming to the probability calculus. However, it is possible to construct more sophisticated forms of probabilism that escape this objection. These theories characterize epistemic justification in terms of probabilities, but they do not simply identify degree of justification with degree of probability. For example, recall Keith Lehrer's coherence theory. Its central thesis is:

P is justified for S if and only if for each proposition Q competing with P, S believes P to be more probable than Q.

This is a doxastic theory because its appeal to probability is only via beliefs about probability, but it could be converted into a nondoxastic theory by appealing to the probabilities themselves:

P is justified for S if and only if P is more probable than each proposition competing with P.

Supplementing this central criterion with a definition of competition will yield a version of probabilism more complicated than the simple rule. We might adopt Lehrer's definition of competition, or we might adopt another definition. Marshall Swain [1981] follows essentially this course. A slightly simplified version of his definition of competition is as follows:

Q is a competitor of P for S if and only if either:
(1) (a) P and Q are contingent,
    (b) Q is negatively relevant to P, and
    (c) Q is not equivalent to a disjunction of propositions one of whose disjuncts, R, is both (i) irrelevant to P and (ii) such that the probability of R is greater than or equal to the probability of P; or
(2) P is noncontingent and Q is ~P. [p. 133]

Swain's theory is just one example of a sophisticated kind of probabilism that escapes the objection to the simple rule that the structure of epistemic justification is too complicated to be captured by the probability calculus. Thus the formal objections to the simple rule do not refute probabilism in general.

Still, two general points can be made about all versions of probabilism. First, there appears to be no appropriate kind of probability for use in probabilist theories of knowledge. Such theories require a definite probability. They are circular if formulated in terms of epistemic probability. Only three other kinds of definite probability have been discussed in the literature: subjective probability, mixed physical/epistemic probability, and propensities. I have argued that the very concept of subjective probability is ill-defined—subjective probabilities do not exist. I regard mixed physical/epistemic probabilities as unproblematic, but they cannot be used in the analysis of epistemic justification because they already presuppose epistemic justification. Propensities are not sufficiently well understood to be of much use anywhere. Furthermore, a common view among propensity theorists is that nontrivial propensities only exist in nondeterministic worlds, but it seems pretty clear that any probabilist analysis of epistemic probability must proceed in terms of a variety of probability that can take values intermediate between 0 and 1 even in deterministic worlds. It seems inescapable that there is no appropriate kind of probability for use in probabilist theories of knowledge.

The second point to be made about probabilist theories concerns not their truth but their motivation. The original motivation for probabilism came from the intuition that what the epistemic evaluation of beliefs should be trying to ensure is that our beliefs are probable. If the simple rule were defensible, it would capture that intuition. But the simple rule is not defensible, and more complicated versions of probabilism do not capture this intuition. In fact, they are incompatible with the intuition—insofar as they diverge from the simple rule, they will have the consequence that we can be justified in believing improbable propositions and unjustified in believing probable propositions.

The intuition that we should only believe things when they are probable is a powerful one. It seems to lead directly to the simple rule, but there are overwhelming objections to the simple rule. What, then, should we make of this intuition? As I have indicated, I believe that it is epistemic probability that is involved in this intuition. In ordinary non-philosophical English, 'probable' is used to express epistemic probability at least as often as it is used to express other kinds of probability, and it is a truism that a belief is justified if and only if its epistemic probability is sufficiently high. But, of course, epistemic probability is defined in terms of epistemic justification, so this provides no analysis of epistemic justification and no support for probabilism.

What should we conclude about probabilism at this point? Decisive objections can be raised against existing probabilist theories of knowledge, and they militate strongly against there being any defensible kind of probabilism. At the very least, the probabilist owes us an account of the kind of probability in terms of which he wants his theory to be understood, and there is good reason for being skeptical about there being any appropriate kind of probability. The most rational attitude to adopt towards probabilism at this point is healthy skepticism, but it cannot be regarded as absolutely certain that no probabilist theory can succeed. In chapter five, I will eventually present arguments that purport to show that no externalist theory of any kind can be correct, and those arguments should lay probabilism to rest for good.

4. Reliabilism

Reliabilism differs from probabilism in that it attempts to analyze epistemic justification in terms of indefinite probabilities rather than definite probabilities. Existing reliabilist theories do this by appealing to the reliability of cognitive processes. I call this *process reliabilism*. The basic idea behind process reliabilism is that a belief is justified if and only if it is produced by a reliable cognitive process.[23] For example, the reliabilist explains why perceptual beliefs are justified by pointing to the fact that, in the actual world, perception is a reliable cognitive process. Similarly, deduction is a reliable cognitive process, so beliefs deduced from other justified beliefs will be justified. On the other hand, wishful thinking is not a reliable cognitive process, so beliefs produced by wishful thinking are not justified. The reliability of a cognitive process is the indefinite probability of beliefs produced by it being true. This is a perfectly respectable notion. Unlike probabilism, we cannot fault process reliabilism for making illegitimate use of probability. Let us consider then just how a reliabilist theory might be formulated. To this end, I will give a sketch of Alvin Goldman's theory, as presented in his article "What is justified belief?" (For Goldman's most recent views, see his [1986].)

4.1   Goldman's Theory

Goldman begins by distinguishing between two kinds of cognitive processes—*belief dependent* processes such as reasoning that take beliefs

23. Reliabilist theories of *knowing* predate reliabilist theories of justification. The first such theories were those of Frank Ramsey, David Armstrong, and W. V. O. Quine. Perhaps the first formulation of a reliabilist theory of justification is due to Wilfrid Sellars [1963], but he formulated it only to reject it. Current forms of reliabilist theories of justification take their impetus from the work of Alvin Goldman. See his [1979], [1981], and [1986]. In this book, I will confine the term 'reliabilism' to reliabilist theories of epistemic justification.

as inputs, and *belief independent* processes such as perception that do not. Focusing first on beliefindependent processes, Goldman writes:

> Consider some faulty process of belief-formation, i.e., processes whose beliefoutputs would be classed as unjustified. Here are some examples: confused reasoning, wishful thinking, reliance on emotional attachment, mere hunch or guesswork, and hasty generalization. What do these faulty processes have in common? They share the feature of *unreliability*: they tend to produce *error* a large proportion of the time. By contrast, which species of belief-forming (or belief-sustaining) processes are intuitively justification-conferring? They include standard perceptual processes, remembering, good reasoning, and introspection. What these processes seem to have in common is *reliability*: the beliefs they produce are generally reliable. [pp. 9–10.]

In light of this diagnosis, Goldman proposes the following:

> If S's belief in p at t results ("immediately") from a belief-independent process that is reliable, then S's belief in p at t is justified.

Turning to belief-dependent processes, Goldman defines such a process to be *conditionally reliable* if and only if it tends to produce true beliefs when the input beliefs are true. For example, deduction and induction are both conditionally reliable belief-dependent processes. Goldman then makes the provisional proposal:

> If S's belief in p at t results ("immediately") from a belief-dependent process that is (at least) conditionally reliable, and if the beliefs (if any) on which this process operates in producing S's belief in p at t are themselves justified, then S's belief in p at t is justified.

This proposal is only provisional because Goldman goes on to recognize that we must take account of what is in effect defeasibility (although he does not call it that). We might arrive at a belief by employing a relatively simple cognitive process (e.g., color perception), but that belief would be unjustified if there were a more elaborate reliable cognitive process (one taking account of additional information, such as abnormal lighting conditions) such that had we employed the more elaborate process we would not have adopted the belief. This leads Goldman to replace the provisional proposal with the following:

> If S's belief in p at t results from a reliable cognitive process, and there is no reliable or conditionally reliable process available to S which, had it been used by S in addition to the process actually used, would have resulted in S's not believing p, then S's belief in p at t is justified.

Goldman's reliability theory generates a structure of justified beliefs having the same kind of pyramid structure that is embodied in a foundations theory or in direct realism. Perceptual input, by being reliable, produces beliefs that are justified simply by virtue of being produced in that way. Subsequent reasoning then produces further beliefs that are justified by being produced by conditionally reliable cognitive processes that are applied to beliefs already justified. But the theory diverges radically from both foundations theories and direct realism in that it makes the justifiedness of a belief depend not only on the processes that produced it, but also on whether those processes happen to be reliable in the actual world. By contrast, internalist theories would rule that if a particular combination of perceptual inputs, reasoning, and so on, produces justified belief in the actual world then it will produce justified belief in all possible worlds. Internalist theories preclude appeal to external considerations such as reliability in evaluating beliefs.

4.2   Problems for Process Reliabilism

Several different kinds of problems can be generated for reliabilism. The simplest is that, intuitively, reliability has nothing to do with epistemic justification. We would certainly expect those cognitive processes producing justified beliefs to be reasonably reliable, because if they were not the human race would have vanished long ago, but it is not the reliability of the processes that is responsible for the justifiedness of the beliefs. The beliefs are justified just because the believer is "reasoning correctly" (in a broad sense of 'reasoning'). If one makes all the right epistemic moves, then one is justified regardless of whether his belief is false or nature conspires to make such reasoning unreliable. To me, this objection seems to have considerable intuitive force, but reliabilists deny the intuition. Internalists have tried to make this objection more precise by arguing that reliabilist theories give assessments of justifiedness that are intuitively wrong in some cases. A favorite example is that of a brain in a vat. Recall poor Harry, whom we met in chapter one. He had his brain removed and wired into a computer that directly stimulated his visual cortex so that he had normal-seeming sensory experiences but they were totally unrelated to his physical surroundings. For Harry, perception became an unreliable cognitive process, and thus the reliabilist is committed to regarding Harry's perceptual beliefs as unjustified. But this seems wrong. Harry has no reason to suspect that anything is amiss, so if he takes reasonable care in forming perceptual judgments we will regard them as justified.

At this point, the debate between the internalists and the reliabilists often reduces to a shoving match of conflicting intuitions, each insisting that *his* intuitions support *his* theory. Such a conflict of intuitions is hard to resolve. There is, however, an argument due to Stewart Cohen [1984] that appears to weigh heavily in favor of the internalist. Cohen notes that even in the case of a brain in a vat, we would distinguish between reasonable and unreasonable epistemic behavior. To illustrate, we noted earlier that perceptual beliefs may be unjustified when the perceiver fails to take account of features of the perceptual situation that he knows or believes to adversely affect the reliability of perception. Consider a person who knows all about the way in which colored lights can affect apparent color. He will be unjustified in judging color on the basis of apparent color when he believes that what he sees is bathed in colored lights. Harry presumably knows all about such phenomena (from before his brain was removed from his skull and installed in the vat), so if he judges something to be red under circumstances that appear normal to him he will be justified, but if he makes the same judgment under circumstances in which he thinks the object is illuminated by red lights then he will be unjustified. We would insist upon making such epistemic discriminations despite the fact that his perceptual judgments are uniformly unreliable.

Goldman [1986] formulates a reliabilist theory that is explicitly intended to avoid brain-in-a-vat and evil demon cases. He defines a *normal world* to be one consistent with our *general* beliefs about the actual world, and then proposes that justification requires production by cognitive processes that are reliable in normal worlds (but not necessarily in the actual world). A simple objection to this theory is that it puts no constraints on how we get our general beliefs. If they are unjustified, then it seems that reliability relative to them should be of no particular epistemic value. Goldman himself ([1986], p. 102) raises basically the same objection to epistemic decision theory based upon subjective probabilities. To paraphrase that objection and apply it to Goldman's own theory:

> Apparently the [general beliefs] may be formed in any fashion at all, including hunch, fancy and the like. But if a belief is based on [a process reliable only relative to general beliefs] of that ilk, there are no grounds for regarding the belief as justified. It certainly is not justified in any sense that links up closely with knowledge.

Note in particular that if our general beliefs are not formed by processes reliable in the actual world, then there is no reason to regard beliefs formed by processes reliable relative to those general beliefs as being probably true. Thus this strategy for avoiding brain-in-a-vat counterexamples appears to forsake the general intuitions that made reliabilism attractive in the first place.

I turn now to a way of attacking process reliabilism that raises very fundamental difficulties for the theory. We have taken it for granted that our ordinary cognitive processes such as color vision are reliable, but are they? Color vision is reliable under some circumstances (e.g., standard lighting conditions) and unreliable under other circumstances (e.g., illumination by colored lights). Judgments of reliability are usually made relative to rather narrowly circumscribed circumstances. We *can* talk about reliability in the universe at large, but the lighting conditions on earth are quite unusual by universe-wide standards. *In the universe at large, color vision is unreliable.* As that does not incline us to regard our normal color judgments as unjustified, it must be concluded that it is not reliability in the universe at large that is relevant. It must instead be reliability in the circumstances in which we actually find ourselves. But what does this mean? We find ourselves in many circumstances. We find ourselves in the universe at large, and we also find ourselves on earth viewing things in ordinary daylight. Relative to which set of circumstances are we to judge reliability? Obviously, the latter, but why? The intuitive answer is "Because it takes account of more relevant information."

It might first be proposed that in judging the reliability of a cognitive process in a particular instance we should take account of *everything* about the circumstances in which it is used. If it makes any sense at all to talk about the reliability of the cognitive process "under the present circumstances" (in all their specificity), it seems that it must be the indefinite probability of producing a true belief, conditional on everything true of the present circumstances. But the present circumstances are infinitely specific and include, among other things, the truth value of the belief being produced by the cognitive process and the fact that that is the belief being produced. Consequently, this indefinite probability must go the same way as objective definite probabilities and be either 1 or 0 depending upon whether the belief in question is true or false. Thus this reliabilist criterion entails the absurd consequence that in order for a belief to be justified it must be true.

Perhaps we can avoid this untoward result by appealing to reliability under less than totally specific circumstances. But how do we decide how specific to make the circumstances short of total specificity? The following seems initially hopeful. Although we cannot talk about the reliability of a cognitive process under the present circumstances in all their specificity without trivializing things, we can talk about the reliability under different general conditions satisfied by the present circumstances. Consider a belief P produced by the cognitive process M. If the present circumstances are of some general type C under which M is reliable, that might incline us to regard P as justified. For instance, M might be color vision and circumstances C might consist of viewing things in white light. But, given reliabilist intuitions, we would retract this judgment of justifiedness if the present circumstances were also of some more specific type C* under which M is unreliable. For example, C* might consist of viewing things in very dim white light. In other words, in evaluating M we need not appeal to totally specific circumstances, but we cannot ignore features of the present circumstances that would make M unreliable. This suggests that we should regard P as justified if and only if (1) there is a description C of the present circumstances such that M is reliable in circumstances of type C, and (2) there is no more specific description C* of the present circumstances such that M is unreliable in circumstances of type C*. Unfortunately, this does not resolve our problem. Suppose P is false. One condition satisfied by the present circumstances is that the process M is currently producing belief in the proposition P and P is false. The probability of a belief being true given that it is produced by M and M is currently producing belief in the proposition P and P is false is 0. Thus the reliabilist criterion once more entails that a belief is justified only if it is true.

Rather than relativizing reliability to circumstances, reliabilists have tended to rely upon gerrymandering processes. For instance, upon observing that color vision is unreliable in the universe at large, they might appeal to the gerrymandered process colorvision-in-white-light. It is important to realize that this is actually equivalent to relativizing reliability to circumstances and is subject to exactly similar problems. For example, for a reliabilist, justification would have to require not just that a belief be produced by a reliable process M, but also that there be no "more specific" process M* (e.g., color-vision-in-dim-white-light) such that the belief is also produced by M* and M* is unreliable. But then we can reproduce the above argument, noting that if a belief P is true and it is produced by a process M then it is also produced by the gerrymandered process M-under-circumstances-in-which-the-belief-produced-is-P-and-P-is-true. Analogously, if P is false and it is produced by M then it is also produced by the gerrymandered process M-under-circumstances-in-which-the-belief-produced-is-P-and-P-is-false. Given any cognitive process producing P, there is a more specific gerrymandered process of one of these two sorts that also produces P, and it is reliable if and only if P is true. So again we get the absurd result that a belief is justified if and only if it is true. The only way to avoid this is to impose some kind of restriction on gerrymandering, but there does not appear to be any non-ad hoc way of doing that.

I can see no way around this problem. In evaluating reliability relative to circumstances (or in gerrymandering processes) it cannot be reasonable to appeal to less specific descriptions of the circumstances in preference to more specific descriptions. That would amount to gratuitously throwing away information. But then the above problem is unavoidable. What is really happening here is that in trying to use reliability (which is an indefinite probability) to evaluate individual beliefs we are encountering the problem of direct inference all over again, and just as before, there is no way to obtain an objective assessment of the individual belief short of its truth value. Reliability is an indefinite probability and there is no way to get an objective definite probability out of it, but only an objective definite probability would be of any ultimate use to process reliabilism. It follows that process reliabilism is essentially bankrupt. It seems that reliabilists have made the mistake of supposing that if they just wave their hands and mutter vague things about probability somebody will be able to come along and fill in the details, but there is no way to do that.

I can see no way around this problem. In evaluating reliability relative to circumstances (or in gerrymandering processes) it cannot be reasonable to appeal to less specific descriptions of the circumstances in preference to more specific descriptions. That would amount to gratuitously throwing away information. But then the above problem is unavoidable. What is really happening here is that in trying to use reliability (which is an indefinite probability) to evaluate individual beliefs we are encountering the problem of direct inference all over again, and all just as before, there is no way to obtain an objective assessment of the individual belief short of its truth value. Reliability is an indefinite probability and there is no way to get an objective definite probability out of it, but only an objective definite probability would be of any ultimate use to process reliabilism. It follows that process reliabilism is essentially bankrupt. It seems that reliabilists have made the mistake of supposing that if they just wave their hands and mutter vague things about probability somebody will be able to come along and fill in the details, but there is no way to do that.

A final objection to process reliabilism concerns its motivation. Externalists were originally motivated by the intuition that in evaluating beliefs, what we want is to ensure that our beliefs are probable. Probabilist theories, proceeding as they do in terms of the definite probabilities of beliefs, attempt to capture this intuition fairly directly. Process reliabilism immediately diverges from the original intuition just by ceasing to talk about the probabilities of beliefs and talking instead about the indefinite probabilities of cognitive processes. Once enough structure is added to process reliabilism to accommodate the difference between belief-dependent and beliefindependent processes, defeasible reasoning, and so on, the resulting theory becomes at least as complicated as an internalist theory. If we can object to internalist theories that they are ad hoc attempts to produce criteria that pick out the intuitively right beliefs as justified, we can surely object to process reliabilism on the same grounds. Such reliabilist theories provide no greater insight into what epistemic justification is all about than do their internalist competitors.

4.3   Other Forms of Reliabilism

Externalist theories take the justifiability of a belief to be determined in part by external considerations. Reliabilists propose that central among those external considerations is some kind of reliability. Existing reliabilist theories are all versions of process reliabilism, which appeals to the reliability of cognitive processes. The above methodological problems seem to me to constitute a decisive refutation of process reliabilism. There is simply no way to coherently formulate such a theory. This has gone overlooked because philosophers have been content to make sloppy use of probability, and that must be rectified.

We must not be too hasty in concluding that because process reliabilism cannot be made to work, no form of reliabilism can be made to work. No other forms of reliabilism have actually been proposed,[24] but that does not mean that other forms of reliabilism are impossible. They would appeal to the reliability of something other than cognitive processes. At this point it may be hard to imagine what such an alternative form of reliabilism might look like, but it will emerge in the next chapter that there is a quite natural theory of this sort that will have to be taken seriously.

It is worth recalling at this point that externalism was originally recommended as a way of avoiding the ad hoc character of internalism. But as externalist theories are made increasingly complex, they can no longer be regarded as capturing the simple idea that in forming beliefs what we should be trying to do is make it probable that our beliefs are true. Externalist theories become just as ad hoc as their internalist competitors, although in a different way. The internalist theories are ad hoc because they proceed piecemeal, propounding an array of unconnected epistemic principles whose only recommendation is that they seem required to legitimize our intuitive reasoning. Complex externalist theories avoid this difficulty by proposing a general analysis of epistemic justification from which all

24. Goldman [1981] hints at a version of what I will call 'norm reliabilism' in the next chapter, but he does not formulate it clearly.

epistemic rules should be derivable. But the complex analyses proposed by such theories are themselves ad hoc for much the same reason as the internalist theories—the only motivation for the details of the analyses is that they (hopefully) allow the analyses to avoid intuitive counterexamples and capture what is intuitively the right reasoning. It seems that despite initial appearances, any externalist theory that has any hope of being correct is going to be just as ad hoc as the internalist theories it seeks to replace.

Despite all this, it must be acknowledged that a correct externalist analysis of epistemic justification would be a significant achievement. But with the failure of any *simple* analyses there ceases to be any compelling reason to believe that a correct externalist analysis is possible. I believe that the above remarks should be regarded as having successfully disposed of all existing externalist theories, but the criticisms presented are specific to the theories discussed and do nothing to refute externalism as such. It remains an open question whether some other kind of externalist theory may be defensible. This question will be taken up in the next chapter, where it will eventually be concluded that no externalist theory can be correct and the true epistemological theory must be a form of direct realism.

5

EPISTEMIC NORMS

1. Recapitulation

W E HAVE SURVEYED existing theories of knowledge and concluded that most are subject to fatal objections. Doxastic theories, both foundationalist and coherence, fail because they cannot accommodate perception and memory. These are cognitive processes that produce beliefs in us, and the beliefs are sometimes justified and sometimes unjustified, but whether they are justified is not just a function of one's other beliefs. It follows that justifiability is a function of more than doxastic states, and hence the true epistemological theory must be a nondoxastic theory. Nondoxastic theories can be internalist or externalist. I have sketched an internalist nondoxastic theory—direct realism—and one of my ultimate purposes in this book is to defend a variety of direct realism. This will be done by arguing against externalist theories. If all externalist theories can be rejected, the only remaining theories are internalist nondoxastic theories, and I take it that direct realism is the most plausible such theory. Existing externalist theories are all versions of either probabilism or process reliabilism. These theories fail for a variety of reasons specific to them. But it remains possible at this stage that some other form of externalism might succeed, so a more general argument against externalism is required if we are to defend direct realism in this way.

All of the theories thus far discussed are subject to a common objection. This is that they fail to give illuminating general accounts of epistemic justification. Although they may start with simple and intuitive ideas, when confronted with detailed objections they are forced to complicate those simple ideas and, in the end, they propound complex and convoluted criteria of justifiedness. Even if some such complex criterion were correct, we would be left wondering why such a concept of epistemic justification should be of interest to us. It has been objected that foundations theories and direct realism propose ad hoc lists of epistemic rules whose only defense is that they seem to be required for the justifiedness of those beliefs we antecedently regard as justified. As formulated, those theories give no principled account of epistemic justification from which this medley of rules might be derived. But we have found that much the same objection can be raised to all the other theories we have discussed as well. The final versions of these theories leave us with such complicated criteria that they cannot be regarded as explanations of what epistemic justification is all about.

To sort this out we need a general account of epistemic justification, and it will be the purpose of this chapter to provide such an account. Once we have a better understanding of epistemic justification it will become possible to dismiss all externalist theories for deep reasons having to do with the general nature of epistemic justification. Basically the same considerations will also necessitate the rejection of a wide variety of internalist theories, including most coherence theories. The general account of epistemic justification that will be proposed here has the further virtue that it is a naturalistic account, in the sense that it integrates the concept of epistemic justification into a naturalistic view of man as a biological machine.

2. Epistemic Norms

What are we asking when we ask whether a belief is justified? What we want to know is whether it is all right to believe it. Justification is a matter of "epistemic permissibility". It is this normative character of epistemic justification that I want to emphasize. That epistemic justification is a normative notion is not a novel observation. The language of epistemic justification is explicitly normative, and a recurrent theme has been that justification is connected with the "ethics of belief". This has played a role in the thought of a number of epistemologists: Chisholm ([1977] and chapter one of [1957]) has repeatedly stressed the normative character of epistemic terms, several recent philosophers have proposed analyzing epistemic justification in terms of the maximization of epistemic values,[1] and a few philosophers have appealed to the normative character of justification in other ways.[2] Thus I will think of epistemic justification as being concerned with questions of the form, "When is it permissible (from an epistemological point of view) to believe P?" This is the concept of epistemic justification that I am concerned to explore.

Norms are general descriptions of the circumstances under which various kinds of normative judgments are correct. Epistemic norms are norms describing when it is epistemically permissible to hold

1. See for example Isaac Levi [1967], Keith Lehrer [1974], p. 146ff., and p. 204ff., and [1981], p. 75ff., and Alvin Goldman [1981], pp. 27–52.
2. See for example Hilary Kornblith [1983]. See also William Alston [1978], Roderick Firth [1978], John Heil [1983], and J. Meiland [1980].

various beliefs. A belief is justified if and only if it is licensed by correct epistemic norms. We assess the justifiedness of a belief in terms of the cognizer's reasons for holding it, and our most fundamental epistemic judgments pertain to reasoning (construing reasoning in the broad manner required by direct realism). Thus we can regard epistemic norms as the norms governing "right reasoning". Epistemic norms are supposed to guide us in reasoning and thereby in forming beliefs. The concept of epistemic justification can be explained by explaining the nature and origin of the epistemic norms that govern our reasoning. I have called this "the reason-guiding concept of epistemic justification". There may be other concepts that can reasonably be labeled "epistemic justification", but it is the reason-guiding concept that is the focus of the present book and is involved in traditional epistemological problems.

Much of recent epistemology has been concerned with describing the contents of our epistemic norms, but the nature and source of epistemic norms has not received much attention. Epistemologists have commonly supposed that epistemic norms are much like moral norms and that they are used in evaluating reasoning in the same way moral norms are used in evaluating actions. One of the main contentions of this chapter will be that this parallel is not at all exact and that epistemologists have been misled in important ways by supposing the analogy to be better than it is. A proper understanding of epistemic norms will provide us with a radically new perspective on epistemology, and from the point of view of this perspective new light can be thrown on a number of central epistemological problems.

An account of epistemic norms must answer two different questions. First, it must describe the correct epistemic norms. Second, it must tell us what makes them correct. The first question concerns the content of epistemic norms, and the second question concerns their justification. By distinguishing between these questions we can see the internalism/externalism distinction in a new light. A belief is justified if and only if it is held in conformance with correct epistemic norms. Externalism is the view that the justifiedness of a belief is a function in part of external considerations. Thus if externalism is right, external considerations must play a role in determining whether a belief is held in conformance with correct epistemic norms. This could arise in either of two ways. On the one hand, external considerations could enter into the formulation of correct epistemic norms. On the other hand, it might be granted that epistemic norms can only appeal to internal considerations, but it might be insisted that external considerations are relevant to determining which set of internalist norms is correct. Thus we are led to a distinction between two kinds of externalism. *Belief externalism* insists that correct epistemic norms must be formulated in terms of external considerations. A typical example of such a proposed norm might be "It is permissible to hold a belief if it is generated by a reliable cognitive process." In contrast to this, *norm externalism* acknowledges that the content of our epistemic norms must be internalist, but employs external considerations in the selection of the norms themselves. The distinction between belief and norm externalism is analogous to the distinction between act and rule utilitarianism. Externalism (simpliciter) is the disjunction of belief externalism and norm externalism. A number of philosophers who are usually considered externalists appear to vacillate between belief externalism and norm externalism. The difference between these two varieties of externalism will prove important. In the end, both must be rejected, but they are subject to different difficulties.[3]

According to internalism, the justifiedness of a belief is a function exclusively of internal considerations, so internalism implies the denial of both belief and norm externalism. That is, the internalist maintains that epistemic norms must be formulated in terms of relations between beliefs or between beliefs and nondoxastic internal states (e.g., perceptual states), and he denies that these norms are subject to evaluation in terms of external considerations. Typically, the internalist has held that whatever our *actual* epistemic norms are, they are necessarily correct and not subject to criticism on any grounds (externalist or otherwise), but I have not built that into the definition of internalism.

There is one respect in which the internalism/externalism distinction remains to be made clear. The distinction is formulated in terms of an undefined notion of an internal state. It is fairly clear what kinds of states people have had in mind when they have talked about internalism and externalism, but it is hard to give a general characterization of them. I will return to this matter in section four.

3. How Do Epistemic Norms Regulate?

In order to get a grasp of the nature of epistemic norms, let us begin by asking their purpose. It is important to distinguish between two uses of norms (epistemic or otherwise). On the one hand, there are third-person uses of norms wherein we use the norms to evaluate the behavior of others. Various norms may be appropriate for third-person evaluations, depending upon the purpose we have in making

3. Alvin Goldman [1981] and [1986] seems to be one of the few externalists who is clear on this distinction. He distinguishes between two senses of 'epistemic justification' (see section five) and adopts belief externalism with regard to one and norm externalism with regard to the other.

the evaluations. For example, we may want to determine whether a person is a good scientist because we are trying to decide whether to hire him. To be contrasted with third-person uses of norms are first-person uses. First-person uses of norms are, roughly speaking, action-guiding.[4] For example, I might appeal to *Fowler's Modern English Usage* to decide whether to use 'that' or 'which' in a sentence. Epistemological questions are inherently first-person. The traditional epistemologist asks, 'How is it possible for me to be justified in my beliefs about the external world, about other minds, about the past, and so on?' These are questions about what to believe. Epistemic norms are the norms in terms of which these questions are to be answered, so these norms are used in a first-person reason-guiding capacity.

If reasoning is governed by epistemic norms, just how is it governed? There is a model of this regulative process that is often implicit in epistemological thinking, but when we make the model explicit it is *obviously* wrong. This model assimilates the functioning of epistemic norms to the functioning of explicitly articulated norms. For example, naval officers are supposed to "do it by the book", which means that whenever they are in doubt about what to do in a particular situation they are supposed to consult explicit regulations governing all aspects of their behavior and act accordingly. Explicitly articulated norms are also found in driving manuals, etiquette books, and so on. Without giving the matter much thought, there is a tendency to suppose that all norms work this way, and in particular to suppose that this is the way epistemic norms work. I will call this 'the intellectualist model'.[5] It takes little reflection to realize that epistemic norms cannot function in accordance with the intellectualist model. If we had to make an explicit appeal to epistemic norms in order to acquire justified beliefs we would find ourselves in an infinite regress, because to apply explicitly formulated norms we must first acquire justified beliefs about how they apply to this particular case. For example, if we are to reason by making explicit appeal to a norm telling us that it is permissible to move from the belief that something looks red to us to the belief that it is red, we would first have to become justified in believing that that norm is included among our epistemic norms and we would have to become justified in believing that we believe that the object looks red to us. In order to become

4. We can also make "third-person evaluations" of our own past behavior, but that is different from what I am calling "first-person uses" of norms.

5. Many philosophers appear to adopt the intellectualist model, although it is doubtful that any of them would seriously defend it if challenged. For example, Alvin Goldman [1981] appears to assume such an account of epistemic norms. The intellectualist model pervades Hilary Kornblith's [1983] discussion. Unfortunately, it is also prominent in my own [1979] discussion.

justified in holding those beliefs, we would have to apply other epistemic norms, and so on *ad infinitum*. Thus it is clear that epistemic norms cannot guide our reasoning in this way.[6]

If the intellectualist model is wrong, then how do epistemic norms govern reasoning? At this point we might raise the possibility that they do not. Perhaps epistemic norms are only of use in third-person evaluations. But it cannot really be true that epistemic norms play *no role at all* in first-person deliberations. We can certainly subject our reasoning to self-criticism. Every philosopher has detected invalid arguments in his own reasoning. This might suggest that epistemic norms are only relevant in a negative way. Our reasoning is innocent until proven guilty. We can use reasoning to criticize reasoning, and hence we can use reasoning in applying epistemic norms to other reasoning, but we cannot be required to reason about norms *before* we can do any reasoning. This would avoid the infinite regress.

But as theoretically attractive as the "innocent until proven guilty" picture might be, it cannot be right. It entails the view, already discussed and rejected in chapter three, according to which all beliefs are prima facie justified. This view cannot handle the fact that epistemic norms guide the acquisition of beliefs and not just their after-the-fact evaluation. This was illustrated by the observation that even in the perceptual acquisition of beliefs about physical objects, the resulting beliefs are sometimes unjustified. More generally, there are a number of natural processes that lead to belief formation. Among these are such "approved" processes as vision, inductive reasoning, deductive reasoning, and memory, and also some "unapproved" but equally natural processes such as wishful thinking. The latter is just as natural as the former. Recall the example I gave earlier. My daughter had gone to a football game, the evening had turned cold, and I was worried about whether she took a coat. I found myself thinking, "Oh, I am sure she is wearing a coat". But then on reflection I decided that I had no reason to believe that—my initial belief was just a matter of wishful thinking. The point here is that wishful thinking is a natural belief-forming process, but we do not accord it the same status as some other belief-forming processes like vision. Although we have a natural tendency to form beliefs by wishful thinking, we also seem to "naturally" know better. This is not just a matter of after-the-fact criticism. We know better than to indulge in wishful thinking at the very time we do it. It seems that *while* we are reasoning we are being guided by epistemic norms that preclude wishful thinking but permit

6. This point has been made several times. I made it in my [1974], and James Van Cleve [1979] made it again. Despite this, I do not think that epistemologists have generally appreciated its significance. (At least, I did not.)

belief formation based upon perception, induction, and so on. This is of more than casual significance, because it might be impossible to rule out wishful thinking by after-the-fact reasoning. This is because the after-the-fact reasoning might include wishful thinking again, and the new wishful thinking could legitimize the earlier wishful thinking. If epistemic norms play no regulative role in our reasoning while it is going on, there is no reason to think they will be able to play a successful corrective role in after-the-fact evaluations of reasoning. In order for the corrective reasoning to be successful it must itself be normatively correct. Epistemic norms must, and apparently do, play a role in guiding our epistemic behavior at the very time it is occurring. But how can they?

Epistemic norms cannot play a merely negative, corrective, role in guiding reasoning, nor can they function in a way that requires us to already make judgments before we can make judgments. What is left? I think that our perplexity reflects an inadequate understanding of the way action-guiding norms usually function. The case of making an explicit appeal to norms in order to decide what to do is the exception rather than the rule. You may make reference to a driving manual when you are first learning to drive a car, but once you learn how to drive a car you do not look things up in the manual anymore. You do not usually give any explicit thought to what to do—you just do it. This does not mean, however, that your behavior is no longer guided by those norms you learned when you first learned to drive. Similarly, when you first learned to ride a bicycle you were told to turn the handlebars to the right when the bicycle leaned to the right. You learned to ride in accordance with that norm, and that norm still governs your bike-riding behavior but you no longer have to think about it. The point here is that *norms can govern your behavior without your having to think about them.* The intellectualist model of the way norms guide behavior is almost always wrong. This is an obvious point, but it has been insufficiently appreciated. It is of major importance in understanding epistemic norms. Reasoning is more like riding a bicycle than it is like being in the navy.

What makes it possible for your bike-riding behavior to be governed by norms without your thinking about the norms is that you *know how* to ride a bicycle. This is *procedural knowledge* rather than *declarative knowledge.* Having procedural knowledge of what to do under various circumstances does not involve being able to give a general description of what we should do under those circumstances. This is the familiar observation that knowing how to ride a bicycle does not automatically enable one to write a treatise on bicycle riding. This is true for two different reasons. First, knowing how to ride a bicycle requires us to know what to do in each situation *as it arises,* but it does not require us to be able to say what we should do before the fact. Second, even when a situation has actually arisen, our knowing what to do in that situation need not be propositional knowledge. In the case of knowing that we should turn the handlebars to the right when the bicycle leans to the right, it is plausible to suppose that most bicycle riders do have propositional knowledge of this; but consider knowing how to hit a tennis ball with a tennis racket. I know how to do it—as the situation unfolds, at each instant I know what to do—but even at that instant I cannot give a description of what I should do. Knowing what to do is the same thing as knowing to do it, and that need not involve propositional knowledge.

We are now in a position to give a rough explanation of how action-guiding norms can govern behavior in a non-intellectualist manner. When we learn how to do something X, we "acquire" a plan of how to do it. That plan might (but need not) start out as explicit propositional knowledge of what to do under various circumstances, but then the plan becomes internalized. Using a computer metaphor, psychologists sometimes talk about procedural knowledge "being compiled". When we subsequently undertake to do X, our behavior is automatically channeled into that plan. This is just a fact of psychology. We form habits or conditioned reflexes. Norms for doing X constitute a description of this plan for doing X. The sense in which the norms guide our behavior in doing X is that the norms describe the way in which, once we have learned how to do X, our behavior is automatically channeled in undertaking to do X. The norms are not, however, just descriptions of what we do. Rather, they are descriptions of what we *try* to do. Norms can be hard to follow and we follow them with varying degrees of success. Think for example, of an expert golfer who knows how to swing a golf club. Nevertheless, he does not always get his stroke right. It is noteworthy, and it will be important later, that when he does not get his stroke right he is often able to tell that by something akin to introspection. When he does it wrong it "feels wrong". The ability to tell in this way whether one is doing something right is particularly important for those skills governing performances (like golf swings) that take place over more than just an instant of time, because it enables us to correct or fine tune our performance as we go along. The distinction between knowing how to do something and actually doing it is the same as the competence/performance distinction in linguistics. Our linguistic knowledge is procedural knowledge. We know how to use language, but we do not always use language correctly.

The internalization of norms results in our having "automatic" procedural knowledge that enables us to do something without having to think about how to do it. It is this process that I am calling 'being guided by the norm without having to think about the norm'. This may be a slightly misleading way of talking, because it suggests that somewhere in our heads there is a mental representation of the norm and that mental representation is doing the guiding. Perhaps it would be less misleading to say that our behavior is being guided by our procedural knowledge and the way in which it is being guided is described by the norm. What is important is that this is a particular way of being guided. It involves nonintellectual psychological mechanisms that both guide and correct (or fine tune) our behavior.

What we know in knowing how to ride a bicycle can be given a normative description. This procedural knowledge consists of knowing what to do under various circumstances, e.g., knowing to turn right when the bike leans to the right. This can equally be described as knowing what we *should* do under those circumstances. The point of using normative language to describe internalized norms is to contrast what the norms tell us to do with what we *do*. The simple fact of the matter is that even when we know how to do something (e.g., swing a golf club) we do not always succeed in following our norms. This use of 'should' in describing procedural knowledge is interesting. Moral philosophers have talked about different senses of 'should', distinguishing particularly between moral uses of 'should' and goal-directed uses of 'should'. An example of the latter is 'If you want the knife to be sharp then you should sharpen it on the whetstone.' But the use of 'should' in 'In riding a bicycle, when the bicycle leans to the right you should turn the handlebars to the right' is of neither of these varieties. It is perhaps more like the goal-directed kind of 'should', but we are not saying that that is what you should do to achieve the goal of riding a bicycle. Rather, that is part of what is involved *in* riding a bicycle—that is *how* to ride a bicycle. Insofar as we can talk about a goal here at all, it is *defined* by the norms.

Now let us apply this to epistemic norms. We know how to reason. That means that under various circumstances we know what to do in reasoning. This can be described equivalently by saying that we know what we should do. Our epistemic norms are just the norms that describe this procedural knowledge. The way epistemic norms can guide our reasoning without our having to think about them is no longer mysterious. They describe an internalized pattern of behavior that we automatically follow in reasoning, in the same way we automatically follow a pattern in bicycle riding. This is what epistemic norms are. They are the internalized norms that govern our reasoning. Once we realize that they are just one more manifestation of the general phenomenon of automatic behavior governed by internalized norms, epistemic norms should no longer seem puzzling. We would like to have a better understanding of the psychological process wherein behavior is generated in conformance with internalized norms, and I will say more about this below. But in the meantime, much of the mystery surrounding epistemic norms evaporates once we recognize that the governing process is a general one and its application to epistemic norms and reasoning is not much different from its application to any other kind of action-guiding norms. Of course, unlike most norms our epistemic norms may be innate, in which case there is no process of internalization that is required to make them available for use in guiding our reasoning.[7]

My proposal is that epistemic norms are to be understood in terms of procedural knowledge involving internalized rules for reasoning. This proposal has a close kin in much recent work in psychology and artificial intelligence (AI). Researchers in these fields often model human cognition in terms of *production systems*. These are computational systems described by "condition/action rules", which tell the system to perform certain actions whenever certain conditions are satisfied.[8] As I have described them, epistemic norms are condition/action rules and they jointly comprise a production system governing rational belief change.

I have described how our epistemic norms work. This is to describe our *actual* epistemic norms. Internalists typically assume that whatever our actual epistemic norms are, they are the correct epistemic norms. I have taken it to be part of the definition of internalism that our epistemic norms are at least not subject to criticism on externalist grounds. Of course, this is precisely where internalists disagree with norm externalists. Let us turn then to a reconsideration of externalism in the light of our new understanding of epistemic norms.

---

7. There has been a lot of recent work in psychology concerning human irrationality. Psychologists have shown that in certain kinds of epistemic situations people have an almost overpowering tendency to reason incorrectly. (Much of the psychological material can be found in Daniel Kahneman, Paul Slovic, and Amos Tversky [1982], and R. E. Nisbett and L. Ross [1980].) It might be tempting to conclude from this that, contrary to what I am claiming, people do not know how to reason. The short way with this charge is to note that if we did not know how to reason correctly in these cases, we would be unable to discover that people reason incorrectly. To say that we know how to reason is to invoke a competence/performance distinction. It in no way precludes our making mistakes. It does not even preclude our almost always making mistakes in specific kinds of reasoning. All it requires is that we can, in principle, discover the errors of our ways and correct them. (This is pretty much the same as the assessment offered by Jonathan Cohen, [1981]. See also the critique in Alvin Goldman [1986].)

8. See, for example, Newell [1972], [1973], [1980], Newell and Simon [1972], and John Anderson [1976], [1983].

4. The Refutation of Externalism

4.1 *Belief Externalism*

Now that we understand how epistemic norms work in guiding our reasoning, it is easy to see that they must be internalist norms. This is because when we learn how to do something we acquire a set of norms for doing it and these norms are internalized in a way enabling our central nervous system to follow them in an automatic way without our having to think about them. This has implications for the content of our norms. For example, I have been describing one of our bike-riding norms as telling us that if the bicycle leans to the right then we should turn the handlebars to the right, but that is not really what we learn when we learn to ride a bicycle. The automatic processing systems in our brain do not have access to whether the bicycle is leaning to the right. What they do have access to are things like (1) our *thinking* that the bicycle is leaning to the right, and (2) certain balance sensations emanating from our inner ear. What we learn is (roughly) to turn the handlebars to the right if we either experience those balance sensations or think on some other basis that the bicycle is leaning to the right. In general, the circumstance-types to which our norms appeal in telling us to do something in circumstances of those types must be directly accessible to our automatic processing systems. The sense in which they must be directly accessible is that our automatic processing system must be able to access them without our first having to make a *judgment* about whether we are in circumstances of that type. We must have non-epistemic access.[9]

This general observation about action-guiding norms has immediate implications for the nature of our epistemic norms. It implies that reason-guiding epistemic norms cannot appeal to external considerations of reliability. This is because such norms could not be internalized. Like *leaning to the right*, considerations of reliability are not directly accessible to our automatic processing systems. There is in principle no way that we can learn to make inferences of various kinds only if they are *in fact* reliable. Of course, we could learn to make certain inferences only if we *think* they are reliable, but that

---

9. It might be insisted that this is at least sometimes a misleading way of talking—if our norms for doing X tell us to do Y whenever we *think* it is the case that C, we might better describe our norms as telling us to do Y when it *is* the case that C. I do not care if one chooses to talk that way, but it must be realized that it has the consequence that although the reformulated norm says to do Y when it is the case that C, knowing how to do X will really only result in our doing Y when we *think* it is the case that C. This will be important. (And, of course, norms appealing to internal states other than beliefs could not be reformulated in this manner anyway.)

would be an internalist norm appealing to *thoughts* about reliability rather than an externalist norm appealing to reliability itself.[10] Similar observations apply to any externalist norms. Consequently, it is in principle impossible for us to actually employ externalist norms. I take this to be a conclusive refutation of belief externalism.

I introduced the internalism/externalism distinction by saying that internalist theories make justifiedness a function exclusively of the believer's internal states, where internal states are those that are "directly accessible" to the believer. The notion of direct accessibility was purposely left vague, but it can now be clarified. I propose to define internal states as those states that are directly accessible to the mechanisms in our central nervous system that direct our reasoning. The sense in which they are *directly* accessible is that access to them does not require us first to have beliefs about them. This definition makes the internalist/externalist distinction precise in a way that agrees at least approximately with the way it has generally been used, although it is impossible to make it agree with everything everyone has said about it because philosophers have drawn the distinction in different ways.

The epistemic norms endorsed by an internalist theory must appeal only to properties of and relations between internal states of the believer. This is not yet enough to characterize internalist norms, however, because an externalist theory might also appeal only to properties of and relations between internalist states of the believer. For instance, probabilism appeals only to the probability of the beliefs held by the believer, and the probability of a belief is a property of it. Internalist theories make the justifiability of a belief a function of the internal states of the believer, in the sense that if we vary anything but his internal states then the justifiability of the belief does not vary. Thus the only properties of and relations between internal states to which internalist norms can appeal are those that cannot be varied without varying the internal states themselves. In other words, they are logical properties of and logical relations between internal states. For instance, if S_1 is the state of believing (P & Q) and S_2 is the state of believing P, then S_1 and S_2 are logically related by the fact that being in S_1 involves believing a conjunction whose first conjunct is believed if one is in state S_2. Thus we can characterize internalist theories as those proposing epistemic norms that appeal only to logical properties of and logical relations between internal states of the believer.

I have characterized internalist theories in terms of direct accessi-

10. It would also be a wholly implausible theory. We do not invariably have beliefs about the reliability of our inferences whenever we make them, and if norms *requiring* us to have such beliefs also require those beliefs to be justified then they lead to an infinite regress.

bility, but I have not said anything in a general way about which properties and relations are directly accessible. It seems clear that directly accessible properties must be in some sense "psychological", but I doubt that we can say much more than that from the comfort of our armchairs. What properties are directly accessible is an empirical question to be answered by psychologists. Despite the fact that we do not have a general characterization of direct accessibility, it is perfectly clear in many specific cases that particular properties to which philosophers have appealed are not directly accessible. In light of this, the preceding refutation of belief externalism can be applied to a remarkably broad spectrum of theories, and it seems to me to constitute an absolutely conclusive refutation of those theories. I have indicated how it applies to theories formulating epistemic norms in terms of reliability. It applies in the same way to probabilist theories. For example, we saw that many probabilists endorse the *simple rule*:

A belief is epistemically permissible if and only if what is believed is sufficiently probable.

If the simple rule is to provide us with a reason-guiding norm then the probability of a belief must be a directly accessible property of it. No objective probability can have that property. Thus it is impossible to use the simple rule, interpreted in terms of objective probabilities, as a reason-guiding norm. This objection could be circumvented by replacing the simple rule with its "doxastic counterpart":

A belief is epistemically permissible if and only if the epistemic agent believes it to be highly probable.

But this rule formulates an internalist norm (albeit, an implausible one).[11]

It might be supposed that we could breathe life back into the simple rule by interpreting it in terms of subjective probability. Here we must be careful to distinguish between subjective probability as actual degree of belief and subjective probability as rational degree of belief. Interpreted in terms of actual degrees of belief, the simple rule would amount to the claim that a belief is justified if and only if it is firmly held, which is an internalist norm, but a preposterous one. Interpreted in terms of rational degrees of belief it becomes an externalist norm. Rational degree of belief is the unique degree of belief one rationally ought to have in a proposition given one's overall doxastic state, and this is to be understood in terms of prudentially

11. We do not ordinarily have any beliefs at all about the probabilities of what we believe. Furthermore, even if we did they would presumably not render our beliefs justified unless the probability beliefs were themselves justified, so we would be threatened by an infinite regress.

rational betting behavior. As I have indicated, I have serious doubts about the intelligibility of this notion. But even if we waive this objection, ascertaining what this unique rational degree of belief should be is immensely difficult. It seems extremely unlikely that the rational degree of belief one ought to have in a proposition is a directly accessible property of it. If it is not then this version of the simple rule also succumbs to our general objection to belief externalism.

Many other epistemological theories succumb to this objection to belief externalism. For example, Keith Lehrer's coherence theory is an internalist theory, but it was pointed out in the last chapter that an externalist theory can be modeled on it. According to this externalist theory, a person is justified in believing a proposition if and only if that proposition is more probable than each proposition competing with it. But a proposition's being more probable than any of its competitors is not a directly accessible property of it, and hence the objective version of Lehrer's theory becomes incapable of supplying us with a reason-guiding norm.

These considerations are efficient in dispatching a wide variety of epistemological theories. All belief-externalist theories succumb to this objection, and a surprising number of internalist theories succumb to it as well. Recall that an internalist theory is any theory proposing epistemic norms that appeal only to logical properties of and logical relations between internal states of the believer. We can make a distinction between properties and relations that are directly accessible and those that are not. A directly accessible property or relation is one to which our automatic processing system has access without our having beliefs about what things have the property or stand in the relation. Not all logical properties or relations are directly accessible, and hence not all internalist theories propose epistemic norms that are internalizable. For instance, a holistic coherence theory adopts a holistic view of reasons according to which a belief is licensed if it is suitably related to the set of *all* the beliefs one holds. A holistic coherence theory requires a relationship between a justified belief and the set of all the beliefs one holds, but that will not normally be a directly accessible property of the justified belief, and hence although the norm proposed by the holistic theory will be an internalist norm, it will not be internalizable. Thus it cannot be reason-guiding.

The general point emerging from all this is that there is a remarkably wide range of epistemological theories succumbing to the simple objection that non-internalist epistemic norms cannot be internalized in the way required in order for them to be reason-guiding. Accordingly, they cannot serve as epistemic norms. No non-internalist theory can provide us with epistemic norms that we could actually use. Correct epistemic norms must be internalist. On the other hand, we have also seen that they must appeal to more than the cognizer's doxastic state. They must also appeal to his perceptual and memory states. Thus the correct epistemological theory must endorse some kind of nondoxastic internalist norms.

The endorsement of nondoxastic norms amounts to the rejection of the doxastic assumption, but that has often seemed puzzling. How is it be possible for nondoxastic states to justify beliefs when we are not aware that we are in them? We are now in a position to understand how nondoxastic norms are possible. They only seem puzzling because we are implicitly assuming the intellectualist model of the way epistemic norms regulate belief. Given the way epistemic norms actually operate, all that is required is that the input states be directly accessible. Belief states are directly accessible, but so are a variety of nondoxastic states like perceptual states and memory states. Thus there is no reason why epistemic norms cannot appeal to those states, and the rejection of the doxastic assumption and the move to direct realism ceases to be puzzling.

Is there any way to salvage belief externalism in the face of the objection that it cannot give reasonable accounts of first-person reason-guiding epistemic norms? The possibility remains that belief externalism might provide norms for third-person evaluations. I think it is noteworthy in this connection that externalists tend to take a third-person point of view in discussing epistemology. If externalist norms played a role in third-person evaluations, we would then have both externalist and internalist norms that could be applied to individual beliefs and they might conflict. What would this show? It would not show anything—they would just be different norms evaluating the same belief from different points of view. I can imagine a persistent externalist insisting, "Well, if the two sets of norms conflict, which way should we reason—which set of norms should we follow?" But that question does not make any sense. Asking what we should do is asking for a normative judgment, and before we can answer the question we must inquire to what norms the 'should' is appealing. To make this clearer consider an analogous case. We can evaluate beliefs from both an epistemic point of view and a prudential point of view. Recall Helen who has good reason for believing that her father is Jack the Ripper. Suppose that if she believed that, it would be psychologically crushing. Then we might say that, epistemically, she should believe it, but prudentially she should not. If one then insists upon asking, "Well, should she believe it or not?", the proper response is, "In what sense of 'should'—epistemic or prudential?" Similarly, if externalist and internalist norms conflict and one asks, "Which way should we reason?", the proper response is to ask to which set of norms the 'should' is appealing. The point is that different norms serve different purposes, and when they conflict that does not show that there is something wrong with one of the sets of norms—it just shows that the different norms are doing different jobs. The job of internalist norms is reason-guiding, and as such they are the norms traditionally sought in epistemology. Externalist norms (if any sense can be made of them) may also have a point, but they cannot be used to solve traditional epistemological problems pertaining to epistemic justification.

4.2 Norm Externalism

Recall that there are two kinds of externalism. Belief externalism advocates the adoption of externalist norms. I regard belief externalism as having been decisively refuted by the preceding considerations. Norm externalism, on the other hand, acknowledges that we must employ internalist norms in our reasoning, but proposes that alternative sets of internalist norms should be evaluated in terms of external considerations. For example, it may be alleged that one set of internalist norms is better than another if the first is more reliable in producing true beliefs. Both internalism and norm externalism endorse internalist norms, but they differ in that the internalist alleges that our epistemic norms are not subject to criticism on externalist grounds. It is hard to see how they could be subject to criticism on internalist grounds, so the internalist has typically assumed that our epistemic norms are immune from criticism—whatever our actual epistemic norms are, they are the correct epistemic norms. That, however, seems odd. On the surface, it seems it must be at least logically possible for two people to employ different epistemic norms. They could then hold the same belief under the same circumstances and on the basis of the same evidence and yet the first could be conforming to his norms and the second not conforming to his. If a person's epistemic norms are always beyond criticism, it would follow that the first person is justified in his beliefs and the second is not, despite the fact that their beliefs are based upon the same evidence. That would at least be peculiar. Because it seems that it must be possible for different people to employ different epistemic norms, this makes a strong prima facie case for norm externalism.

Action-guiding norms are not generally immune from criticism. Typically, action-guiding norms tell us how to do one thing *by* doing something else.[12] For example, knowing how to ride a bicycle consists

---

12. The *by* relation is what Alvin Goldman [1976a] calls *level-generation*.

of knowing what more basic actions to perform—leg movements, arm movements, and the like—by doing which we ride the bicycle. An action that is performed by doing something else is a *nonbasic* action. Norms describing how to perform nonbasic actions can be subject to external evaluation. There may be more than one way to perform the nonbasic action, and some ways may be better (more efficient, more reliable, and so on) than others. If I know how to do it in one way and you know how to do it in another way, you know how to do it better than I if the norms governing your behavior are better than the norms governing mine. For example, we may both know how to hit the target with a bow and arrow, but you may know how to do it more reliably than I.[13] It thus becomes an empirical question whether acting in accordance with a proposed norm will constitute your doing what you want to be doing and whether another norm might not be better.

Reasoning is not, strictly speaking, an action, but it is something we do, and we do it by doing other simpler things. We reason by adopting new beliefs and rejecting old beliefs under a variety of circumstances. Our norms for reasoning tell us when it is permissible or impermissible to do this. It seems that the norms we actually employ should be subject to external criticism just like any other norms. The norm externalist proposes that we should scrutinize them and possibly replace them by other norms. Because of the direct accessibility problem, we cannot replace them by norms making explicit appeal to reliability, but what we might discover is that (1) under certain circumstances inferences licensed by our natural norms are unreliable, and (2) under certain circumstances inferences not licensed by our natural norms are highly reliable. The norm externalist proposes that we should then alter our epistemic norms, adopting new internalist norms allowing us to make the inferences described under (2) and prohibiting those described under (1).

We must distinguish between two construals of the norm externalist's proposal. He might be telling us that when we *discover* old reasoning patterns to be unreliable or new reasoning patterns to be reliable then we should alter our norms and our reasoning accordingly. Alternatively, he might be telling us that if old patterns simply *are* unreliable and new patterns *are* reliable, independently of our knowing or believing that they are, then we should alter our reasoning. The first construal seems like an eminently reasonable proposal, and it is one that has been made explicitly by various externalists. For example, in discussing how reliabilist considerations bear on reasoning, Goldman [1981] writes:

---

13. Alternatively, we may have the same norms but your physical skills make you better able to conform to them.

> At the start a creature forms beliefs from automatic, preprogrammed doxastic processes. . . . Once the creature distinguishes between more and less reliable belief-forming processes, it has taken the first step toward doxastic appraisal. . . . The creature can also begin doxastic self-criticism, in which it proposes *regulative* principles to itself. (p. 47)

But this involves a fundamental misconception. Our epistemic norms are not subject to criticism in this way. Particular instances of reasoning are subject to such criticism, and the criticism can dictate changes in that reasoning, but this does not lead to changes in our epistemic norms. This is because unlike other norms, our epistemic norms already accommodate criticism based on reliability. The point is twofold. First, discovering that certain kinds of inferences are unreliable under certain circumstances constitutes a defeater for those inferences and hence makes us unjustified in reasoning in that way, and this is entirely in accordance with our natural unmodified epistemic norms. For example, we discover that color vision is unreliable in dim lighting, and once we discover this we should cease to judge colors on that basis under those circumstances. But this does not require an alteration of our epistemic norms, because color vision only provides us with defeasible reasons for color judgments, and our discovery of unreliability constitutes a defeater for those reasons. This is entirely in accordance with the norms we already have. Second, discovering that some new inferences are reliable under certain circumstances provides us with justification for making those inferences under those circumstances, but this is licensed by the norms we already have. That is precisely what induction is all about. For example, I might discover that I am clairvoyant and certain kinds of "visions" provide reliable indications of what is about to happen. Once I make this discovery it becomes reasonable for me to base beliefs about the future on such visions. Again, this is entirely in accordance with the norms we already have and does not require us to alter those norms in any way. The general point is that the kinds of reliability considerations to which the norm externalist appeals can lead us to reason differently (refrain from some old inferences and make some new inferences), but this does not lead to any change in our epistemic norms. Epistemic norms are unique in that they involve a kind of built-in feedback having the result that the sort of external criticism that could lead to the modification of other action-guiding norms does not necessitate any modification of epistemic norms.

I have had several externalists respond to this objection by protesting that they do not see the point of distinguishing between considerations of reliability leading us to alter our reasoning and those considerations leading us to alter our norms. But if all the externalist means is that considerations of reliability can lead us to alter our reasoning, then he is not disagreeing with anyone. In particular, he is not disagreeing with paradigmatic internalists like Chisholm and myself. Norm externalism becomes nothing but a pretentious statement of a platitude.

The alternative construal of norm externalism takes it to be telling us that if old patterns of reasoning are unreliable and new patterns are reliable, then regardless of whether we *know* these facts about reliability, we should not reason in accordance with the old patterns and we should reason in accordance with the new patterns. What is the meaning of 'should' in this claim? It cannot be taken as a recommendation about how to reason, because it is not a recommendation anyone could follow. We can only alter our reasoning in response to facts about reliability if we are apprised of those facts. However, normative judgments do not always have the force of recommendations. That is, they are not always intended to be action-guiding. This is connected with the distinction that is often made in ethics between subjective and objective senses of 'should'. To say that a person subjectively should do X is to say, roughly, that given what he believes (perhaps falsely) to be the case he has an obligation to do X. To say that he objectively should do X is to say, roughly, that if he were apprised of all the relevant facts then he would have an obligation to do X. Judgments about what a person subjectively should do can serve as recommendations, but judgments about what a person objectively should do can only serve as external evaluations having some purpose other than guiding behavior.[14] The subjective/objective distinction can be regarded as a distinction between evaluating the person and evaluating his act. The subjective sense of 'should' has to do with moral responsibility, while the objective sense has to do with what act might best have been performed.

We can draw a similar subjective/objective distinction in epistemology. The epistemic analogue of moral responsibility is epistemic justification. A person is being "epistemically responsible" just in case his beliefs are justified. In other words, epistemic justification corresponds to *subjective* moral obligation. What determines whether a belief is justified is what else the epistemic agent *believes* about the world (and what other directly accessible states he is in)—not what is in fact true about the world. This seems to show that whatever considerations of de facto reliability may bear upon, it is not epistemic justification. They must instead bear upon the epistemic analogue of objective obligation. What is that analogue? There is one clear analogue—objective epistemic justification is a matter of what you should

14. They may serve as recommendations in an indirect fashion by conveying to a person that there are relevant facts of which he is not apprised.

believe if you were apprised of all the relevant truths. But what you should believe if you were apprised of all the relevant truths is just *all the truths*. In other words, the epistemic analogue of objective justification is *truth*. There is nothing here to give solace to a norm externalist.

Goldman [1981] draws a somewhat different distinction between two senses of 'justified' in epistemology. He distinguishes between "theoretical" evaluations of reasoning and "regulative" evaluations (the latter being reason-guiding). He suggests that the theoretical sense of justification is the sense required for knowledge and that it is to be distinguished from the reason-guiding sense. He suggests further that his reliabilist theory concerns the theoretical sense. The proposal is that it is knowledge that provides the point of a norm externalist's evaluation of epistemic norms in terms of considerations of reliability unknown to the epistemic agent. I do not believe that, but even if it were true it would not affect my overall point. The sense of epistemic justification with which I am concerned in this book is the reason-guiding sense, and if it is acknowledged that norm externalism bears only upon another sense of justification then my main point has been conceded.

4.3   *Epistemological Relativism and the Individuation of Concepts*

The apparent failure of norm externalism, leaves us with a puzzling problem. Internalists have typically assumed that whatever epistemic norms we actually employ are automatically correct. But that seems hard to reconcile with the seemingly obvious fact that it is at least logically possible for different people to employ different norms. Surely, if Smith and Jones believe P for the same reasons, they are either both justified or both unjustified. There is no room for their justification to be relative to idiosyncratic features of their psychology resulting in their employing different epistemic norms. This seems to imply that there is just one set of correct epistemic norms, and the norms a person actually employs may fail to be correct. This conclusion would seem to be obvious if it were not for the fact that there is no apparent basis for criticizing a person's norms. That is precisely what norm externalism tries unsuccessfully to do. The reliabilist considerations to which the norm externalist appeals are the only plausible candidates for considerations of use in criticizing and correcting epistemic norms, and we have seen that our epistemic norms cannot be corrected in this way. Of course, I might criticize Jones' norms simply because they disagree with mine, but he could equally criticize mine because they disagree with his. Are we committed to a thorough-going epistemological relativism then? That is at least unpalatable.

The solution to the problem of relativism can be found by turning to a different problem. This is the problem of how concepts are individuated. The standard view takes concepts to be individuated by their truth conditions. The claim of this theory is that what makes a concept the concept that it is are the conditions that must be satisfied for something to exemplify that concept. These conditions comprise its truth conditions. The precise content of the truth condition theory of concepts deserves closer inspection than it usually receives. There is one sense in which the truth condition theory of concepts is correct but also completely trivial and uninteresting. The truth condition of the concept *red* is the condition of *being red*, and the truth condition of the concept *blue* is the condition of *being blue*. The following is undeniable:

red = *blue* if and only if *being red* = *being blue*

but it is hardly illuminating. Rather than explaining the concepts, the truth conditions presuppose the concepts. We might just as well define the "identity condition" of a physical object to be the condition of *being that object* and then claim that physical objects are individuated by their identity conditions. That is about as unilluminating as a theory can be.

Typically, philosophical logicians slide back and forth between the vacuous claim that concepts are individuated by their truth conditions and the considerably more contentious claim that concepts can be informatively characterized by (and only by) giving truth condition analyses of them. A truth condition analysis of a concept is an informative statement of necessary and sufficient conditions for something to exemplify the concept. I think it is fair to say that many philosophical logicians do not clearly distinguish between the vacuous claim and the contentious claim, or at least take the vacuous claim to somehow directly support the contentious claim. But I see no reason to think there is any connection between the two claims.

There is another strand to this story. Traditionally, the only logical relations between concepts that were recognized by philosophers were entailment relations. Concepts, as "logical items", were supposed to be individuated by their logical properties, and it seemed that the only logical properties concepts possessed were those definable in terms of their entailment relations to other concepts. This generates the picture of a "logical space" of concepts, the identity of a concept being determined by its position in the space, and the latter being determined by its entailment relations to other concepts. The claim that concepts must have definitions is just a more specific version of this general picture—one alleging that the position of a concept in logical space is determined not just by one-way entailments but by two-way logical equivalences. Some version of this picture has been prevalent throughout much of twentieth century philosophy, and it still plays a prominent role in philosophical logic. I will call this general picture of the individuation of concepts *the logical theory of concepts*. It has typically been either confused with or identified with the truth condition theory.

The simplest objection to all of this is that most concepts do not have the kind of definitions required by the logical theory of concepts. Analytic philosophy in the mid-twentieth century concerned itself almost exclusively with the search for such definitions, and if we can learn anything from that period it is that the search was largely in vain. It is a very rare concept that can be given an informative definition stating truth conditions. The importance of this simple objection cannot be overemphasized. Most concepts do not have definitions. For reasons I find mysterious, many philosophers seem to just ignore this and go on pretending that the logical theory of concepts is correct.

We can also raise a more purely epistemological problem for the logical theory of concepts, and I will now spend some time developing this problem. In general, the logical theory cannot make sense of reasons. To see this, let us begin with prima facie reasons. The logical theory appears to lead directly to the impossibility of prima facie reasons. I assume that what makes something a good reason for holding a belief is a function of the content of the belief. If the content of the belief is determined by entailment relations, then those entailment relations must also determine what are good reasons for holding that belief. The only kinds of reasons that can be derived from entailment relations are reasons that are themselves entailments—conclusive reasons. Thus we are forced to the conclusion that all reasons must be entailments. But this must be wrong, because we have seen that we cannot solve epistemological problems in terms of conclusive reasons. Justified belief makes essential appeal to defeasible reasoning.

We might try distinguishing between 'formal reasons' that derive from principles of logic and apply equally to all concepts, and 'substantive reasons' that are specific to individual concepts and reflect the contents of those concepts. The preceding argument is really only an argument that the logical theory of concepts is incompatible with there being nonconclusive substantive reasons. Thus we could render the logical theory of concepts compatible with defeasible reasoning if it could be maintained that all legitimate defeasible reasons are formal reasons. The only plausible way of defending this claim is to maintain that the only legitimate defeasible reasons are inductive reasons and to insist that inductive reasons are formal reasons. This is to take induction to be a species of logic. On this view, there are two kinds of logic—deductive and inductive—and each generates formal reasons that pertain to all concepts and hence need not be derivable from the contents of individual concepts. For example, a conjunction (P & Q) gives us a reason for believing its first conjunct P regardless of what P and Q are. Similarly, it was traditionally supposed that inductive reasons are formal reasons pertaining equally to all concepts. This absolves us from having to derive inductive prima facie reasons from the essential properties of the concepts to which the reasons apply.

Unfortunately, this attempt to render the logical theory of concepts compatible with induction fails. It was pointed out in chapter one that induction does not apply equally to all concepts. Inductive reasoning must be restricted to projectible concepts. There is no generally accepted theory of projectibility, but it is generally recognized that what makes a concept projectible is not in any sense a "formal" feature of it. The simplest argument for this was given long ago by Nelson Goodman [1955]. Define:

x is *grue* if and only if either (1) x is green and first examined before the year 2000, or (2) x is blue and not first examined before the year 2000.

x is *bleen* if and only if either (1) x is blue and first examined before the year 2000, or (2) x is green and not first examined before the year 2000.

'Grue' and 'bleen' are not projectible. For example, if we now (prior to the year 2000) examine lots of emeralds and find that they are all green, that gives us an inductive reason for thinking that all emeralds are green. Our sample of green emeralds is also a sample of grue emeralds, so if 'grue' were projectible then our observations would also give us a reason for thinking that all emeralds are grue. These two conclusions together would entail the absurd consequence that there will be no emeralds first examined after the year 2000. It follows that 'grue' is not projectible. Now the thing to notice is that 'blue' and 'green' are definable in terms of 'grue' and 'bleen' in the precisely the same way 'grue' and 'bleen' were defined in terms of 'blue' and 'green':

x is green if and only if either (1) x is grue and first examined before the year 2000, or (2) x is bleen and not first examined before the year 2000.

x is blue if and only if either (1) x is bleen and first examined before the year 2000, or (2) x is grue and not first examined before the year 2000.

Thus the *formal* relationships between the pair 'blue', 'green' and the pair 'grue', 'bleen' are symmetrical, and hence we cannot distinguish the projectible from the nonprojectible by appealing only to formal properties of the concepts. Projectibility seems to have essentially to do with the content of the concepts. Therefore, any explanation for the existence of inductive prima facie reasons must make reference to the particular concepts to which the reasons apply, and hence, on the logical theory of concepts, inductive prima facie reasons become as mysterious as any other prima facie reasons.

There is of course the further point, defended earlier, that epistemology requires more prima facie reasons than just inductive ones. Thus even if inductive reasons had turned out to be formal reasons, that would not entirely solve the problem of the possibility of prima facie reasons.

The next thing to notice is that the logical theory of concepts makes conclusive reasons just as mysterious as prima facie reasons. This has generally been overlooked, but it is really rather obvious. Epistemologists have noted repeatedly that logical entailments do not always constitute reasons. Some entailments are conclusive reasons and others are not reasons at all. The latter is because P may entail Q without the connection between P and Q being at all obvious. For example, mathematicians have proven that the Axiom of Choice entails Zorn's Lemma. These are abstruse mathematical principles apparently dealing with quite different subject matters, and just looking at them one would not expect there to be any connection between them. If, without knowing about the entailment, one were so perverse as to believe Zorn's lemma on the basis of the Axiom of Choice, one would not be justified in this belief. Once the entailment is known, you can become justified in believing Zorn's Lemma *partly* by appeal to the Axiom of Choice, but your full reason for believing Zorn's Lemma will be the conjunction of the Axiom of Choice and the proposition that if the Axiom of Choice is true then Zorn's Lemma is true. You are believing Zorn's Lemma on the basis of this conjunction rather than just on the basis of the Axiom of Choice. You can never become justified in believing Zorn's Lemma on the basis of the Axiom of Choice alone, so the latter is not a reason for the former.

On the other hand, some entailments do provide reasons. If I justifiably believe both P and $(P \supset Q)$, I *can* justifiably believe Q on the basis of these other two beliefs. In this case I do not have to believe Q on the basis of the more complicated belief:

P and $(P \supset Q)$ and if $[P \& (P \supset Q)]$ then Q.

To suppose that each instance of reasoning in accordance with *modus ponens* must be reconstructed in this way would lead to an infinite regress.[15] Thus some entailments are conclusive reasons and others are not. But the logical theory of concepts gives us no way to make this distinction. It characterizes concepts in terms of their entailment relations to other concepts, but, *a fortiori*, all entailment relations are entailment relations. There is nothing about the entailment relations themselves that could make some of them reasons and others not. Thus conclusive reasons become just as mysterious as prima facie reasons on the logical theory of concepts. This seems to indicate pretty conclusively that the logical theory of concepts is wrong. There has to be more to concepts than entailment relations.

To argue that the logical theory of concepts is wrong is not yet to say what is right. The theory I want to endorse in its place is *the epistemological theory of concepts*. This theory begins by noting that concepts are both logical and epistemological items. That is, concepts are the categories whose interrelationships are studied by logic, and they are also the categories in terms of which we think of the world. The interrelationships studied by logic can all be reduced to entailment relations. Thus logic need not take note of any other features of concepts. Logic can get along with a cruder picture of concepts than can epistemology. But a complete account of concepts must accommodate both logic and epistemology. There is good reason to think that the role of concepts in epistemology is fundamental. Not all entailment relations are conclusive reasons, but it seems likely that all entailment relations derive from "simple" entailment relations, where the latter are just those that are conclusive reasons. Thus a theory of concepts adequate for epistemology will very likely be adequate for logic as well. The question then becomes, 'What kind of theory of concepts is adequate for epistemology?' In epistemology, the essential role of concepts is their role in reasoning. They are the categories in terms of which we think of the world, and we think of the world by reasoning about it. This suggests that concepts are individuated by their role in reasoning. What makes a concept the concept that it is is the way we can use it in reasoning, and that is described by saying how it enters into various kinds of reasons, both conclusive and prima facie. Let us take the *conceptual role* of a concept to consist of (1) the reasons (conclusive or prima facie) for thinking that something exemplifies it or exemplifies its negation, and (2) the conclusions we can justifiably draw (conclusively or prima facie) from the fact that something exemplifies the concept or exemplifies the negation of the concept. My proposal is that concepts are individuated by their conceptual roles. The essence of a concept is to have the conceptual role that it does. If this is right, the explanation for how there can be

15. This was apparently first noted by Lewis Carroll.

such things as prima facie reasons becomes trivial. Prima facie reasons are primitive constituents of the conceptual roles that characterize concepts. Prima facie reasons need not have an origin in something deeper about concepts, because there is nothing deeper. In an important sense, there is nothing to concepts over and above their conceptual role. To describe the conceptual role of a concept is to give an analysis of that concept, although not a truth condition analysis.[16]

I think it is undeniable that concepts are individuated by their conceptual roles, and not (at least in any non-vacuous way) by their truth conditions. But some further explanation for all of this is required. *Why* are concepts individuated in this way? I will shortly propose an answer to this question. For the moment, however, I will simply take it as established that concepts are individuated in this way. The importance of this theory of concepts for the matters at hand is that it lays to rest the spectre of epistemological relativism. Epistemological relativism is the view that (1) different people could have different epistemic norms that conflict in the sense that they lead to different assessments of the justifiedness of the same belief being held on the same basis, and (2) there is no way to choose between these norms. The epistemological theory of concepts enables us to escape any such relativism. Because concepts are individuated by their conceptual roles, it becomes impossible for people's epistemic norms to differ in a way that makes them conflict with one another. The epistemic norms a person employs in reasoning determine what concepts he is employing because they describe the conceptual roles of his concepts. If two people reason in accordance with different sets of epistemic norms, all that follows is that they are employing different concepts. Thus it is impossible for two people to employ different epistemic norms in connection with the same concepts. Their conceptual frameworks are determined by their epistemic norms. Epistemological relativism is logically false.[17]

16. This view of concepts is reminiscent of the verification theories of the logical positivists. I first defended a theory of this sort in my [1968], and in more detail in my [1974], although in those publications I talked about "justification conditions" rather than conceptual roles, and used the term a bit more narrowly. This view of concepts is also related to the somewhat cruder views expressed by Michael Dummet [1975] and [1976] and Hilary Putnam [1979] and [1984].

17. The conclusion that if different people employ different epistemic norms then they employ different concepts may seem puzzling because it appears to make it inexplicable how such people could communicate with each other. But two points should be made here. First, I doubt that there really is any variation in epistemic norms from person to person. I suspect that epistemic norms are species specific. But even if that conjecture is false, it need create no difficulty for communication. I have argued at length in two recent books that concepts play only an indirect role in communication. (My entire theory of language is developed in my [1982]. A briefer sketch of the theory can be found in chapter two of my [1984]. The reader who is concerned with this question should consult those books.)

4.4   *Conclusions*

To summarize the discussion of externalism, one can be an externalist by being either a belief externalist or a norm externalist. These exhaust the ways in which externalist considerations might be brought to bear on our epistemic norms. The belief externalist tries to formulate epistemic norms directly in terms of externalist considerations, but it is impossible to construct reason-guiding norms in this way. The norm externalist proposes instead to recommend changes in reason-guiding norms on the basis of considerations of reliability. But this appeal to reliability is redundant because it is already accommodated by our unmodified internalist norms. Thus, as far as I can see, externalism has nothing to contribute to the solution to traditional epistemological problems. Justified beliefs are those resulting from normatively correct reasoning. Consequently, any evaluation of the justifiedness of a belief must be reason-guiding and hence must be beyond the pale of externalism.

5. Man as a Cognitive Machine

I have described how epistemic norms work and how they are related to concepts, but we may be left wondering why all of this should be the case. A fuller understanding of the nature of epistemic norms can be obtained by seeing how they are integrated into the broader picture of man as a cognitive machine. I take it for granted that man is a kind of biological information processor. Considerable light can be thrown on human epistemology by reflecting on the workings of cognitive machines in general.

Suppose we were undertaking the feat of building an "intelligent machine" that could interact with its surroundings, learn from experience, and survive in a reasonably hostile environment. Let's call our machine 'Oscar'. What would we have to put into Oscar to make him work? At the very least we would have to provide him with ways of sensing the environment and thinking about the world. It is worth pursuing some of the details.

5.1   *Oscar I*

We must begin by incorporating sensors much like our sense organs so that Oscar can respond to states of the environment, and we might even call these sensors 'sense organs'. We must also incorporate "reasoning" facilities, both deductive and inductive. And we must incorporate some sort of conative structure to provide goals for Oscar to attempt to realize. If Oscar is to survive in a hostile environment, it would also be wise to provide sensors that respond to conditions under which he is in imminent danger of damage or destruction. We might call these 'pain sensors'. Oscar could then have built-in "fight or flight" responses elicited by the activation of his pain sensors.

I have described Oscar as thinking about the world. That involves a system of mental representation—what we might call a 'language of thought'.[18] For Oscar to have a thought is for him to "entertain" a sentence in his language of thought and treat it in a certain way. Without going into details, we can suppose abstractly that for Oscar to have a thought is for him to have a sentence in his language of thought residing in his "B-box".[19] Adopting a computer metaphor, we can think of the latter as a memory location. Oscar's thoughts and beliefs must be causally related to his environment and his behavior. On the one hand, Oscar must be constructed in such a way that the stimulation of his sensory apparatus tends to cause him to acquire certain beliefs. On the other hand, Oscar's having appropriate beliefs must tend to cause him to behave in corresponding ways. To describe these causal connections will be to describe his facilities for "pure reasoning" (his epistemology) and his facilities for practical reasoning.

Let us call the machine resulting from this stage of design 'Oscar I'.[20]

5.2   Oscar II

Oscar I could function reasonably well in a congenial environment. But in an environment that is both reasonably complex and reasonably hostile, Oscar I would be doomed to early destruction. He would be easy meat for wily machinivores. The difficulty is this. To be effective in avoiding damage, Oscar I must not only be able to *respond* to the stimulation of his pain-sensors when that occurs—he must also be able to *predict* when that is apt to occur and avoid getting into such situations. He must be able to exercise "foresight". As we have constructed him, Oscar I has the ability to form generalizations about his environment as sensed by his sense organs, but he has no way to form generalizations about the circumstances in which his pain-sensors are apt to be activated. This is because Oscar I has no direct way of knowing when his pain-sensors are activated—he has no way of "feeling pain". As I have described them, the pain-sensors cause behavioral responses directly and do not provide input to Oscar's

18. This term comes from Jerry Fodor [1975].
19. The "B-box" metaphor is due to Stephen Schiffer [1981].
20. Oscar I is is pretty much the same as the machines discussed by Hilary Putnam [1960].

cognitive machinery. If Oscar is to be able to avoid pain rather than merely respond to it, he must be able to tell when he is in pain and be able to form generalizations about pain. To do this he needs another kind of sensor—a "pain-sensor sensor" that detects when the pain-sensors are activated. (Of course, the pain-sensors can themselves be pain-sensor sensors if they send their outputs to more than one place. We do not need a separate organ to sense the operation of the first organ.) Suppose we build these into Oscar I, renaming him Oscar II. This gives him a rudimentary kind of self-awareness. If the conative structure of Oscar II is such that he is moved to avoid not only the current activation of his pain-sensors but their anticipated activation as well, then this will enable him to avoid getting into situations that would otherwise result in his early demise.

It is illuminating to note that the difference between Oscar I and Oscar II is roughly the difference between an amoeba and a worm. Amoebas only *respond* to pain (or more conservatively, what we can regard as the activation of their pain-sensors)—worms can learn to avoid it. The learning powers of worms are pretty crude, proceeding entirely by simple forms of conditioning, but we have said nothing about Oscar that requires him to have greater learning powers.

Beginning with Oscar II we can distinguish between two kinds of sensors. First, Oscar II has *external sensors* to sense the world around him. These are of two kinds. He has ordinary perceptual sensors, and he also has pain-sensors that respond to environmental stimuli that tend to indicate impending damage to his body. Oscar II also has an *internal sensor* to sense the operation of his pain-sensors. His internal sensor could be described as a 'higher-order sensor' because it senses the operation of another sensor.

5.3   Oscar III

Oscar II is still a pretty dumb brute. I have described him as sensing his physical environment and forming generalizations on that basis. But he does not do a very good job of that. The trouble is that he can only take his perception of the environment at face value. If his "red sensor" provides the input 'red' to his cognitive machinery, he can relate that to various generalizations he has formed concerning when there are red things about, and he can also use the input to form new generalizations.But the generalizations at which he will arrive will be crude affairs. He will have no conception of the environment fooling him. For example, he will be unable to distinguish between a machine-eating tiger and a mirror image of a machine-eating tiger. All he will be able to conclude is that some tigers are dangerous and others are not. We, on the other hand, know that all tigers are dangerous, but that sometimes there is no tiger there even though it looks to us like there is. Oscar II has no way of learning things like this. He has no way of discovering, for example, that his red sensor is not totally reliable. This is because, at least until he learns a lot about micromechanics, he has no way to even know that he has a red sensor or to know when that sensor is activated. He responds to the sensor in an automatic way, just as Oscar I responded to his pain-sensors in an automatic way. If Oscar II is to acquire a sophisticated view of his environment, he must be able to sense the activation of his red sensor.[21] That will enable him to discover inductively that his red sensor is sometimes activated in the absence of red objects.

This point really has to do with computing power. Given sufficient computing power, Oscar might be able to get by, forming all of his generalizations directly on the basis of the output of his external sensors. His generalizations would parallel the kind of "phenomenalistic generalizations" required by the phenomenalist epistemologies championed in the first half of this century by such philosophers as Rudolf Carnap, Nelson Goodman, and C. I. Lewis.[22] The most salient feature of such generalizations would be their extraordinary complexity. Just imagine what it would be like if instead of thinking about physical objects you had to keep track of the world entirely in terms of the way things appear to you and your generalizations about the world had to be formulated entirely in those terms. You could not do it. Human beings do not have the computational capacity required to form and confirm such complex generalizations or to guide their activities in terms of them. Instead, human beings take perceptual input to provide only prima facie reasons for conclusions about their physical environment. This allows them to split their generalizations into two parts. On the one hand they have generalizations about the relations between their perceptual inputs and the state of their environment, and on the other hand they have generalizations about regularities within the environment that persist independently of perception of the environment. The advantage of dividing things up in this way is that the two sets of generalizations can be adjusted in parallel to keep each manageably simple under circumstances in which purely phenomenalistic generalizations would be unmanageable. Epistemologically, we begin by trusting our senses and taking their pronouncements to be indicative of the state of the world. More

21. Putnam [1960] overlooks this.
22. See Rudolf Carnap [1967], Nelson Goodman [1951] and C. I. Lewis [1946].

formally, appearance provides us with prima facie reasons for judgments about the world and, initially, we have no defeaters for any of those judgments. Making initial judgments in this way we find that certain generalizations are approximately true. If (a) we can make those generalizations exactly true by adjusting some of our initial judgments about the world, and (b) we can do it in such a way that there are simple generalizations describing the circumstances under which things are not as they appear, we take that as a defeater for the initial perceptual judgments that we want to overturn and we embrace the two sets of generalizations (the generalizations about the environment and the generalizations about the circumstances under which perception is reliable). The result is a considerable simplification in the generalizations we accept and in terms of which we guide our activities.[23] A secondary effect is that once we acquire evidence that a generalization is approximately true, there is a "cognitive push" toward regarding it as exactly true.

The logical form of what goes on here is strikingly similar to traditional accounts of scientific theory formation. On those accounts we begin with a set of data and then we "posit theoretical entities" and construct generalizations about those entities with the objective of constructing a theory that makes correct predictions about new data. There is a formal parallel between this picture and our thought about physical objects. Physical objects play the role of theoretical entities, our sensory input provides the data, and we try to adjust the generalizations about physical objects and the "bridge rules" relating physical objects and sensory input, in such a way that we can make correct predictions about future sensory input. Of course, all of this is to over-intellectualize what goes on in human thought. We do not invent physical objects as theoretical entities designed to explain our sensory inputs. We just naturally think in terms of physical objects, and our conceptual framework makes that epistemologically legitimate independent of any reconstruction of it in terms of scientific theory formation. My point is merely that the logical structure is similar. From an information-processing point of view, the adoption of such a logical structure gives us an additional degree of freedom (the physi-

23. Philosophers of science have long been puzzled by the role of simplicity in scientific confirmation. When two theories would each explain the data but one is significantly simpler than the other, we take the simpler one to be confirmed. But this is puzzling. What has simplicity got to do with truth? I think that the explanation for the role simplicity plays in confirmation probably lies in the kinds of considerations I have been describing. Its importance has to do with minimizing computational complexity, and its legitimacy has to do with the fact that, in a sense, the objects the generalizations are about are "free floating" and can be adjusted to minimize complexity. This is a bit vague, but I find it suggestive.

cal objects, or the theoretical entities) that can be adjusted to simplify the associated generalizations and thus minimize the computational complexity of using those generalizations to guide activity.[24]

The point of all this is that to acquire the kind of manageable generalizations about the environment that will enable him to keep functioning and achieve his built-in goals, an intelligent machine must be able to sense the operation of his own sensors. Only in that way can he treat the input from these sensors as defeasible and form generalizations about their reliability, and the need to treat them this way is dictated by considerations of computational complexity. Let's build such second-order sensors into Oscar II and rename him 'Oscar III'. He thus acquires a further degree of self-awareness. The difference between Oscar II and Oscar III may be roughly parallel to the difference between a bird and a cat. Kittens quickly learn about mirror images and come to ignore them, but birds will go on attacking their own reflections until they become exhausted.

Although Oscar III has second-order sensors sensing the operation of his first-order "perceptual" sensors, this does not mean that he can respond to his perceptual sensors only by sensing their operation— that is the mistake of the foundations theorist. In the ordinary course of events Oscar III can get along fine just responding mechanically to his perceptual sensors. To attend to the output of a sensor is to utilize (in cognition) the output of a higher order sensor that senses the output of the first sensor. Oscar III need not attend to the output of his perceptual sensors under most circumstances because doing so would not alter his behavior (except to slow him down and make him less efficient). He need attend only to the output of his second-order sensors under circumstances in which he has already discovered that his first-order sensors are sometimes unreliable.[25] This is related to

24. There is an interesting purely formal question here that, I guess, lies in the domain of theoretical computer science. That is the question of the extent to which and the circumstances under which computational complexity can be decreased by introducing such "intervening variables". It is obvious that this can sometimes be achieved, but it would be interesting to have a general account of it.

25. Oscar would be more like human beings if we supplied him with a "preprocessor" that modifies the input from his perceptual sensors in accordance with simple generalizations he has made about perceptual error. If he has acquired no relevant generalizations then the preprocessor will pass the input from the perceptual sensors through to his cognitive machinery unchanged, but if Oscar has acquired relevant generalizations then a red input from the perceptual sensors might be changed to orange by the preprocessor, and so on. Oscar's second-order sensors might then sense the output of the preprocessor rather than the output of the perceptual sensors themselves. This would be computationally more efficient, allowing Oscar to direct the full power of his intellect at his perceptual input only when his preprocessor cannot make sense of it. This is roughly the way people work. It involves a feedback loop from the machinery used for high-level cognitive processing to a preprocessor that lies between the sense organs and the high-level machinery.

the fact that Oscar III will automatically have reason to believe that sense perception is generally reliable. (Of course, he might be wrong about this.)

The cognitive role of the pain-sensors is a bit different from that of the perceptual organs. Oscar III will function best if he almost always attends to the output of his pain-sensors. These play a different kind of role than the perceptual sensors. Their role is not just one of fine-tuning. Except in "emergency situations" in which all cognitive powers are brought to bear to avoid a permanent systems crash, Oscar III should always be on the lookout for new generalizations about pain, and this requires that he almost always be aware of when his pain-sensors are activated. This parallels the fact that in human beings we are much more aware of our pains than of our visual sensations. We generally "look through" our visual sensations at the world and do not think about the sensations themselves.

I have attributed two kinds of self-awareness to Oscar III—he has the ability to sense the activation of his pain-sensors and also to sense the activation of his perceptual organs. These proceed via "internal" or "higher order" sensors. The important thing to realize is that there are simple explanations for why such self-awareness will make an intelligent machine work better. Other kinds of self-awareness may also be either desirable or necessary. I have not described Oscar III as having any awareness of what goes on internally after he acquires perceptual input or pain stimuli. In particular, I have not described him as having any way of sensing the operation of those cognitive processes whereby he forms generalizations on the basis of his per-ceptual inputs and pain stimuli. But such awareness seems to be required for two reasons. First, consider defeasible reasoning. In defeasible reasoning we reason to a conclusion, and then subsequent reasoning may lead to new conclusions that undercut the original reasoning and cause us to retract the original conclusion. In order for such negative feedback to work, the cognitive agent must be able to sense and keep track of his reasoning processes. Actually, humans are not terribly good at this. We forget our reasons rather rapidly, and we often fail to make appropriate corrections even when we remember our reasons.[26] We would probably work better if we could keep better track of our reasoning processes. At any rate, the general point seems clear. The ability to sense his own reasoning processes will be required in order for Oscar to indulge in defeasible reasoning, and defeasible reasoning seems to be required by any kind of sophisticated epistemo-logy.

26. Recent psychologists have delighted in documenting human subjects' failure to make corrections to reasoning in light of new information. The first of these studies is apparently that of L. Ross, M. R. Lepper, and M. Hubbard [1975].

There is another reason a well-functioning cognitive agent must be able to sense his own reasoning processes to some extent. A cognitive agent does not try to gather information at random—he normally seeks to answer specific questions (motivated ultimately by conative considerations). Built-in epistemic norms will determine what kind of reasoning he is *permitted* to pursue, but they do not dictate what reasoning he *must* pursue. Effective problem solving (at least in humans) involves the use of reasoning strategies rather than random permissible reasoning, and we acquire such strategies by learning about how best to search for solutions to various kinds of problems. To learn such things we must be aware of how we proceed in particular cases so that we can make generalizations about the efficacy of the search procedures employed.

5.4 *Mental Representations*

I described the Oscarites as having a language of thought to encode information. This language of thought is a representational system. It must, among other things, provide ways of thinking about particular objects and ascribing properties to them. I will call ways of thinking of objects *mental representations*. Philosophy has traditionally adopted a rather parochial view of mental representations, often recognizing only one way of thinking of an object—as the unique object having a certain combination of properties. This is to think of an object "under a description". In fact, this is one of the least common ways of thinking of objects. This is most easily seen by considering how often you can actually find a description that uniquely picks out an object without the description itself involving a way of thinking about another object. For instance, I can think of my mother as 'the mother of me', but that only works insofar as I already have some way of thinking of myself. It is often fairly easy to propound descriptions that pick out objects uniquely as long as we are allowed to build into the descriptions relations to other objects. But to get such descriptions going in the first place, we must begin with some other ways of thinking of at least some objects. Those other ways could involve descriptions provided those descriptions did not make reference to further objects, but I challenge the reader to find even one such description. If we cannot find such descriptions, then it seems clear that they do not constitute the mental representations in terms of which we think of objects.

The unavoidable lesson to be learned from the paucity of descriptions is that we have nondescriptive ways of thinking of at least some objects. We do not have to look very far to find some of those nondescriptive mental representations. First, consider perception. When I see an object and make a judgment about it, I do not usually think of that object under a description—not even a description like 'the object I am seeing' (I am typically seeing many different objects at any one time). Instead, I just focus my attention on the object and have a thought whose closest expression in English is something like 'That is a table'. In a case like this, my visual experience involves what we might call a 'percept' of an object, and I think of the object in terms of that percept. That percept is my mental representation of the perceived object, and it is a constituent of my thought.[27] Percepts are not descriptions, so this is an example of a nondescriptive mental representation.

A percept can only represent an object while that object is being perceived. If I later see another object that looks precisely the same way to me, then precisely the same percept will recur, but this time it will represent the new object. I can, however, continue to think about the original object after I am no longer perceiving it. When I do that I am no longer thinking of it in terms of the percept, so I must be employing a different kind of mental representation. This new mental representation still need not be a description. Once I have become able to think about an object in some way or other, I can continue to think about it even when that original mental representation is no longer available to me. This is clear in the case of objects originally represented by percepts, but it is equally true of objects originally thought about under descriptions. Thinking of an object under a description, I may acquire a wide variety of beliefs about it, but I may eventually forget the original description. For instance, I might have first come to think of Christopher Columbus under some description like 'The man my teacher is talking about', but I can no longer remember just what description I might have used and I may no longer remember that Christopher Columbus satisfies that description. Such forgetfulness does not deprive me of my ability to think of Christopher Columbus. I have a nondescriptive way of thinking of Christopher Columbus. Such nondescriptive ways of thinking of an object are parasitic on originally having some other way of thinking of the object (either perceptual or descriptive), but they are distinct from those other ways. I call these nondescriptive ways of thinking of objects '*de re* representations', and I have written about them at length elsewhere.[28]

The above remarks are largely remarks about the phenomenology

27. For related accounts of mental representation in perception, see: Kent Bach [1982], Romane Clark [1973], and David Woodruff Smith [1984] and [1986].

28. See my [1981] and [1982] p. 60ff. Those publications go into some detail in describing the workings of *de re* representations, but those details are largely irrelevant to the present discussion. Related discussions occur in Diana Ackerman's [1979], [1979a] and [1980]. I have proposed that a number of Keith Donnellan's [1972] well-known examples are best understood as illustrating the occurrence of *de re* representations in our thought.

of human thought. They amount to the observation that we rarely think of objects under descriptions, but we do have both perceptual and nonperceptual nondescriptive ways of thinking of objects. As a remark about human psychology, this seems obviously correct, but it may also seem philosophically puzzling. How can there be such nondescriptive ways of thinking of objects? I think, however, we can make the puzzlement go away by reflecting on Oscar. Mental representations are just singular terms in the language of thought. If it can be shown that there is no obstacle to constructing Oscar in such a way that his language of thought contains such singular terms, then there should be no reason to be suspicious of the claim that human beings employ such mental representations. From an information-processing point of view we can think of *de re* representations as pigeon holes (memory locations) into which we stuff properties as we acquire reasons to believe that the objects represented have those properties. Properties may drop out of the pigeon holes if they are not used occasionally (i.e., we forget). In order to establish a pigeon hole as representing a particular object we must begin by thinking of the object in some other way, and that initial way of thinking of the object will be the first thing to be put into the pigeon hole. For example, we might begin by thinking of an object under a description, from that acquire a *de re* representation of the object, and then we might eventually forget the original description and only be able to think of the object under the *de re* representation. From an information-processing point of view there are good reasons (having to do with the efficient use of memory) for incorporating something like *de re* representations into the language of thought used by an intelligent machine, and we would be well advised to equip Oscar with some such device.

Another important representational device is that involved in first-person beliefs. Numerous philosophers have observed that, although we can think of ourselves in more familiar ways (e.g., under descriptions, or perceptually), we can also have thoughts about ourselves in which we do not think of ourselves in any of those ways.[29] I will follow David Lewis in calling these *de se* beliefs.[30] The mental representations employed in *de se* beliefs will be called *de se* representations. The

---

29. See H. N. Castaneda [1966], [1967], and [1968], Roderick Chisholm [1981a], David Lewis [1979], John Perry [1977] and [1979], and my [1981] and [1982], p. 13ff. This has also played a role in some recent work in artificial intelligence. See Creary and Pollard [1985], and Rapaport [1984] and [1984a].

30. The existence of *de se* beliefs raises numerous philosophical questions about the analysis of what is believed. Hector-Neri Castaneda and I have both argued that in *de se* belief one believes a proposition containing a particular kind of designator—what I

existence of *de se* representations is illustrated by the following example (due to John Perry [1979]):

> I once followed a trail of sugar on a supermarket floor, pushing my cart down the aisle on one side of a tall counter and back the aisle on the other, seeking the shopper with the torn sack to tell him he was making a mess. With each trip around the counter, the trail became thicker. But I seemed unable to catch up. Finally, it dawned on me. I was the shopper I was trying to catch.

What happened when Perry realized that he was the shopper with the torn sack? He came to believe an identity, viz., that the shopper with the torn sack was the same person as he himself. This identity involves thinking of the same individual (himself) in two different ways (with two different mental representations) and believing that they *are* the same individual. The first mental representation is a straightforward descriptive representation—Perry thinks of himself as 'the shopper with the torn sack'. But the second representation, in which he thinks of himself as 'me, myself', is a unique representation different from the kinds of representations we can employ in thinking of other things. I can think of myself under a description, or perceptually (e.g., I may see myself in a mirror), or in terms of a *de re* representation, but whenever I think of myself in one of those ways I may fail to realize that it is myself that I am thinking of. To realize that I am thinking of myself is to relate the mental representation I am employing to a special way of thinking of myself—my *de se* representation of myself.

Why do I have such a special way of thinking of myself? *De se* representations are essential elements of the language of thought of any sophisticated cognizer (human or otherwise). This is most easily illustrated by considering the conative aspects of Oscar. The purpose of providing Oscar with cognitive powers is to enable him to achieve built-in goals. This is accomplished by combining his beliefs with a conative structure consisting of preferences, desires, aversions, and so

previously called a "personal designator", but what might more aptly be called a "*de se* designator". Roderick Chisholm, David Lewis, and John Perry, on the other hand, have all urged that *de se* belief does not take a propositional object. They claim that the object of *de se* belief is instead a property or concept and *de se* belief involves a unique form of self-attribution. Fortunately, we need not get involved in this mare's nest at the moment. I doubt there is any substantive difference between the two accounts. Without some further constraints on what it is for something to be an object of belief, we can describe *de se* belief in either way. For example, Lewis' arguments to the contrary turn upon the assumption that any cognitive agent can, in principle, entertain any proposition. My own endorsement of *de se* propositions led me to deny that and insist instead that some propositions are logically idiosyncratic. But there appears to be no way to substantiate either position without *first* resolving the question whether belief must take a propositional object.

on, and natural inclinations to behave in specifiable ways in the presence of particular combinations of beliefs and conations. The problem now is to construct appropriate behavioral tendencies of the latter sort in a creature lacking *de se* beliefs. I claim that it cannot be done. Practical reasoning consists of forming the intention to do something under specified circumstances, forming the belief that you are in such circumstances, and then performing the action. We must supply the cognitive agent with rules for the formation of appropriate intentions and beliefs. The intentions are *conditional* intentions to do something *if* some particular condition is satisfied. To be useful, the conditions must concern the agent's situation and not just the general state of the universe. They must involve the *agent's* being in the specified circumstances. The rules for the formation of such conditional intentions must be constructed in such a way that the condition involves a mental representation of the agent. The representation cannot be one that just happens to represent the agent, because the rules must be constructed prior to any contingent knowledge of the world. For instance, the rules for intention formation cannot proceed in terms of definite descriptions that just happen to represent the agent, because it cannot be predicated ahead of time which of these will represent the agent. The rules themselves must require that the intentions involve a mental representation of the agent, and at the time the rules are being constructed it cannot be predicted what mental representations will represent the agent as a matter of contingent fact, so the rules for intention formation must employ a mental representation that represents the agent necessarily. That is precisely what *de se* representations are.

It is illuminating to illustrate this by considering chess-playing programs. Sophisticated chess-playing programs learn and get better as they play. Existing programs do not involve any kind of *de se* representation, and that may seem to be a counterexample to the claims just made. But the reason such programs need not involve *de se* representation is that, in the appropriate sense, everything in their vocabulary describes the situation of the chess-playing computer, and so there is no distinction to be drawn between its situation and the general state of the universe. Contrast this with a computer running a more sophisticated kind of chess-playing program that learns not just by playing but also by witnessing games played by other computers. In this case the computer must be able to distinguish between its own game and games it is merely witnessing. Its own game must somehow be tagged *as* its own. In effect, this involves *de se* representation.

My conclusion is that practical reasoning requires an agent to form beliefs about his *own* current situation and form intentions about what to do if his current situation is of a particular sort. It does no good to have general existential beliefs about the state of the universe if those beliefs cannot be related to the agent, and it is precisely the latter that cannot be done without *de se* beliefs. *De se* representations are required in order to make conation and intellection mesh properly. Thus *de se* beliefs are essential in the construction of a sophisticated cognitive/conative machine. I take it that that is why they play a central role in human thought.

It is somewhat illuminating to consider just what we have to do to equip Oscar with *de se* thought. It might seem that in order to do this we have to provide him with a Cartesian ego and a way of perceiving it. But it takes little reflection to see that that is wrong. Providing his language of thought with *de se* representations is just a matter of including a primitive singular term in his language of thought and then wiring him up in such a way that sensory input results in his having *de se* beliefs, and rational deliberation results in *de se* intentions. There is nothing mysterious about this. It is all a matter of programming (or wiring). In particular, we do not have to equip Oscar with "ghost" in his machine.

5.5 *Belief Formation*

The purpose of having a language of thought is to mediate Oscar's behavioral response to his environment. Sensory input results in behavioral output, and an important part of the connection is provided by thought. The thought processes constitute reasoning and are governed by rules for reasoning—both pure reasoning and practical reasoning. The rules for pure reasoning constitute epistemic norms. In effect, epistemic norms comprise a "program" for the manipulation of sentences in the language of thought in response to sensory input.

Insofar as a cognitive agent's reasoning conforms to his epistemic norms, his beliefs are justified. At this point, it might be wondered why it is possible for human beings to reason unjustifiedly. Why not just "hardwire" a cognitive agent in such a way that he *must* reason in conformance with his epistemic norms? The answer to this seems to have to do with the existence of multiple systems of information processing. *Intellection* is the process whereby we indulge in explicit reasoning and form conclusions on that basis. But intellection is slow and consumes large amounts of our limited computational capacity. To get around this we also have a number of "quick-and-dirty" systems that allow us to form conclusions or to respond to environmental input quickly in cases in which we do not have time to deliberate. These systems are quick but "dirty" in the sense that they sometimes make mistakes in ways that can only be corrected through explicit reasoning. To illustrate, suppose you are dealt four cards that are colored on one side and numbered on the other. The exposed faces of the cards contain a two, a three, a red face, and a black face. To test the hypothesis that all cards with even numbers on one side are black on the other, which cards must you turn over? Almost all subjects say initially that you must turn over the card with a two showing and the card with a black face showing. But a little logical reflection indicates that it is not the card with the black face that you must turn over, but rather the card with the red face. Intellection leads to the right answer, but we have a strong initial tendency to give the wrong answer. Because the tendency to give the wrong answer is so uniform across subjects (even among logicians if they do not explicitly reason it out), this appears to illustrate the operation of a quick-and-dirty system that goes wrong in this case.[31]

Epistemic norms govern intellection, but in many cases we want to be able to form beliefs on the basis of our quick-and-dirty systems instead. If that is to be possible, it must be possible for us to circumvent our epistemic norms. That is why conformance to epistemic norms is not hardwired, and it is why we are able to hold unjustified beliefs. I think it is noteworthy, however, just how difficult it is to generate intuitive examples of people holding unjustified beliefs. That almost never happens. Except in cases driven by the quick-and-dirty systems, people almost always conform to their epistemic norms. It generally requires some kind of extreme psychological pressure to contravene those norms.

The operation of quick-and-dirty systems goes on "under the surface"—it is not introspectible. Only the output of the quick-and-dirty systems is introspectible. This contrasts with intellection, whose operation is introspectible. The reason for this difference is that intellection involves defeasible reasoning, and as we have seen, defeasible reasoning requires us to be aware of our own reasoning. By contrast, the operation of the quick-and-dirty systems does not involve the same kind of negative feedback and so does not require introspective awareness. On the other hand, intellection must always be available for the correction of the output of quick-and-dirty systems, so that output must be introspectible.

5.6   Reason, Truth, and the Individuation of Concepts

We are now in a position to further understand the account of the individuation of concepts that was proposed above and was used to

31. The details of these experiments can be found in P. C. Wason and P. M. Johnson-Laird [1972].

fend off epistemological relativism. According to the logical theory of concepts, all but the most basic concepts have nontrivial definitions in terms of more basic concepts, where these definitions state necessary and sufficient conditions for objects to exemplify the concepts. The simplest objection to the logical theory of concepts is that such definitions almost never exist. It is a very rare concept that can be given an informative definition of this sort. I have urged instead that concepts are individuated by their conceptual roles, where these are their roles in reasoning. This is the epistemological theory of concepts. Thus far I have argued *that* the epistemological theory of concepts is correct, but now we are in a position to see *why* it is correct.

Thought consists of the manipulation of sentences in the language of thought. What do we have to do to make it possible for Oscar to think? Correct reasoning consists of manipulating sentences in the language of thought in conformance with our epistemic norms. Thus all we have to do is to provide Oscar with epistemic norms and appropriate dispositions to conform to them. Providing Oscar with epistemic norms amounts to supplying conceptual roles for the primitive terms in his language of thought. Once we have done that, there is nothing further we need to do by way of interpreting his language of thought. In particular, there is no need to somehow "supply truth conditions". That does not even make sense. There is nothing we could do that would constitute supplying truth conditions. There is no role for truth conditions to play in cognition. Once we have provided epistemic norms, Oscar can reason and his reasoning can mediate his behavioral response to sensory input. That is the only role there is for his language of thought to play.

It follows that the "semantics" of Oscar's language of thought is completely described by describing the conceptual roles of the primitive terms of his language of thought. Those primitive terms express concepts, and I want to conclude from this that the same thing is true of concepts—concepts are characterized by their conceptual roles. Here, I understand the conceptual role of a concept to be the conceptual role of a term in the language of thought that expresses that concept. One must not jump to this conclusion too hastily, however. Concepts are Platonic items whereas terms in the language of thought are mental items. Concepts are constituents of propositions, and propositions are what we think when we have thoughts. Thought consists of the manipulation of sentences in the language of thought. General terms in the language of thought express concepts. This suggests that in constructing a semantics for the language of thought we begin with concepts and then attach them to terms from the language of thought. But I think that this is misleading. What is basic is the language of thought itself, and talk of concepts and propositions is to be explained in terms of it rather than the other way around. Concepts and propositions are forced into our ontology by the nature of defeasible reasoning. Defeasible reasoning requires us to be able to think about our thoughts. I must, for example, be able to recognize that one thought was my reason for another thought. Thinking about my thoughts in this way, I must also be able to assign truth values to them so that I can judge, for instance, that my reason for one thought involved another thought that I now know to be false. It is possible to think about our thoughts in ways that are related only contingently to their contents. For example, if I woke up thinking that it was a beautiful day, I can think about that thought as the first thought I had this morning. But such contingent ways of thinking of thoughts are not sufficient for defeasible reasoning. In defeasible reasoning I must be able to judge that some thought I had was false, and in order to do that I must know what it was that I was thinking. For example, I cannot judge (except indirectly) that the first thought I had this morning was false unless I know that it was the thought that it was a beautiful day. In other words, I must be able to think about my thoughts in terms of their contents. This is to think about them in terms of the propositions that are thought. Thus a cognitive agent endowed with the power of defeasible reasoning must have a language of thought that contains what we can regard as ways of thinking about propositions.

The preceding suggests that defeasible reasoning requires ontologically suspicious presuppositions. But in an important sense, that is wrong. The language of thought is the vehicle for reasoning. Once we have enabled Oscar to reason by providing him with epistemic norms we have done all we need to do by way of integrating his language of thought into his cognitive machinery. In doing this, we will, among other things, have taught Oscar how to use mental representations of propositions in reasoning. But note that in enabling Oscar to reason with these mental representations we do not have to tell him what they represent—all we have to do is tell him what moves are legitimate in using them in reasoning. This is a matter of wiring or programming—not ontology. On the other hand, once we have wired him or programmed him to reason in the right ways, he then has the power to do what we call 'thinking about propositions'. But in order for him to do this, we do not have to first "supply propositions for him to think about". Looking at all this from the outside, whether there really are any propositions for him to be thinking about is totally irrelevant to his reasoning.

But next note that we can also look at this from the inside. After all, we too are cognitive agents endowed with defeasible reasoning. We regard Oscar as thinking about propositions because he is doing what

we do when we have thoughts that we regard as being about propositions. Is there something illegitimate about what we are doing? Surely
not. We are conforming to our epistemic norms, and those norms
make it the case that we are justified in concluding that there are
propositions. This follows from the kinds of judgments we must be
able to make in defeasible reasoning. For instance, I must be able to
conclude that I assumed something false in reasoning in a certain
way. The "something false" was a proposition. That is just what we
mean by 'proposition'. It follows (in accordance with my epistemic
norms) from the fact that I assumed something false that *there was*
something false, i.e., there was a false proposition, and hence there
was a proposition. Thus belief in propositions is mandated by our
epistemic norms, which are in turn constitutive of our conceptual
framework. Hence we cannot be faulted for believing in propositions
and concepts. We are completely justified in such beliefs.

My conclusion is that an ontology of propositions and concepts is
forced upon us by our epistemic norms, or equivalently, by the
semantics of our language of thought. That semantics is constituted
by our epistemic norms. Concepts are, in effect, created to be the
contents of general terms in the language of thought. The general
terms are basic, and concepts are to be understood in terms of them
rather than the other way around. Those general terms are characterized by their conceptual roles, so the concepts are equally characterized by their conceptual roles. This I take it is the ultimate and deep
explanation for the epistemological theory of concepts.

If we do not need truth conditions for the functioning of concepts,
it might be wondered why we even have the concept of truth. The
answer is that this concept is required for defeasible reasoning. We
can *think* a thought, and we can also *think about* a thought. To think a
thought is to think about whatever the thought is about. On the other
hand, to think about the thought is to think about a proposition. In
what we might call 'first-order reasoning' we just think thoughts,
reasoning from one to the next without thinking about the thoughts.
But in correcting defeasible reasoning we must also think about our
thoughts, judging, for instance, that something we used in getting to a
particular conclusion was false. We do not need the concept of truth
in order to affirm a thought while thinking that thought. The affirma-
tion is part of the thinking. But in order to affirm a thought while
thinking about it, we do need the concept of truth. The ability to
ascend a level and think about our thoughts is required for the
operation of defeasible reasoning, and that in turn requires that we
have the evaluative concepts of truth and falsity.

The way in which we ascend levels and ascribe truth values to
propositions is dictated by our epistemic norms. If P is a proposition I

am able to entertain, then my language of thought must contain a mental representation 'P' of P, and my epistemic norms must license reasoning something like the following:

What I believed was 'P'.
P
Therefore, what I believed was true.[32]

Just to have a label, I will call this *disquotational reasoning*. I write the mental representation 'P' using quotation marks because this is suggestive of the way the representation works. The quotation marks cannot be taken altogether seriously, because we are not forming the quotation name of a sentence but rather a mental representation of a proposition. But there is a strong and important parallel between the mental representation 'P' and quotation names of sentences. We can refer to a sentence in terms of some property it has contingently, e.g., as 'the first sentence on page 137'. In contrast to this, quotation names are noncontingent ways of referring to sentences. The rules of English dictate that enclosing a sentence in quotation marks generates a term designating that sentence and no other sentence. Similarly, we can think of a proposition in different ways. For example, I might think of a proposition under the contingent description 'The first proposition entertained by Bertrand Russell on the morning of April 3, 1921'. But I will not ordinarily be able to ascribe truth or falsity to the proposition so conceived unless I know what proposition it is. To know what proposition it is is to be able to think of it in another way, "in terms of its content", and know that the two propositions are the same. This is to think of the proposition in a "direct" fashion that is necessarily a way of thinking of that particular proposition. This point can be put more clearly in terms of the above schema of disquotational reasoning. That schema is supposed to be dictated by our epistemic norms. But in order for our epistemic norms to dictate any such schema, it must be predetermined that 'P' designates P. Thus 'P' cannot designate P just accidentally. 'P' must designate P necessarily. (This is precisely analogous to the observation that practical reasoning requires me to have a special way of thinking of myself that is necessarily a way of thinking of myself.) 'P' designates P necessarily because our epistemic norms predetermine that it does, and the way they predetermine that is by licensing the above schema of disquotational reasoning.

Thus far I have been talking about propositions, but similar

---

32. We must beware in formulating this reasoning because we are flirting with the liar paradox.

observations can be made about concepts. I might think of a concept as 'Immanuel Kant's favorite concept' but that will not help me in judging whether Holly exemplifies that concept unless I know what concept it is, and knowing what concept it is involves being able to think of it in another, noncontingent, way. This corresponds to the fact that we employ something like disquotational reasoning in connection with concepts too. For instance, we may move from the observation that the ball is red to the conclusion that the ball exemplifies the concept of being red. Such reasoning requires us to be able to think about the concept in a direct noncontingent way.[33] In logical contexts, when we think of concepts and propositions we usually think of them in this direct fashion.[34]

I have described one way in which defeasible reasoning requires the concepts of truth and falsity. Defeasible reasoning also requires them in another way. This has to do with a general kind of defeater applicable to all prima facie reasons. All prima facie reasons are subject to defeat by "reliability defeaters". If P is a prima facie reason for Q, and I believe Q on this basis, my reasoning is defeated by the discovery that I am in some kind of circumstances C under which P's being true is not a reliable indicator of Q's being true. For example, suppose I believe that the sheet of paper before me is red on the basis of its looking red. This reasoning is defeated by the discovery that the paper is illuminated by red lights and under such circumstances something's looking red is not a reliable indicator of its being red. The concept of reliability presupposes truth. The reliability of P as an indicator of Q under circumstances of type C is just the probability of Q's *being true* under circumstances of type C given that P *is true*. Thus this is another way in which defeasible reasoning requires us to be able to think about propositions and their truth.

The concept of truth is required for defeasible reasoning, but it is just one more concept in our ratiocinative arsenal. The concept of truth is characterized by its role in reasoning just like any other concept. Rather than truth being fundamental and rules for reasoning being derived from it, the rules for reasoning come first and truth is characterized by the rules for reasoning about truth.

33. In my [1984] I argued that the distinction between modal operators and modal properties turns essentially on our having such noncontingent ways of thinking of propositions and concepts.

34. This is why ordinary language objections to philosophers' use of terms like 'directly aware' seem beside the point. Philosophers are using these terms to express concepts they are thinking about directly. They are not thinking about those concepts under contingent descriptions like 'the concept ordinarily expressed by the phrase "directly aware" in English', and accordingly the objection that the way they are using the term 'directly aware' does not conform to ordinary usage is simply irrelevant.

6. A Naturalistic Internalism

One of the main purposes of this book is to defend a nondoxastic internalism of the sort described in chapter four under the label 'direct realism'. To my mind the most serious objection (other than falsehood) to all existing epistemological theories is that they are radically incomplete. Although they might give correct descriptions of some of our epistemic norms, they provide no systematic account of epistemic justification. They do not tell us what epistemic justification is all about and they do not explain why we have the epistemic norms we have. This objection can now be met. Epistemic justification consists of holding beliefs in conformance to correct epistemic norms. But as we have seen, our epistemic norms are constitutive of the concepts we have and hence it is a necessary truth that our actual epistemic norms are correct. Thus we can give an entirely adequate analysis of epistemic justification as follows:

A person's belief is justified if and only if he holds it in conformance to his epistemic norms.

In understanding this analysis we must distinguish between doing something in accordance with norms and doing it in conformance to the norms. The analysis proceeds in terms of the latter. To say that you act in accordance with a norm is just to say that your behavior does not violate the norm. This is compatible with your doing it for some reason unrelated to the norm. To say that you act in conformance with the norm is to say not only that you act in accordance with the norm but also that your behavior is guided by the norm. Justification requires conformance—not just accordance.

This is a naturalistic analysis of epistemic justification. Reasoning is a natural process. It is something we know how to do. To say that we know how to do it is to say that it is governed by norms. Our epistemic norms are, by definition, the norms that actually govern our reasoning. This, I claim, is a naturalistic definition of 'epistemic norm'. Of course, I have not proposed an informative logical analysis of the governance process which forms the basis of these definitions, but that should not be expected. This is a natural process that we can observe in operation, not just in reasoning but in all cases of internalized procedural knowledge, and its nature can be clarified by psychological investigations. I take it that the preceding remarks about the role of epistemic norms in a cognitive machine go some distance towards clarifying all of this. But it must be emphasized that the only clarification that can be expected here is empirical clarification. We can no more provide an informative logical analysis of the governance process than we can provide an informative logical analysis of electrons or magnetism. These are natural kinds and natural processes that we discover in the world, and their nature is revealed by empirical investigation—not logical analysis.

No doubt some philosophers will be disturbed by the fact that my analysis of epistemic justification does not characterize justified beliefs in terms of a single general property (like reliability) intrinsic to the beliefs, but instead characterizes justified beliefs in terms of the reasoning underlying them. That, however, is just the way things are. What makes a belief justified is its being supported by reasoning of an approved sort, and there is no reason to think there are general intrinsic properties of beliefs that determine whether that is possible. This is connected with the charge that internalist theories give piecemeal characterizations of epistemic justification. That is only a difficulty if there is something more to be given and hence something is being left out. To clarify this point, let us distinguish between a characterization of epistemic justification in the sense of an analysis of epistemic justification, and a characterization in the sense of an epistemological theory. I gave an analysis above. I will understand an epistemological theory, on the other hand, to be a theory that attempts to describe our epistemic norms. There is nothing piecemeal about my analysis of epistemic justification, but an epistemological theory will automatically be piecemeal. This is a consequence of the nature of reason-guiding (or more generally, action-guiding) norms. Such norms tell us that under certain circumstances we are permitted to do various things and not permitted to do other things. These norms have to be rather specific because, as we saw above, they must take as input only features of the present circumstances that are directly accessible to our automatic processing systems. This precludes the possibility of the norms appealing to sweeping general features of the circumstances (features such as the belief being produced by a reliable process). Compare the norms for bicycle riding. These are going to be very specific, including such things as, 'If you feel yourself losing momentum then push harder on the pedal' and 'If you think you are falling to the right then turn the handlebars to the right'. Epistemic norms will be equally specific, telling us things (approximately) such as 'If something looks red to you and you have no reason for thinking it is not red then you are permitted to believe it is red'. There is no more reason to think that we can combine all epistemic norms into one simple general formula than there is for thinking there is a single simple formula governing the use of the pedals, the handlebars, the brakes, and so on, in bicycle riding. Action-guiding norms cannot work that way.

It is illuminating to contrast this account of epistemic norms with more conventional internalist formulas. Internalists have been inclined to say instead that our epistemic norms describe the way we *actually reason*. This claim has played an important role in internalist epistemology, because it tells us how to find out what proper epistemic norms are—just examine the way we actually reason.[35] But this is at least misleading. We do not always reason correctly, and what epistemic norms describe is *correct* reasoning. We might similarly be inclined to say that our bike-riding norms describe the way we actually ride a bicycle, but even when we know how to ride a bicycle we sometimes make mistakes and fail to conform to our norms—I might be distracted by a pretty girl and lose my balance. Thus we might more accurately say that our bike-riding norms describe the way we actually ride a bicycle when we do it correctly. This formulation, however, sounds vacuous. After all, riding a bicycle correctly or reasoning correctly just is to conform to the norms. This creates a real puzzle for traditional accounts of actionguiding norms. The puzzle is resolved by seeing how norms for doing something are connected with knowing how to do it. The best way to describe the connection between norms and actual behavior is to say, as I did above, that our bike-riding norms and our epistemic norms are the norms that *actually guide us* in riding bicycles and reasoning. This is similar, in a very important respect, to the more customary claim that our epistemic norms describe the way we actually reason. In each case, norms are to be elicited from what we actually do and not from some mysterious criterion, separate from our actual behavior, that tells us what we should do. But there is also an important difference between the present formulation and the traditional formulation. The present formulation does not take our reasoning behavior at face value. It recognizes that we can reason incorrectly. That need not confound us in formulating epistemic norms because, by virtue of knowing how to reason, we know how to evaluate reasoning, and so we can recognize correct and incorrect reasoning when we see it (although not necessarily with perfect reliability). This recognition process is part of the internal "non-intellectual" process whereby our norms govern our behavior. The process is non-intellectual in the sense that it does not involve our making any conscious explicit comparison of our behavior with some explicitly formulated paradigm. The process goes on under the surface. But even though we cannot consciously monitor the process, we can make use of the results by noting that under certain circumstances we judge some behavior to be permissible and other behavior to be impermissible. On the basis of these individual (normative) observations we can try to construct a general theory of right reasoning or correct bicycle riding.

35. Chisholm [1977] endorsed this under the label "critical cognitivism", and I endorsed it (in my [1974]) and called it "descriptivism".

This general account of epistemic norms and epistemological theories has important implications for philosophical methodology. Epistemological theories are supposed to give general accounts of "right reasoning"—that is, they purport to describe our epistemic norms. It is a contingent psychological fact that we have the norms we have. Equivalently, it is a contingent psychological fact that we employ the conceptual framework we actually employ. Does this mean that epistemological theories are contingent? This is a rather complicated question. The answer is, "Partly 'yes', and partly 'no'." Part of what we do in epistemology is to elicit our actual epistemic norms, and that really is a contingent matter. But our ultimate conclusions are to the effect that particular concepts have conceptual roles of certain sorts. The conceptual role of a concept is a necessary feature of that concept, so it seems that our ultimate conclusions are, if true, necessarily true. Let us take this a bit more slowly, looking at each step of what transpires in an epistemological analysis.

We begin with a question such as, 'How are we justified in forming beliefs about the colors of objects?', that is, 'What are the conceptual roles of color concepts?' We begin our investigation by trying to determine how we actually make such judgments. This is a matter of eliciting the epistemic norms we actually employ. That is a question about human psychology. But this does not mean that the best way to go about answering it is by performing laboratory experiments. To illustrate, consider a simpler case. Typing is an excellent example of something we learn to do automatically. When we learn to type we internalize norms telling us what to do and then we follow those norms automatically. Now suppose we want to describe those norms. Consider the question, "What finger do you use to type 'w'?" We *could* try to answer that question by designing a laboratory experiment in which we observe people typing 'w's under a wide variety of circumstances, but that would be silly. There is a much easier way to do it. We can *imagine* typing a 'w' and observe what we do. Touch typists find themselves using their left ring finger. How can this work as a way of eliciting our norms? After all, we are not just asking what finger a person uses on a particular occasion, and people do not always type correctly. What we want to know is what finger our typing norms prescribe using to type a 'w'. The reason we can answer this question by performing our thought experiment is that there is an introspectible difference between conforming to one's internalized norms and not conforming. It is this fact that led us to the discovery of epistemic norms in the first place. We could perversely type the 'w' with our right index finger, but if we did we would know that we were not doing it the way we learned to do it. The explanation for the introspectibility of this difference is something we have already observed. Namely, it is required in order for action-guiding norms to be able to correct ongoing behavior. For example, in swinging a tennis racket I monitor my swing, I can tell at each instant whether I am too high or too low, and I can correct my swing accordingly. Thus it is important to the operation of action-guiding norms that conformance to them be introspectible.

Now consider the epistemological question, 'How do we judge that something is red?', where this is intended to be a question about our epistemic norms. Sometimes we reflect upon actual judgments we observe ourselves making. More often we *imagine* making such judgments under normal circumstances and see what goes on. For example, suppose we are considering the hypothesis that something's looking red to us gives us a prima facie reason for thinking it is red. We imagine being in situations in which things look red to us and note that if there are no "intervening" considerations we will come to believe that the object is red. This is not just an observation about what actually happens. It is an observation about what we know *to do* in judging colors, that is, an observation about how our automatic processing system actually guides us in reasoning about colors. It is the introspectibility of conforming to a norm that makes this observation possible. Next, suppose it is asked whether, in acquiring justification from this prima facie reason, it suffices to merely believe no defeaters, or if we must instead have the positive belief that there are no true defeaters. We might imagine being in situations in which we believe no defeaters but have not given the matter any thought and so have no beliefs one way or the other about whether there are any true defeaters. Again, by introspecting on whether we would be conforming to norms by making various judgments in these imagined circumstances, we find that under such circumstances we would be conforming to our norms by judging the object to be red on the basis of its looking red to us, and so we conclude that our epistemic norms permit us to make the inference without having the belief that there are no true defeaters.

This illustrates what goes on in epistemological analysis. Our basic data concern what inferences we would or would not be permitted to make under various circumstances, real or imaginary. This data concerns individual cases and our task as epistemologists is to construct a general theory that accommodates it. Epistemologists have often supposed that our epistemic rules should be, in some sense, self-evident.[36] I have been arguing that many of the individual bits of data on which our epistemological theory is founded will, in a certain sense, be self-evident (more accurately, introspectible). By virtue of

---

36. This is what Ernest Sosa [1981] calls "methodism".

knowing how to reason we know how to tell right reasoning when we see it, and that provides us with our data. But that does not guarantee that it will be easy to construct theories describing our epistemic norms or that such theories will be obviously right once we have them. One complication both in the use of thought experiments and in interpreting our data is that because our automatic processing system operates in a non-intellectual way without any conscious monitoring, it need not be obvious to us what makes a particular belief justified even when it is evident to us that it is justified. Our data consists in the fact that various beliefs *are* justified—not *why* they are justified. This can be illustrated by reflecting upon the fact that we have a much better account of perceptual knowledge than we do of many other kinds of knowledge. I have urged that our being appeared to in various ways provides us with prima facie justification for holding beliefs about our physical surroundings. The defense of this claim assumes that our beliefs in normal perception arise psychologically from our being appeared to in various ways. This is a contingent psychological thesis and cannot be regarded as a self-evident philo- sophical datum. Nevertheless, we regard it as a well established psychological fact, and so have no misgivings about assuming it in constructing an account of our epistemic norms.

Contrast epistemological theories of perceptual knowledge with those of a priori knowledge. We have no very good theories of a priori knowledge despite the fact that we have no difficulty telling which beliefs are justified and which are not when we are actually doing mathematics or logic. In other words, we know how to proceed in a priori reasoning, and hence we have the same kind of basic data as in the case of perception—we can recognize some beliefs as justified and others as not. What we lack in the case of a priori knowledge is a psychological account of what is going on when we have justified beliefs. We do not know the psychological source of such beliefs, and this hamstrings us in the attempt to construct theories of justification. This illustrates both the way in which our basic epistemological data are self-evident and the importance of contingent nonself-evident psychological facts in the construction of epistemological theories. In an important sense, describing our actual epistemic norms is part of psychology. This does not mean that it is best carried out in the laboratory, but neither can it be denied that the results of laboratory investigations can be relevant.

It is interesting to compare the epistemological methodology I have just described with the standard methodology in linguistics. In con- structing grammatical theories for their own languages, linguists typically rely upon their own intuitions regarding grammaticality. They make what they call 'the competence/performance distinction', according to which it is assumed that speakers of a language know how to judge grammaticality even if they do not always produce grammatical sentences, and then they rely upon their own ability to judge grammaticality to provide them with data concerning the grammaticality of particular sentences. They then seek general theories of grammaticality to accommodate this data. What is happpening here is precisely parallel to what goes on in the construction of an epistemological theory. In each case, we have procedural knowledge. In the one case we know how to reason, and in the other case we know how to talk. Because the conformance to internalized norms is introspectible, this procedural knowledge enables us to recognize particular instances of correct reasoning and correct talking, and then we can use those particular instances as data upon which to build a general theory.

The contingent enterprise of describing our actual epistemic norms is not all there is to epistemology. From a description of our epistemic norms, we want to draw conclusions about the conceptual roles of various concepts, and that is a matter of conceptual analysis. But conceptual analysis is supposed to provide us with necessary truths. How is it possible to derive necessary truths from contingent psychological generalizations? In order to answer this question, note first that true statements about the necessary properties of things need not be necessarily true. To take a well-worn example, nine is the number of planets, and nine is necessarily such that it is odd, so it follows that the number of planets is necessarily such that it is odd; but the latter is only contingently true. This is because the necessity involved is *de re* rather than *de dicto*. Similarly, a statement describing the necessary properties of a concept must refer to the concept in some way, and if the mode of reference is only contingently a way of referring to that particular concept then even though the property ascribed to the concept is a necessary property of the concept, the resulting statement will be contingent. Applying this to epistemology, in describing epistemic norms we are describing necessary properties of concepts, but this does not mean that our epistemological pronouncements are themselves necessary truths. It depends upon how we are thinking of the concepts. For example, we might be thinking of the concept *red* under some description such as 'what is ordinarily expressed by the word "red" in English'. The meaning of an English word is a contingent matter, and so the claim that the concept *red*, so conceived, has such-and-such a conceptual role, will be a contingent claim about necessary properties of concepts.

Although conceptual analyses need not be expressed by necessary truths, there will be necessary truths lurking in the wings. We can think of propositions and concepts in terms of contingent descriptions of them, but I pointed out above that disquotational reasoning requires that we also have noncontingent ways of thinking of propositions and concepts. This involves the use of mental representations that are predetermined by our epistemic norms to designate the propositions or concepts that they do designate. If you think about a concept in this direct fashion and you ascribe a necessary property to it, then your belief is necessarily true. A conceptual analysis describes necessary properties of concepts, so if the conceptual analysis is expressed by a proposition that is about the concept directly then that proposition is necessarily true. Thus conceptual analyses do generate necessary truths. But they are not a priori truths. The analyses describe the conceptual roles of concepts, and our knowledge of those conceptual roles is derived from the discovery of contingent psychological generalizations regarding what epistemic norms we employ in reasoning. Thus the ultimate issue of epistemology is necessary *a posteriori* conceptual analyses.

Naturalistic epistemology is usually associated with externalism, but the present internalism is thoroughly naturalistic and, to my mind, gives epistemology much firmer roots in psychology than do existing externalist theories. Epistemology and psychology become firmly wedded.

7. Direct Realism

Having proposed a general account of the nature of epistemic norms and epistemic justification, I will end this book with a sketch of what I regard as the correct set of epistemic forms. I have argued that (1) the correct epistemic norms must be nondoxastic, and (2) they cannot be externalist. Thus what we must have is a nondoxastic internalist theory. Specifically, our epistemic norms must license inferences directly from perceptual states to physical-object beliefs without mediation by beliefs about the perceptual states. A theory of this sort is what I have called 'direct realism'. Direct realism can have a structure very much like a foundations theory. My own view is that the foundations theory sketched in chapter two got things almost right. Where it went wrong was in adopting the doxastic assumption and thereby assuming that perceptual input must be mediated by epistemologically basic beliefs. Epistemic norms must be able to appeal directly to our being in perceptual states and need not appeal to our having beliefs to that effect. In other words, there can be "half-doxastic" epistemic connections between beliefs and nondoxastic states that are analogous to the "fully doxastic" connections between beliefs and beliefs that we call 'reasons'. I propose to call the half-doxastic connections 'reasons' as well, but it must be acknowledged that this is stretching our ordinary use of the term 'reason'. The motivation for this terminology is that the logical structure of such connections is completely analogous to the logical structure of ordinary prima facie reasons. That is, the half-doxastic connections convey justification defeasibly, and the defeaters operate like the defeaters proposed by the foundations theory formulated in chapter two.

The treatment of reasons adopted in chapter two took reasons to be the propositions believed rather than the states of believing those propositions. As long as we are concerned exclusively with reasoning from beliefs, that is unassailable. But reasoning from nondoxastic states must be described differently because nondoxastic states do not have propositional content in the same way belief states do. If I believe that I am appeared to redly then my belief states has as its content the proposition that I am appeared to redly. But if I am merely appeared to redly, that perceptual state does not similarly have a propositional content. Reasoning from the perceptual state must appeal to the perceptual state itself rather than to a (nonexistent) content. When one makes a perceptual judgment on the basis of a perceptual state, I want to say that the perceptual state itself is one's reason. For the sake of uniformity, I will say the same thing about belief states, taking the belief state rather than the content of the belief state to be the reason. This involves the following modifications to our earlier definitions of 'reason' and 'defeater':

DEFINITION:
A state M of a person S is a *reason* for S to believe Q if and only if it is logically possible for S to become justified in believing Q by believing it on the basis of being on the state M.

DEFINITION:
If M is a reason for S to believe Q, a state M* is a *defeater* for this reason if and only if it is logically possible for S to be in the combined state consisting of being in both the state M and the state M* at the same time, and this combined state is not a reason for S to believe Q.

Reasons are always reasons *for* beliefs, but the reasons themselves need not be beliefs. We can modify our definitions of 'rebutting defeater' and 'undercutting defeater' similarly. A mental state is a *prima facie reason* for a belief if and only if it is a reason for which there can be defeaters.

Direct realism can adopt the same basic structure of epistemic justification as does the foundations theory of chapter two, with the exception that epistemologically basic beliefs are replaced by "epistemologically basic mental states", the latter being mental states that constitute reasons for various kinds of judgments. Among these mental states will be perceptual states, memory states, and perhaps some others. For instance, direct realism can handle the problem of perception by adopting nondoxastic prima facie reasons such as the following:

x's looking red to S is a prima facie reason for S to believe that x is red.

This means that the perceptual state itself is the reason, and not a belief about the perceptual state.

An initially puzzling feature of direct realism emerges from the observation that although we do not usually have beliefs about our perceptual states, we *sometimes* have such beliefs. When we do they are relevant to what perceptual judgments we are justified in making. For example, if x looks red to me, but I believe that x does not look red to me, then I am not justified in taking x to be red on the basis of the perceptual state. Other doxastic and nondoxastic combinations are also possible. For instance, I might believe that x looks red to me when in fact it does not. Reflection on such cases seems to indicate that they justify one in judging that x is red. These examples indicate that when we have them, beliefs about nondoxastic states take precedence over the nondoxastic states themselves in determining what we are justified in believing. This can be explained by recalling the corrective role of intellection in belief formation. Intellection is always available to correct the output of both quick-and-dirty systems and intellection itself. Ordinarily, we move directly from perceptual states to judgments about physical objects, without forming any beliefs about what perceptual states we are in. What we are now noting is that in those unusual cases in which we do form such beliefs, the beliefs about the perceptual states take precedence over the states themselves in determining what conclusions are justified. This is a direct reflection of the corrective role of intellection. An efficient cognitive agent must be able to function mechanically for the most part by employing systems that are quick but dirty. Intellection is available by correcting the dirty systems when they go wrong. In order to do that, intellection must have the power to override other systems. Intellection functions in terms of beliefs, so beliefs about input states must be given precedence over the input states themselves.

Giving beliefs about perceptual states precedence over the perceptual states themselves can be handled by taking the above nondoxastic reason to supplement the doxastic reason described in chapter two rather than replacing it. That doxastic reason must now be reformulated as follows:

S's believing that x looks red to him is a prima facie reason for S
to believe that x is red.

Then we adopt the following defeater for the nondoxastic reason:

S's believing that x does not look red to him is a defeater for x's
looking red to S as a prima facie reason for S to believe that x is
red.

Memory can be handled analogously be supplementing the doxastic mnemonic prima facie reason described in chapter two with the
following nondoxastic mnemonic prima facie reason and accompany-
ing defeater:

S's seeming to remember P is a prima facie reason for S to
believe P; S's believing that he does not seem to remember P is a
defeater for this prima facie reason.

This is only a crude sketch of the structure of reasons embodied in
a plausible formulation of direct realism, but it is enough to give the
flavor of such a theory.[37] It strikes me as a very plausible kind of
theory. It reins the attractive intuitions about the connection between
justification and reasoning that are part and parcel of classical foundations theories, while avoiding the shortcomings of such theories by
giving up the doxastic assumption. Perhaps it is good to close this
book by considering what we can say about the skeptical problem with
which the book began. That was the problem of how and we can know
that we are not brains in vats with all our perceptual experiences
provided by a sophisticated computer. This skeptical problem can be
seen to have a trivial solution. My perceptual experience provides me
with good reasons for believing that I am in my study, typing on my
computer and occasionally gazing out at the mountains. It is a
necessary truth that my perceptual experiences provide me with such
reasons. This necessary truth is a reflection of the necessary features
of my concepts that make them the concepts they are. The structure
of reasons is constitutive of the concepts. That I am in my study,
typing and looking out at the mountains, entails and provides a
conclusive reason for believing that I am not a brain in a vat. Thus I
have perfectly ordinary reasons for thinking that I am in normal
surroundings and hence am not a brain in a vat. The mere logical
possibility of a brain in a vat does not defeat reasons. If I had some
concrete reason for thinking I really was a brain in a vat, then I would
have to take that possibly seriously and I could not lay the spectre of

skepticism to rest so easily. But in fact, I have no such reason and hence need not be seriously concerned about the skeptical hypothesis.

This resolution of the skeptical problem may seem unsatisfying to one enamored of skeptical dilemmas. But recall that our task is not that of proving the skeptic wrong. I take it that we know from the start that the skeptic is wrong. What is wanted is an explanation of *how* we can know that we are not brains in vats rather than a proof (satisfactory to the skeptic) *that* we are not. The general explanation is that perceptual knowledge is acquired on the basis of prima facie reasons. Those reasons do not have to logically entail what they are reasons for. Our being appeared to in various ways does not logically entail that we are not brains in vats, but it does justify us in believing that we are not. End of story.

37. For more details about how to formulate a version of direct realism, see my [1974]. The theory adumbrated there is a sophisticated form of direct realism.

APPENDIX

THE GETTIER PROBLEM

1. Introduction

IT IS RARE in philosophy to find a consensus on any substantive issue, but for some time there was almost complete consensus on what is called 'the justified true belief analysis of knowing'. According to that analysis:

> S knows P if and only if:
> (1) P is true;
> (2) S believes P; and
> (3) S is justified in believing P.

In the period immediately preceding the publication of Gettier's [1963] landmark article "Is justified true belief knowledge?", this analysis was affirmed by virtually every writer in epistemology. Then Gettier published his article and single-handedly changed the course of epistemology. He did this by presenting two clear and undeniable counterexamples to the justified true belief analysis. Recounting the example given in chapter one, consider Smith who believes falsely but with good reason that Jones owns a Ford. Smith has no idea where Brown is, but he arbitrarily picks Barcelona and infers from the putative fact that Jones owns a Ford that either Jones owns a Ford or Brown is in Barcelona. It happens by chance that Brown is in Barcelona, so this disjunction is true. Furthermore, as Smith has good reason to believe that Jones owns a Ford, he is justified in believing this disjunction. But as his evidence does not pertain to the true disjunct of the disjunction, we would not regard Smith as *knowing* that either Jones owns a Ford or Brown is in Barcelona.

Gettier's paper was followed by a spate of articles attempting to meet his counterexamples by adding a fourth condition to the analysis of knowing. The first attempts to solve the Gettier problem turned on the observation that in Gettier's examples, the epistemic agent arrives at his justified true belief by reasoning from a false belief. That suggested the addition of a fourth condition something like the following:

180

S's grounds for believing P do not include any false beliefs.[1]

It soon emerged, however, that further counterexamples could be constructed in which knowledge is lacking despite the believer's not inferring his belief from any false beliefs. Alvin Goldman [1976] constructed the following example. Suppose you are driving through the countryside and see what you take to be a barn. You see it in good light and from not too great a distance, it looks the way barns look, and so on. Furthermore, it is a barn. You then have justified true belief that it is a barn. But in an attempt to appear more opulent than they are, the people around here have taken to constructing very realistic barn facades that cannot readily be distinguished from the real thing when viewed from the highway. There are many more barn facades around than real barns. Under these circumstances we would not agree that you know that what you see is a barn, even though you have justified true belief. Furthermore, your belief that you see a barn is not in any way inferred from a belief about the absence of barn facades. Most likely the possibility of barn facades is something that will not even have occurred to you, much less have played a role in your reasoning.

We can construct an even simpler perceptual example. Suppose S sees a ball that looks red to him, and on that basis he correctly judges that it is red. But unbeknownst to S, the ball is illuminated by red lights and would look red to him even if it were not red. Then S does not know that the ball is red despite his having a justified true belief to that effect. Furthermore, his reason for believing that the ball is red does not involve his believing that the ball is not illuminated by red lights. Illumination by red lights is related to his reasoning only as a defeater, not as a step in his reasoning. These examples, of other related examples,[2] indicate that justified true belief can fail to be knowledge because of the truth values of propositions that do not play a direct role in the reasoning underlying the belief. This observation led to a number of "defeasibility" analyses of knowing.[3] The simplest defeasibility analysis would consist of adding a fourth condition requiring that there be no true defeaters. This might be accomplished as follows:

There is no true proposition Q such that if Q were added to S's beliefs then he would no longer be justified in believing P.[4]

1. See, for example, Michael Clark [1963].
2. See, for example, Brian Skyrms [1967].
3. The first defeasibility analysis was that of Keith Lehrer [1965]. That was followed by Lehrer and Thomas Paxson [1969], Peter Klein [1971], [1976], [1979], [1980], Lehrer [1974], [1979], Ernest Sosa [1974], [1980], and Marshall Swain [1981].
4. This is basically the analysis proffered by Klein [1971].

But Keith Lehrer and Thomas Paxson [1969] presented the following counterexample to this simple proposal:

> Suppose I see a man walk into the library and remove a book from the library by concealing it beneath his coat. Since I am sure the man is Tom Grabit, whom I have often seen before when he attended my classes, I report that I know that Tom Grabit has removed the book. However, suppose further that Mrs. Grabit, the mother of Tom, has averred that on the day in question Tom was not in the library, indeed, was thousands of miles away, and that Tom's identical twin brother, John Grabit, was in the library. Imagine, moreover, that I am entirely ignorant of the fact that Mrs. Grabit has said these things. The statement that she has said these things would defeat any justification I have for believing that Tom Grabit removed the book, according to our present definition of defeasibility. . . .
>
> The preceding might seem acceptable until we finish the story by adding that Mrs. Grabit is a compulsive and pathological liar, that Tom Grabit is a fiction of her demented mind, and that Tom Grabit took the book as I believed. Once this is added, it should be apparent that I did know that Tom Grabit removed the book. (p. 228)

A natural proposal for handling the Grabit example is that in addition to there being a true defeater there is a true defeater defeater, and that restores knowledge. For example, in the Grabit case it is true that Mrs. Grabit reported that Tom was not in the library but his twin brother John was there (a defeater), but it is also true that Mrs. Grabit is a compulsive and pathological liar and John Grabit is a fiction of her demented mind (a defeater defeater). It is difficult, however, to construct a precise principle that handles these examples correctly by appealing to true defeaters and true defeater defeaters. It will not do to amend the above proposal as follows:

> If there is a true proposition Q such that if Q were added to S's beliefs then he would no longer be justified in believing P, then there is also a true proposition R such that if Q and R were both added to S's beliefs then he would be justified in believing P.

The simplest difficulty for this proposal is that adding R may add new reasons for believing P rather than restoring the old reasons. It is not trivial to see how to formulate a fourth condition incorporating defeater defeaters. I think that such a fourth condition will ultimately provide the solution to the Gettier problem, but no proposal of this sort has been worked out in the literature.[5] I will pursue this further in the next section.

---

5. A good survey of the literature on the Gettier problem, going into much more detail than space permits here, can be found in Shope [1983].

2. Objective Epistemic Justification

The Gettier problem has spawned a large number of proposals for the analysis of knowledge. As the literature on the problem has developed, the proposals have become increasingly complex in the attempt to meet more and more complicated counterexamples to simpler analyses. The result is that even if some very complex analysis should turn out to be immune from counterexample, it would seem *ad hoc*. We would be left wondering why we employ any such complicated concept. I will suggest that our concept of knowledge is actually a reasonably simple one. The complexities required by increasingly complicated Gettier-type examples are not complexities in the concept of knowledge, but instead reflect complexities in the structure of our epistemic norms.

In the discussion of externalism I commented on the distinction between subjective and objective senses of 'should believe' and how that pertains to epistemology. The subjective sense of 'should believe' concerns what we should believe given what we actually do believe (possibly incorrectly). The objective sense of 'should believe' concerns what we should believe given what is in fact true. But what we should believe given what is true is just the truths, so the objective sense of 'should believe' gets identified with truth. The subjective sense, on the other hand, is ordinary epistemic justification. What I now want to suggest, however, is that there is an intermediate sense of 'should believe', that might also be regarded as objective but does not reduce to truth.

It is useful to compare epistemic judgments with moral judgments. Focusing on the latter, let us suppose that a person S subjectively should do **A**. This will be so *for particular reasons*. There may be relevant facts of which the person is not apprised that bear upon these reasons. It might be the case that even in the face of all the relevant facts, S should still do **A**. That can happen in either of two ways: (1) among the relevant facts may be new reasons for doing **A** of which S has no knowledge; or (2) the relevant facts may, on sum, leave the original reasons intact. What I have been calling 'the objective sense of "should" ' appeals to both kinds of considerations, but there is also an important kind of moral evaluation that appeals only to considerations of the second kind. This is the notion of the original reasons surviving intact, and it provides us with another variety of objective moral evaluation. We appraise a person and his act simultaneously by saying that he has a moral obligation to perform the act (he subjectively should do it) and his moral obligation derives from what are in fact good reasons (reasons withstanding the test of truth). It seems to me that we are often in the position of making such appraisals, although moral language provides us with no simple way of expressing them. The purely objective sense of 'should' pertains more to acts than to agents, and hence does not express moral obligation. Therefore, it should not be confusing if I express appraisals of this third variety artificially by saying that S has an *objective obligation* to do **A** when he has an obligation to do **A** and the obligation derives from what are in fact good reasons (in the face of all the relevant facts).

How might objective obligation be analyzed? It might at first be supposed that S has an objective obligation to do **A** if and only if (1) S subjectively should do **A**, and (2) there is no set of truths **X** such that if these truths were added to S's beliefs (and their negations removed in those cases in which S disbelieves them) then it would not be true that S subjectively should do **A** *for the same reason*. This will not quite do, however. It takes account of the fact that moral reasons are defeasible, but it does not take account of the fact that the defeaters are also defeasible. For example, S might spy a drowning man and be in a position to save him with no risk to himself. Then he subjectively should do so. But suppose that, unbeknownst to S, the man is a terrorist who fell in the lake while he was on his way to blow up a bus station and kill many innocent people. Presumably, if S knew that then he would no longer have a subjective obligation to save the man, and so it follows by the proposed analysis that S does not have an objective obligation to save the man. But suppose it is also the case that what caused the man to fall in the lake was that he underwent a sudden religious conversion that persuaded him to give up his evil ways and devote the rest of his life to good deeds. If S knew this, then he would again have a subjective obligation to save the man, for the same reasons as his original reasons, and so he has an objective obligation to save the man. There is, however, no way to accommodate this on the proposed analysis. On that analysis, if a set of truths defeats an obligation, there is no way to get it undefeated again by appealing to a broader class of truths.

What the analysis of objective obligation should require is that if S were apprised of "enough" truths (all the relevant ones) then he would still be subjectively obligated to do **A**. This can be cashed out as requiring that there is a set of truths such that if S were apprised of them then he would be subjectively obligated in the same way as he originally was, and those are all the relevant truths in the sense that if he were to become apprised of any further truths that would not make any difference. Precisely:

S has an objective obligation to do **A** if and only if:
    (1) S subjectively should do **A**; and

(2) there is a set **X** of truths such that, given any more inclusive set **Y** of truths, necessarily, if the truths in **Y** were added to S's beliefs (and their negations removed in those cases in which S disbelieves them) then it would still be true *for the same reason* that S subjectively should do **A.**

Now let us return to epistemology. An important difference between moral judgments and epistemic judgments is that basic moral judgments concern obligation whereas basic epistemic judgments concern permissibility. This reflects an important difference in the way moral and epistemic norms function. In morality, reasons are reasons for obligations. Anything is permissible that is not proscribed. In epistemology, on the other hand, epistemic justification concerns what beliefs you are permitted to hold (not 'obliged to hold'), and reasons are required for permissibility. Thus the analogy between epistemology and morality is not exact. The analogue of objective moral obligation is "objective epistemic permissibility", or as I will say more simply, *objective epistemic justification*. I propose to ignore our earlier concept of objective epistemic justification because it simply reduces to truth. Our new concept of objective epistemic justification can be defined as follows, on analogy to our notion of objective moral obligation:

S is objectively justified in believing P if and only if:

(1) S is (subjectively) justified in believing P; and

(2) there is a set **X** of truths such that, given any more inclusive set **Y** of truths, necessarily, if the truths in **Y** were added to S's beliefs (and their negations removed in those cases in which S disbelieves them) and S believed P *for the same reason* then he would still be (subjectively) justified in believing P.

Despite the complexity of its definition, the concept of objective epistemic justification is a simple and intuitive one. As is so often the case with technical concepts, the concept is easier to grasp than it is to define. It can be roughly glossed as the concept of getting the right answer while doing everything right. I am construing 'S is justified in believing P' in such a way that it entails that S does believe P, so objective justification entails justified belief. It also entails truth, because if P were false and we added ~P to **Y** then S would no longer be justified in believing P. Thus, objective epistemic justification entails justified true belief.

My claim is now that objective epistemic justification is very close to being the same thing as knowledge. We will find in section three that a qualification is required to turn objective justification into knowledge, but in the meantime it can be argued that the Gettier problem can be resolved by taking objective epistemic justification to be a necessary condition for knowledge. This enables us to avoid the familiar Gettier-type examples that create difficulties for other analyses of knowledge. Consider one of Gettier's original examples. Jones believes, correctly, that Brown owns a Ford. He believes this on the grounds that he has frequently seen Brown drive a particular Ford, he has ridden in it, he has seen Brown's auto registration which lists him as owning that Ford, and so forth. But unknown to Jones, Brown sold that Ford yesterday and bought a new one. Under the circumstances, we would not agree that Jones now knows that Brown owns a Ford, despite the fact that he has a justified true belief to that effect. This is explained by noting that Jones is not objectively justified in believing that Brown owns a Ford. This is because there is a truth—namely, that Brown does not own the Ford Jones thinks he owns—such that if Jones became apprised of it then his original reasons would no longer justify him in believing that Jones owns a Ford, and becoming apprised of further truths would not restore those original reasons.

To take a more complicated case, consider Goldman's barn example. Suppose you are driving through the countryside and see what you take to be a barn. You see it in good light and from not too great a distance, and it looks like a barn. Furthermore, it is a barn. You then have justified true belief that it is a barn. But the countryside here is littered with very realistic barn facades that cannot readily be distinguished from the real thing when viewed from the highway. There are many more barn facades than real barns. Under these circumstances we would not agree that you know that what you see is a barn, even though you have justified true belief. This can be explained by noting that if you were aware of the preponderance of barn facades in the vicinity then you would not be justified in believing you see a barn, and your original justification could not be restored by learning other truths (such as that it is really a barn). Consequently, your belief that you see a barn is not objectively justified.[6]

Finally, consider the Grabit example. Here we want to say that I really do know that Tom Grabit stole the book, despite the fact that Mrs. Grabit alleged that Tom was thousands of miles away and his twin brother John was in the library. That she said this is a true defeater, but there is also a true defeater defeater, viz., that Mrs. Grabit is a compulsive and pathological liar and John Grabit is a fiction of her demented mind. If we include *both* of these truths in the set **X** then I remain justified *for my original reason* in believing that Tom

6. This can be formulated in terms of defeaters and defeater defeaters. 'Most of the things around here that look like barns are not barns' is a true reliability defeater, but there is no true defeater defeater. In particular, 'That really is a barn', although true, does not restore your original justification—instead, it constitutes a new reason for believing that what you see is a barn.

stole the book, so in this case my belief is objectively justified despite the existence of a true defeater.

To a certain extent, I think that the claim that knowledge requires objective epistemic justification provides a solution to the Gettier problem. But it might be disqualified as a solution to the Gettier problem on the grounds that the definition of objective justification is vague in one crucial respect. It talks about being justified, *for the same reason*, in believing P. I think that that notion makes pre-theoretic good sense, but to spell out what it involves requires us to construct a complete epistemological theory. That, I think, is why the Gettier problem has proven so intractable. The complexities in the analysis of knowing all have to do with filling out this clause. The important thing to realize, however, is that these complexities have nothing special to do with knowledge per se. What they pertain to is the structure of epistemic justification and the way in which beliefs come to be justified on the basis of other beliefs and nondoxastic states. Thus even if it is deemed that we have not yet solved the Gettier problem, we have at least put the blame where it belongs—not on knowledge but on the structure of epistemic justification and the complexity of our epistemic norms.

Let us turn then to the task of filling in some of the details concerning epistemic justification. In chapter two, I proposed an analysis of epistemic justification in terms of ultimately undefeated arguments. That analysis proceeded within the context of a subsequently rejected foundationalist theory, but basically the same analysis can be resurrected within direct realism. For this purpose we must take arguments to proceed from internal states (both doxastic and nondoxastic states) to doxastic states, the links between steps being provided by reasons. Within direct realism, reasons are internal states. They are generally doxastic states, but not invariably. At the very least, perceptual and memory states can also be reasons.

Our epistemic norms permit us to begin reasoning from certain internal states without those states being supported by further reasoning. Such states can be called *basic states*. Paramount among these are perceptual and memory states. Arguments must always begin with basic states and proceed from them to nonbasic doxastic states. What we might call *linear arguments* proceed from basic states to their ultimate conclusions through a sequence of steps each consisting of a belief for which the earlier steps provide reasons. It seems likely, however, that we must allow arguments to have more complicated structures than those permitted in linear arguments. Specifically, we must allow "subsidiary arguments" to occur within the main argument. A subsidiary argument can begin with premises that are merely assumed for the sake of the argument rather than because they have already been justified. For instance, in the forms of conditional proof familiar from elementary logic, in establishing a conditional $(P \supset Q)$, we may begin by taking P as a premise (even though it has not been previously established), deriving Q from it, and then "discharging" the assumption of the antecedent to obtain the conditional $(P \supset Q)$. It seems that something similar occurs in epistemological arguments. We can accommodate this by taking *an argument conditional on a set* **X** *of propositions* to be an argument beginning not just from basic states but also from doxastic states that consist of believing the members of **X**. Then an argument that justifies a conclusion for a person may have embedded in it subsidiary arguments that are conditional on propositions the person does not believe. For present purposes we need not pursue all the details of the permissible structures of epistemological arguments, but the general idea of conditional arguments will be useful below.

An argument *supports* a belief if and only if that belief occurs as a step in the argument that does not occur within any subsidiary argument. A person *instantiates* an argument if and only if he is in the basic states from which the argument begins and he believes the conclusion of the argument on the basis of that argument. Typically, in reasoning to a conclusion one will proceed first to some intermediate conclusions from which the final conclusion is obtained. The notion of holding a belief on the basis of an argument is to be understood as requiring that one also believes the intermediate conclusions on the basis of the initial parts of the argument.

Epistemic justification consists of holding a belief on the basis of an ultimately undefeated argument, that is, instantiating an ultimately undefeated argument supporting the belief. To repeat the definition of an ultimately undefeated argument, every argument proceeding from basic states that S is actually in will be *undefeated at level 0* for S. Of course, arguments undefeated at level 0 can embed subsidiary arguments that are conditional on propositions S does not believe. Some arguments will support defeaters for other arguments, so we define an argument to be undefeated at level 1 if and only if it is not defeated by any other arguments undefeated at level 0. Among the arguments defeated at level 0 may be some that supported defeaters for others, so if we take arguments undefeated at level 2 to be arguments undefeated at level 0 that are not defeated by any arguments undefeated at level 1, there may be arguments undefeated at level 2 that were arguments defeated at level 1. In general, we define an argument to be *undefeated at level $n + 1$* if and only if it is undefeated at level 0 and is not defeated by any arguments undefeated at level n. An argument is *ultimately undefeated* if and only if there is some point beyond which it remains permanently undefeated; that is, for some N, the argument remains undefeated at level n for every n > N.

This gives us a picture of the structure of epistemic justification. Many details remain to be filled in, but we can use this picture without further elaboration to clarify the concept of objective epistemic justification. Roughly, a belief is objectively justified if and only if it is held on the basis of some ultimately undefeated argument **A**, and either **A** is not defeated by any argument conditional on true propositions not believed by S, or if it is then there are further true propositions such that the initial defeating arguments will be defeated by arguments conditional on the enlarged set of true propositions. This can be made precise by defining an *argument conditional on* **Y** to be any argument proceeding from basic states S is actually in together with doxastic states consisting of believing members of **Y**. We then say that an argument instantiated by S (not an argument conditional on **Y**) is *undefeated at level n + 1 relative to* **Y** if and only if it is undefeated by any argument undefeated at level n relative to **Y**. An argument is *ultimately undefeated relative to* **Y** if and only if there is an N such that it is undefeated at level n relative to **Y** for every n > N. Then the concept of objective epistemic justification can be made more precise as follows:

> S is objectively justified in believing P if and only if S instantiates some argument **A** supporting P which is ultimately undefeated relative to the set of all truths.

I will take this to be my official definition of objective epistemic justification. I claim, then, that the Gettier-style counterexamples to the traditional definition of knowledge can all be met by taking knowledge to require objective epistemic justification. This makes precise the way in which knowledge requires justification that is either undefeated by true defeaters, or if defeated by true defeaters then those defeaters are defeated by true defeater defeaters, and so on.

A common view has been that the reliability of one's cognitive processes is required for knowledge, and thus reliabilism has a place in the analysis of knowledge quite apart from whether it has a place in the analysis of epistemic justification.[7] The observation that knowledge requires objective epistemic justification explains the appeal of the idea that knowledge requires reliability. Nondefeasible reasons logically entail their conclusions, so they are always perfectly reliable, but defeasible reasons can be more or less reliable under various circumstances. Discovering that the present circumstances are of a

7. See, for example, Alvin Goldman [1981], pp. 28–9.

type in which a defeasible reason is unreliable constitutes a defeater for the use of that reason. Objective justification requires that if a belief is held on the basis of a defeasible reason then there are no true defeaters (or if there are then there are true defeater defeaters, and so on). Thus knowledge automatically requires that one's reasons be reliable under the present circumstances. Reliabilism has a place in knowledge even if it has none in justification. It is worth emphasizing, however, that considerations of reliability are not central to the concept of knowledge. Rather than having to be imposed on the analysis in an *ad hoc* way, they emerge naturally from the observation that knowledge requires objective epistemic justification.

3. Social Aspects of Knowledge

It is tempting to simply identify knowledge with objective epistemic justification. As I have pointed out, objective justification includes justified true belief, and it is immune from Gettier-style counterexamples. It captures the idea underlying defeasibility analyses. The basic idea is that *believed* defeaters can prevent justification, and defeaters that are true but not believed can prevent knowledge while leaving justification intact. However, there are also some examples that differ in important ways from the Gettier-style examples we have discussed so far, and they are not so easily handled in terms of there being true defeaters. These examples seem to have to do with social aspects of knowing. The philosopher most prominently associated with these examples is Gilbert Harman.[8] One of Harman's examples is as follows:

> Suppose that Tom enters a room in which many people are talking excitedly although he cannot understand what they are saying. He sees a copy of the morning paper on a table. The headlines and main story reveal that a famous civil-rights leader has been assassinated. On reading the story he comes to believe it; it is true. . . .
> Suppose that the assassination has been denied, even by eyewitnesses, the point of the denial being to avoid a racial explosion. The assassinated leader is reported in good health; the bullets are said, falsely, to have missed him and hit someone else. The denials occurred too late to prevent the original and true story from appearing in the paper that Tom has seen; but everyone else in the room has heard about the denials. None of them know what to believe. They all have information that Tom lacks. Would we judge Tom to be the only one who knows that the assassination has actually occurred? . . . I do not think so. ([1968], p. 172)

8. See Harman [1968] and [1980]. Harman credits Ernest Sosa [1964] with the original observation that social considerations play a role in knowledge.

This example cannot be handled in the same way as the Grabit example. As in the Grabit example there is a true defeater, viz., that the news media have reported that the assassination did not occur. But just as in the Grabit example, there is also a true defeater defeater, viz., that the retraction of the original story was motivated by an attempt to avoid race riots and did not necessarily reflect the actual facts. The appeal to true defeaters and true defeater defeaters should lead us to treat this example just like the Grabit example, but that gives the wrong answer. The Grabit example is one in which the believer has knowledge, whereas the newspaper example is one in which the believer lacks knowledge.

Harman gives a second kind of example in a recent article:

> In case one, Mary comes to know that Norman is in Italy when she calls his office and is told he is spending the summer in Rome. In case two, Norman seeks to give Mary the impression that he is in San Francisco by writing her a letter saying so, a letter he mails to San Francisco where a friend then mails it on to Mary. This letter is in the pile of unopened mail on Mary's desk before her when she calls Norman's office and is told he is spending the summer in Rome. In this case (case two), Mary does not come to know that Norman is in Italy.
>
> It is important in this case that Mary could obtain the misleading evidence. If the evidence is unobtainable, because Norman forgot to mail the letter after he wrote it, or because the letter was delivered to the wrong building where it will remain unopened, then it does not keep Mary from knowing that Norman is in Italy. ([1981], p. 164)

Again, there is a true defeater, viz., that the letter reports Norman to be in San Francisco. But there is also a true defeater defeater, viz., that the letter was written with the intention to deceive. So Mary's belief is objectively justified. Nevertheless, we want to deny that Mary knows that Norman is in Italy.

Harman ([1981], p. 164) summarizes these examples by writing, "There seem to be two ways in which such misleading evidence can undermine a person's knowledge. The evidence can either be evidence that it would be possible for the person to obtain himself or herself or evidence possessed by others in a relevant social group to which the person in question belongs." We might distinguish between these two examples by saying that in the first example there is a true defeater that is "common knowledge" in Tom's social group, whereas in the second example there is a true defeater that is "readily available" to Mary. I will loosely style these "common knowledge" and "ready availability" defeaters.

It is worth noting that a common knowledge defeater can be defeated by a defeater defeater that is also common knowledge. For example, if it were common knowledge that the news media was disclaiming the assassination, but also common knowledge that the disclaimer was fraudulent, then Tom would retain his knowledge that the assassination occurred even if he were unaware of both the disclaimer and its fraudulence. The same thing is true of ready availability defeaters. If Norman had a change of heart after sending the false letter and sent another letter explaining the trick he played on Mary, and both letters lay unopened on Mary's desk when she called Norman's office, her telephone call would give her knowledge that Norman is in Italy.

What is more surprising is that common knowledge and ready availability defeaters and defeater defeaters can be combined to result in knowledge. For instance, if Norman's trick letter lays unopened on Mary's desk when she makes the call, she will nevertheless acquire knowledge that Norman is in Italy if Norman is an important diplomat and, unbeknownst to her, the news media have been announcing all day that Norman is in Rome but has been trying to fool people about his location by sending out trick letters. This shows that despite the apparent differences between common knowledge and ready availability defeaters, there must be some kind of connection between them.

My suggestion is that these both reflect a more general social aspect of knowledge. We are "socially expected" to be aware of various things. We are expected to know what is announced on television, and we are expected to know what is in our mail. If we fail to know all these things and that makes a difference to whether we are justified in believing some true proposition P, then our objectively justified belief in P does not constitute knowledge. Let us say that a proposition is *socially sensitive for S* if and only if it is of a sort S is expected to believe when true. My claim is that Harman's examples are best handled by taking them to involve cases in which there are true socially sensitive defeaters. This might be doubted on the grounds that not all readily available truths are socially sensitive. For instance, suppose that instead of having his trick letter mailed from San Francisco, Norman had a friend secrete it under Mary's doormat. We are not socially expected to check regularly under our doormats, but nevertheless this is something we can readily do and so information secreted under our doormats counts as readily available. It does not, however, defeat knowledge. If the trick letter were secreted under Mary's doormat, we would regard her as knowing that Norman is in Italy. Suppose, on the other hand, that we lived in a society in which it is common to leave messages under doormats and everyone is expected to check his doormat whenever he comes home. In that case, if the trick letter were under Mary's doormat but she failed to check there before calling Norman's office, we would not regard that call as providing her with knowledge. These examples seem to indicate that it is social sensitivity and not mere ready availability that enables a truth to defeat a knowledge claim.

My suggestion is that we can capture the social aspect of knowledge by requiring a knower to hold his belief on the basis of an argument ultimately undefeated relative not just to the set of all truths, but also to the set of all socially sensitive truths. My proposal is:

S knows P if and only if S instantiates some argument **A** supporting P which is (1) ultimately undefeated relative to the set of all truths, and (2) ultimately undefeated relative to the set of all truths socially sensitive for S.

This proposal avoids both the Gettier problem and the social problems discussed by Harman. At this stage in history it would be rash to be very confident of any analysis of knowledge, but I put this forth tentatively as an analysis that seems to handle all of the known problems.

BIBLIOGRAPHY

Ackermann, Diana
    1979   Proper names, propositional attitudes and non-descriptive connotations. *Philosophical Studies* 35: 55–70.

    1979a   Proper names, essences, and intuitive beliefs. *Theory and Decision* 11: 5–26.

    1980   Thinking about an object: Comments on Pollock. *Midwest Studies in Philosophy*, vol. 5, pp. 501–8. Minneapolis: University of Minnesota Press.

Alston, William
    1978   Meta-ethics and meta-epistemology. In *Values and Morals*, ed. A. I. Goldman and Jaegwon Kim, pp. 275–97. Dordrecht: Reidel.

Anderson, John
    1976   *Language, Memory, and Thought*. Hillsdale, NJ: Lawrence Erlbaum Associates.

    1983   *The Architecture of Cognition*. Cambridge: Harvard University Press.

Armstrong, David
    1968   *A Materialist Theory of Mind*. London: Routledge & Kegan Paul.

Ayer, A. J.
    1946   *Language, Truth, and Logic*. New York: Dover.

Bach, Kent
    1982   *De re* belief and methodological solipsism. In *Thought and Object: Essays on Intentionality*, ed. Andrew Woodfield. Oxford: Oxford University Press.

Bonjour, Laurence
    1976   The coherence theory of empirical knowledge. *Philosophical Studies* 30: 281–312.

    1978   Can empirical knowledge have a foundation? *American Philosophical Quarterly* 15: 1–14.

    1985   *The Structure of Empirical Knowledge*. Cambridge: Harvard University Press.

Carnap, Rudolf
    1962   The aim of inductive logic. In *Logic, Methodology, and the Philosophy of Science*, ed. Ernest Nagel, Patrick Suppes, and Alfred Tarski, pp. 303–18. Stanford: Stanford University Press.

    1967   *The Logical Structure of the World*. London: Routledge & Kegan Paul.

    1971   Inductive logic and rational decisions. In *Studies in Inductive Logic and Probability*, ed. R. Carnap and R. C. Jeffrey. Berkeley: University of California Press.

Castañeda, H. N.
1966   He*: A study in the logic of self-consciousness. *Ratio* 8: 130–57.
1967   Indicators and quasi-indicators. *American Philosophical Quarterly* 4: 85–100.
1968   On the logic of attributions of self-knowledge to others. *Journal of Philosophy* 65: 439–56.
Chisholm, Roderick
1957   *Perceiving*. Ithaca, NY: Cornell University Press.
1966   *Theory of Knowledge*. Englewood Cliffs, NJ: Prentice-Hall.
1977   *Theory of Knowledge*. 2nd ed. Englewood Cliffs, NJ: Prentice-Hall.
1981   A version of foundationalism. *Midwest Studies in Philosophy*, vol. 5, pp. 543–64. Minneapolis: University of Minnesota Press.
1981a   *The First Person*. Minneapolis: University of Minnesota Press.
Clark, Michael
1963   Knowledge and grounds: A comment on Mr. Gettier's paper. *Analysis* 24: 46–48.
Clark, Romane
1973   Sensuous judgments. *Nous* 7: 45–56.
Cohen, L. Jonathan
1981   Can human irrationality be experimentally demonstrated? *The Behavioral and Brain Sciences* 4: 317–70.
Cohen, Stewart
1984   Justification and truth. *Philosophical Studies* 46: 279–96.
Creary, L. G. and C. J. Pollard
1985   A computational semantics for natural language. *Proceedings of the Association for Computational Linguistics*, 1985.
Donnellan, Keith
1972   Proper names and identifying descriptions. In *Semantics of Natural Language*, ed. Donald Davidson and Gilbert Harman. Dordrecht: Reidel.
Doyle, Jon
1979   A truth maintenance system. *Artificial Intelligence* 12: 231–72.
1982   Nonmonotonic logics. In *Handbook of Artificial Intelligence*, vol. 3, ed. Paul R. Cohen and Edward A. Feigenbaum, pp. 114–79. Los Altos, Calif.: William Kaufmann.
Dummett, Michael
1975   What is a theory of meaning? In *Mind and Language*, ed. Samuel Guttenplan. Oxford: Oxford University Press.
1976   What is a theory of meaning? (II). In *Truth and Meaning*, ed. Gareth Evans and John McDowell. Oxford: Oxford University Press.
Eells, Ellory
1983   Objective probability theory theory. *Synthese* 57: 387–442.
Dretske, Fred
1981   *Knowledge and the Flow of Information*. Cambridge: MIT Press.
Fetzer, James
1971   Dispositional probabilities. *Boston Studies in the Philosophy of Science*, vol. 8, pp. 473–82. Dordrecht: Reidel.

1977   Reichenbach, reference classes, and single case 'probabilities'.
            Synthese 34: 185–217.
1981   *Scientific Knowledge. Boston Studies in the Philosophy of Science*, vol.
            69. Dordrecht: Reidel.
Finetti, Bruno de
1937   La prevision: ses lois logiques, ses sources subjectives. *Annales de
            l'Institut Henri Poincaré* 7: 1–68. Translated as "Foresight: Its
            logical laws, its subjective sources" in *Studies in Subjective Proba-
            bility*, ed. Henry Kyburg and Howard Smokler. New York, 1964.
Firth, Roderick
1950   Radical empiricism and perceptual relativity. *The Philosophical
            Review* 59: 164–83, 319–31.
1978   Are epistemic concepts reducible to ethical concepts? In Gold-
            man and Kim [1978].
Fodor, J. A.
1975   *The Language of Thought.* Cambridge: Harvard University Press.
Gettier, Edmund
1963   Is justified true belief knowledge? *Analysis* 23: 121–23.
Giere, Ronald N.
1973   Objective single case probabilities and the foundations of statis-
            tics. In *Logic, Methodology, and Philosophy of Science*, ed. P. Suppes,
            et al. Amsteredam: North Holland.
1973a   Review of Mellor's *The Matter of Chance. Ratio* 15: 149–55.
1976   A Laplacean formal semantics for single-case propensities. *Jour-
            nal of Philosophical Logic* 5: 321–53.
Goldman, Alvin
1976   Discrimination and perceptual knowledge. *Journal of Philosophy*
            73: 771–91.
1976a   *A Theory of Human Action.* Princeton: Princeton University Press.
1979   What is justified belief? In *Justification and Knowledge*, ed.
            George Pappas. Dordrecht: Reidel.
1981   The internalist conception of justification. *Midwest Studies in
            Philosophy*, vol. 5, pp. 27–52. Minneapolis: University of Minne-
            sota Press.
1986   *Epistemology and Cognition.* Cambridge: Harvard University
            Press.
Goldman, Alvin, and Jaegwon Kim, eds.
1978   *Values and Morals.* Dordrecht: Reidel.
Goodman, Nelson
1951   *The Structure of Appearance.* Cambridge: Harvard University
            Press.
1955   *Fact, Fiction, and Forecast.* Cambridge: Harvard University Press.
Hacking, Ian
1965   *Logic of Statistical Inference.* Cambridge: Cambridge University
            Press.
Harman, Gilbert
1968   Knowledge, inference, and explanation. *American Philosophical
            Quarterly* 5: 164–73.
1970   Induction. In *Induction, Acceptance, and Rational Belief*, ed. Mar-
            shall Swain. Dordrecht: Reidel.

1973   *Thought*. Princeton: Princeton University Press.
1980   Reasoning and Explanatory Coherence. *American Philosophical Quarterly* 17: 151–58.
1981   Reasoning and evidence one does not possess. *Midwest Studies in Philosophy*, vol. 5, pp. 163–82. Minneapolis: University of Minnesota Press.
1984   Positive versus negative undermining in belief revision. *Nous* 18: 39–49.
1986   *Change in View*. Cambridge: MIT Press.

Heil, John
1983   Believing what one ought. *Journal of Philosophy* 80: 752–65.

Hempel, Carl
1962   Deductive-Nomological and Statistical Explanation. In *Minnesota Studies in the Philosophy of Science*, vol. 3, ed. Herbert Feigl and Grover Maxwell. Minneapolis: University of Minnesota Press.

Jeffrey, Richard
1965   *The Logic of Decision*. New York: McGraw-Hill.
1970   Dracula Meets Wolfman: Acceptance vs. Partial Belief. In *Induction, Acceptance, and Rational Belief*, ed. Marshall Swain, pp. 157–85. Dordrecht: Reidel.

Kahneman, Daniel, Paul Slovic, and Amos Tversky
1982   *Judgment Under Uncertainty: Heuristics and Biases*. Cambridge: Cambridge University Press.

Kant, Immanuel
1958   *Critique of Pure Reason*. Translated by Norman Kemp Smith. London: Macmillan.

Kaplan, Mark
1985   It's not what you know that counts. *Journal of Philosophy* 92: 350–63.

Kintsch, W.
1974   *The Representation of Meaning in Memory*. Hillsdale, NJ: Lawrence Erlbaum Associates.

Kintsch, W., and J. M. Keenan
1973   Reading rate and retention as a function of the number of the propositions in the base structure of sentences. *Cognitive Psychology* 5: 257–74.

Klein, Peter
1971   A proposed definition of propositional knowledge. *Journal of Philosophy* 68: 471–82.
1976   Knowledge, causality, and defeasibility. *Journal of Philosophy* 73: 792–812.
1979   Misleading "misleading defeaters". *Journal of Philosophy* 76: 382–86.
1980   Misleading evidence and the restoration of justification. *Philosophical Studies* 37: 81–89.

Kornblith, Hilary
1983   Justified belief and epistemically responsible action. *Philosophical Review* 92: 33–48.

Kyburg, Henry, Jr.
 1961   *Probability and the Logic of Rational Belief.* Middletown: Wesleyan
         University Press.
 1970   Conjunctivitis. In *Induction, Acceptance, and Rational Belief,* ed.
         Marshall Swain. Dordrecht: Reidel.
 1974   *The Logical Foundations of Statistical Inference.* Dordrecht: Reidel.
Lehrer, Keith
 1965   Knowledge, truth, and evidence. *Analysis* 25: 168–75.
 1971   How reasons give us knowledge, or the case of the gypsy lawyer.
         Journal of Philosophy 68: 311–13.
 1974   *Knowledge.* Oxford: Oxford University Press.
 1975   Reason and consistency. In *Analyses and Metaphysics,* ed. Keith
         Lehrer, pp. 57–74. Dordrecht: Reidel.
 1979   The Gettier problem and the analysis of knowledge. In *Justifica-
         tion and Knowledge: New Studies in Epistemology,* ed. George Pap-
         pas, pp. 65–78. Dordrecht: Reidel.
 1981   Self-profile. In *Profiles: Keith Lehrer,* ed. R. J. Bogdan.
         Dordrecht: Reidel.
 1982   Knowledge, truth, and ontology. In *Language and Ontology,*
         proceedings of the 6th international Wittgenstein Symposium.
         Vienna: Hölder-Pichler-Tempsky.
Lehrer, Keith, and Thomas Paxson
 1969   Knowledge: Undefeated justified true belief. *Journal of Philoso-
         phy* 66: 225–37.
Levi, Isaac
 1967   *Gambling with Truth: An Essay on Induction and the Aims of Science.*
         New York: Alfred A. Knopf.
 1980   *The Enterprise of Knowledge.* Cambridge: MIT Press.
Lewis, C. I.
 1946   *An Analysis of Knowledge and Valuation.* LaSalle: Open Court.
 1956   *Mind and the World Order.* New York: Dover.
Lewis, David
 1979   Attitudes de dicto and de se. *Philosophical Review* 87: 513–43.
 1980   A subjectivist's guide to objective chance. In *Ifs,* ed. W. L.
         Harper, R. Stalnaker, and G. Pearce, pp. 267–98. Dordrecht:
         Reidel.
Malcolm, Norman
 1963   *Knowledge and Certainty,* pp. 229–30. Englewood Cliffs, NJ:
         Prentice Hall.
Margolis, Joseph
 1973   Alternative strategies for the analysis of knowledge. *Canadian
         Journal of Philosophy* 2: 461–69.
McDermott, D., and Jon Doyle
 1980   Non-monotonic logic I. *Artificial Intelligence* 13: 41–72.
Meiland, J.
 1980   What ought we to believe? Or the ethics of belief revisited.
         American Philosophical Quarterly 17: 15–24.
Mellor, D. H.
 1969   Chance. *Proceedings of the Aristotelian Society,* suppl. vol. 43, pp.
         11–36.
 1971   *The Matter of Chance.* Cambridge: Cambridge University Press.

200   BIBLIOGRAPHY

Moore, G. E.
1903   *Principia Ethica*. Cambridge: Cambridge University Press.
1959   Proof of an external world. In *Philosophical Papers*. London:
          Allen & Unwin.
Neurath, Otto
1932   Protokollsätze. *Erkenntnis* 3: 204–14.
Newell, Allan
1972   A theoretical exploration of mechanisms for coding the stimu-
          lus. In *Coding Processes in Human Memory*, ed. A. W. Melton and
          E. Martin. Washington: Winston.
1973   Production systems: Models of control structures. In *Visual
          Information Processing*, ed. W. G. Chase. New York: Academic
          Press.
1980   Reasoning, problem solving, and decision processes: The prob-
          lem space as a fundamental category. In *Attention and Perform-
          ance VIII*, ed. R. Nickerson. Hillsdale, NJ: Lawrence Erlbaum
          Associates.
Newell, Allan, and H. A. Simon
1972   *Human Problem Solving*. Englewood Cliffs NJ: Prentice-Hall.
          Nisbett, Richard, and Lee Ross
1980   *Human Inference: Strategies and Shortcomings of Social Judgment.*
          Englewood Cliffs, NJ: Prentice-Hall.
Perry, John
1977   Frege on demonstratives. *Philosophical Review* 86: 474–97.
1979   The problem of the essential indexical. *Nous* 13: 3–22.
Pollock, John
1967   Criteria and our knowledge of the material world. *Philosophical
          Review* 76: 28–62.
1968   What is an epistemological problem? *American Philosophical
          Quarterly* 5: 183–90.
1970   The structure of epistemic justification. *American Philosophical
          Quarterly*, monograph series 4: 62–78.
1974   *Knowledge and Justification*. Princeton: Princeton University
          Press.
1979   A plethora of epistemological theories. In *Justification and
          Knowledge*, ed. George Pappas. Dordrecht: Reidel.
1980   Thinking about an object. *Midwest Studies in Philosophy* vol. 5, pp.
          487–500. Minneapolis: University of Minnesota Press.
1981   Statements and propositions. *Pacific Philosophical Quarterly* 62:
          3–16.
1982   *Language and Thought*. Princeton: Princeton University Press.
1983   A theory of direct inference. *Theory and Decision* 15: 29–96.
1983a   Epistemology and probability. *Synthese* 55: 231–52.
1984   *The Foundations of Philosophical Semantics*. Princeton: Princeton
          University Press.
1984a   Nomic probability. *Midwest Studies in Philosophy*, vol. 9, pp. 177–
          204. Minneapolis: University of Minnesota Press.
1984b   A solution to the problem of induction. *Nous* 18: 423–62.
1984c   Reliability and justified belief. *Canadian Journal of Philosophy* 14:
          103–14.

1984d   Foundations for direct inference. *Theory and Decision* 17: 221–
             56.
1986   A theory of moral reasoning. *Ethics* 96: 506–23.
198?a   My brother, the machine. *Nous*, in press.
198?b   Epistemic norms. *Synthese*, in press.
198?c   *Nomic Probability and the Foundations of Induction*, in preparation.
Prichard, H. A.
1950   *Moral Obligation*. Oxford: Oxford University Press.
Putnam, Hilary
1960   Minds and machines. In *Dimensions of Mind*, ed. Sidney Hook.
             New York: New York University Press.
1979   *Meaning and the Moral Sciences*. Cambridge: Cambridge Univer-
             sity Press.
1984   *Reason, Truth, and History*. Cambridge: Cambridge University
             Press.
Quine, W. V. O.
1960   *Word and Object*. Cambridge: MIT Press.
Quine, W. V., and Joseph Ullian
1978   *The Web of Belief*, 2nd edition. New York: Random House.
Rapaport, W. J.
1984   Quasi-indexical reference in propositional semantic networks.
             Proceedings COLING–84.
1984a   Belief representation and quasi-indicators. Technical Report
             215, SUNY Buffalo Department of Computer Science.
Rawls, John
1971   *A Theory of Justice*. Cambridge: Harvard University Press.
Reichenbach, Hans
1949   *A Theory of Probability*. (Original German edition 1935.) Berke-
             ley: University of California Press.
Reiter, Raymond
1978   On reasoning by default. *Theoretical Issues in Natural Language
             Processing*, vol. 2, 210–18.
1980   A logic for default reasoning. *Artificial Intelligence* 13: 81–132.
Rorty, Richard
1979   *Philosophy and the Mirror of Nature*. Princeton: Princeton Univer-
             sity Press.
Ross, L., M. R. Lepper, and M. Hubbard
1975   Perseverance in self-perception and social perception: Biased
             attributional processes in the debriefing paradigm. *Journal of
             Personality and Social Psychology* 32: 880–92.
Ross, David
1930   *The Right and the Good*. Oxford: Oxford University Press.
Russell, Bertrand
1912   *Problems of Philosophy*. Oxford: Oxford University Press.
Salmon, Wesley
1966   *The Foundations of Statistical Inference*. Pittsburgh: University of
             Pittsburgh Press.
Savage, L. J.
1954   *The Foundations of Statistics*. New York: John Wiley.
Schiffer, Stephen
1981   Truth and the theory of content. In *Meaning and Understanding*,
             ed. H. Parret and J. Bouverese. Berlin: Walter de Gruyter.

Schlick, Moritz
1959   The foundations of knowledge. Reprinted in *Logical Positivism*, ed. A. J. Ayer, pp. 224–25. Glencoe, Ill.: Free Press.
Schmitt, Frederick
1984   Reliability, objectivity and the background of justification. *Australasian Journal of Philosophy* 62: 1–15.
Sellars, Wilfrid
1963   Empiricism and the philosophy of mind. Reprinted in *Science, Perception, and Reality*. New York: Humanities Press; London: Routledge & Kegan Paul.
Shope, Robert K.
1983   *The Analysis of Knowing*. Princeton: Princeton University Press.
Skyrms, Brian
1967   The explication of 'X knows that p'. *Journal of Philosophy* 64: 373–89.
Smith, David Woodruff
1984   Content and context of perception. *Synthese* 61: 61–87.
1986   The ins and outs of perception. *Philosophical Studies* 49: 187–212.
Sosa, Ernest
1964   The analysis of 'knowledge that p'. *Analysis* 25: 1–8.
1974   How do you know? *American Philosophical Quarterly* 11: 113–22.
1980   Epistemic presupposition. In *Justification and Knowledge: New Studies in Epistemology*, ed. George Pappas. Dordrecht: Reidel.
1981   The raft and the pyramid: Coherence versus foundations in the theory of knowledge. *Midwest Studies in Philosophy*, vol. 5, pp. 3–26. Minneapolis: University of Minnesota Press.
Squires, Robert
1969   Memory unchained. *The Philosophical Review* 77: 178–97.
Stevenson, Charles L.
1944   *Ethics and Language*. New Haven: Yale University Press.
Strawson, P. F.
1952   *An Introduction to Logical Theory*. London: Methuen.
Suppes, Patrick
1973   New foundations for objective probability: Axioms for propensities. In *Logic, Methodology, and Philosophy of Science*, vol. 5, ed. Suppes et al., 515–29. Amsterdam: North Holland.
Swain, Marshall
1981   *Reasons and Knowledge*. Ithaca, NY: Cornell University Press.
Tye, Michael
1984   The adverbial approach to visual experience. *The Philosophical Review* 93: 195–226.
Unger, Peter
1967   Experience and factual knowledge. *Journal of Philosophy* 64: 152–73.
Van Cleve, James
1979   Foundationalism, epistemic principles, and the Cartesian Circle. *Philosophical Review* 88: 55–91.
Wason, P. C., and P. N. Johnson-Laird
1972   *Psychology of Reasoning: Structure and Content*. London: B. T. Batsford.

Williams, Michael
  1977   *Groundless Belief*. New Haven: Yale University Press.
Winograd, Terry
  1980   Extended inference modes in reasoning by computer systems.
          Artificial Intelligence 13: 5–26.
Wittgenstein, Ludwig
  1953   *The Philosophical Investigations*. 3rd ed. Translated by G. E. M.
          Anscombe. New York: Macmillan.

INDEX